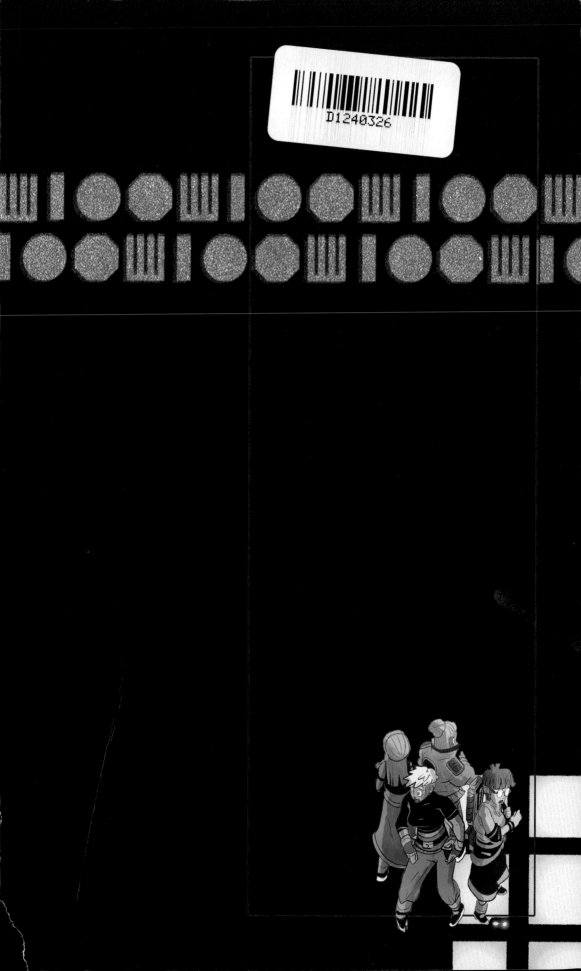

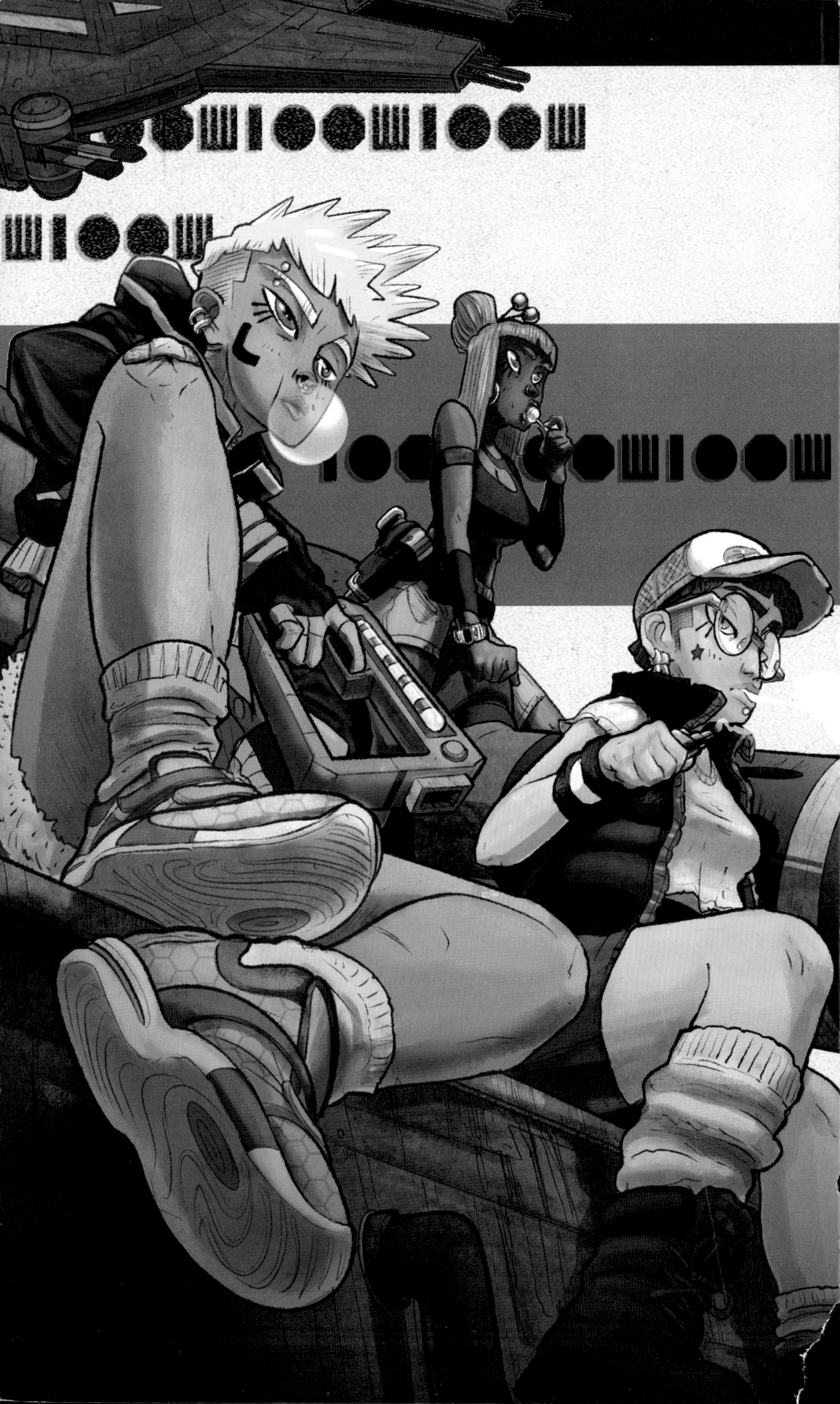

VOLUME 01

BECSTAR™

JOE CORALLO
WRITER

LORENZO COLANGELI
ARTIST

SWEENEY BOO
COVER ARTIST

JOAMETTE GIL
LETTERER

CHRIS FERNANDEZ
EDITOR

MIGUEL ANGEL ZAPATA
LOGO & BOOK DESIGN

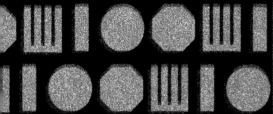
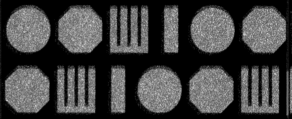

Laura Chacón
Founder

Mark London
CEO and Chief Creative Officer

Giovanna T. Orozco
VP of Operations

Chris Fernandez
Publisher

Chris Sanchez
Editor-in-Chief

Cecilia Medina
Chief Financial Officer

Manuel Castellanos
Director of Sales &
Retailer Relations

Allison Pond
Marketing Director

Miguel Angel Zapata
Design Director

Brian Hawkins
Assistant Editor

Diana Bermúdez
Graphic Designer

David Reyes
Graphic Designer

Adriana T. Orozco
Interactive Media Designer

Nicolás Zea Arias
Audiovisual Production

Frank Silva
Executive Assistant

Stephanie Hidalgo
Office Manager

FOR MAD CAVE COMICS, INC. Becstar™ Published by Mad Cave Studios, Inc. 8838 SW 129 St. Miami, FL 33176. © 2021 Mad Cave Studios, Inc. All rights reserved. Contains materials originally published in single magazine form as Becstar™ (2021) #1-5.

First Printing. Printed in Canada.
ISBN: 978-1-952303-16-6

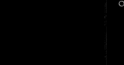

PART 01

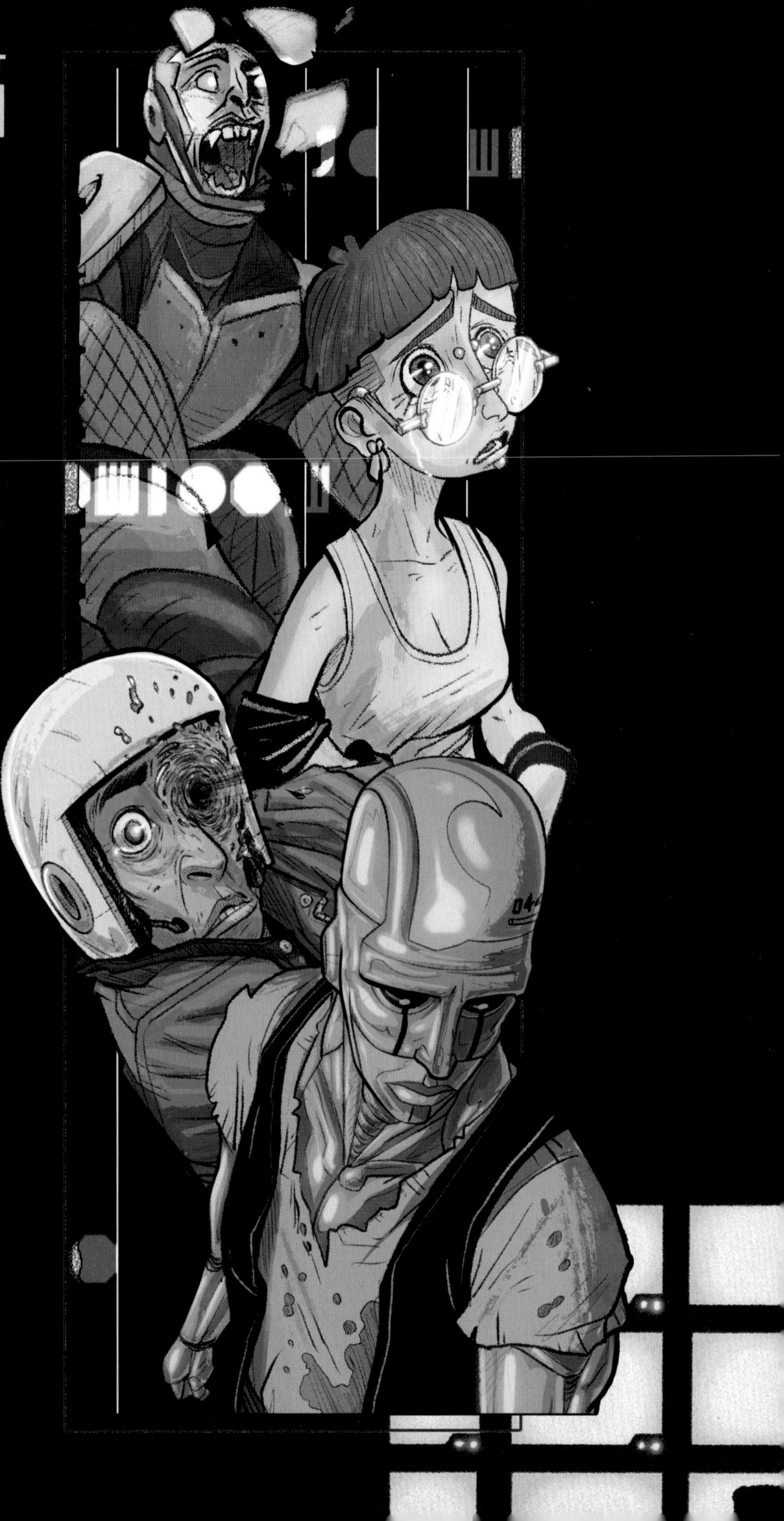

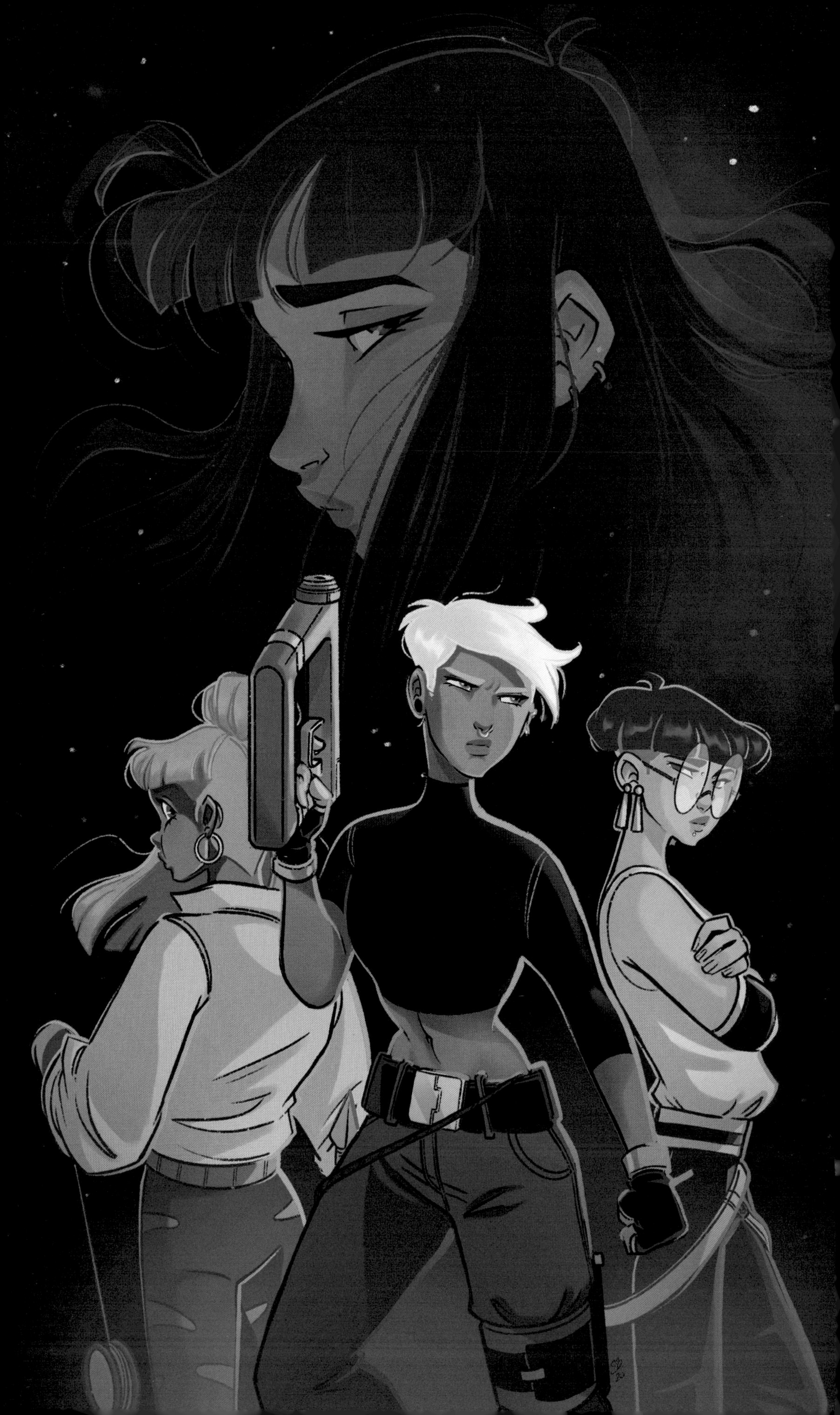

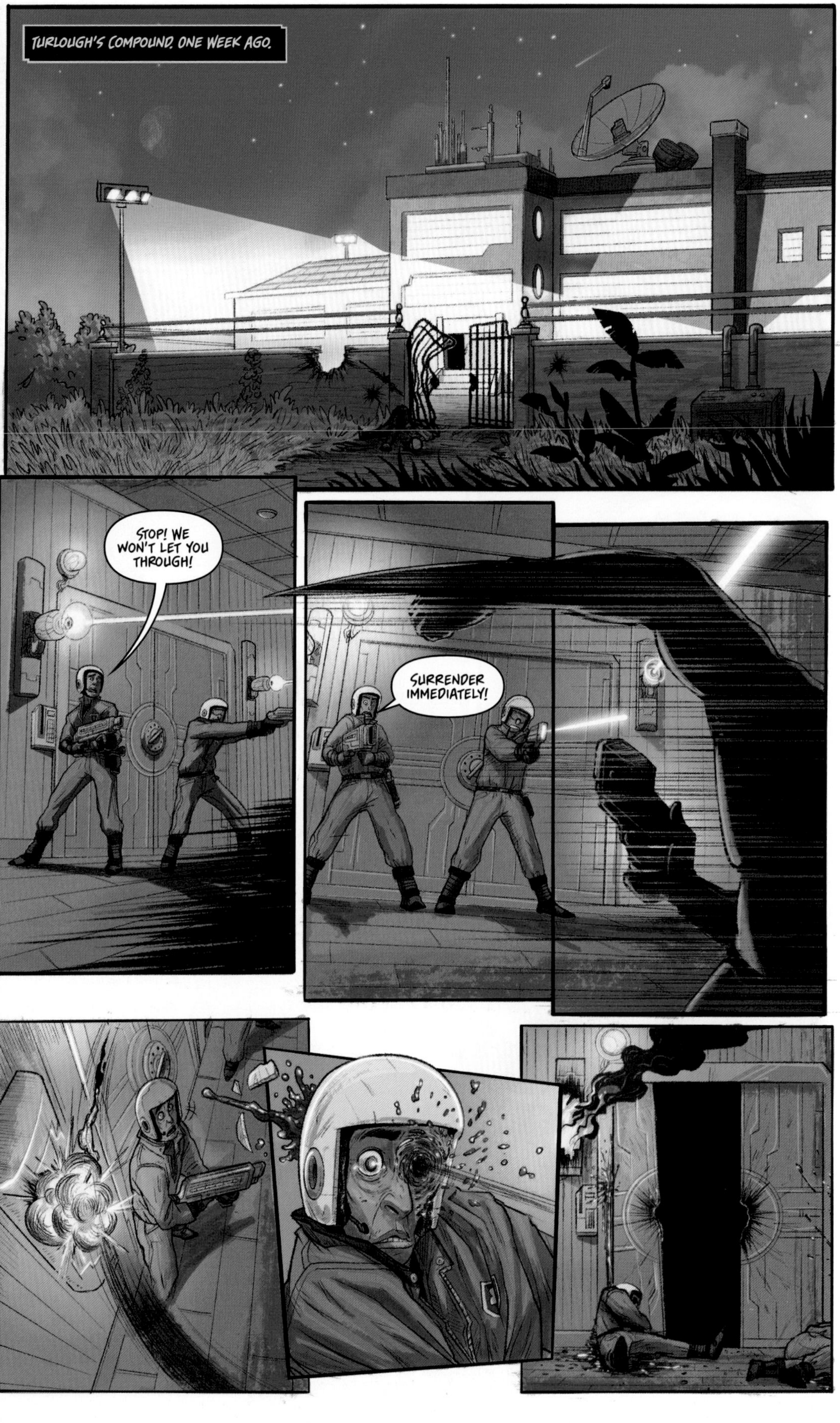
TURLOUGH'S COMPOUND, ONE WEEK AGO.
STOP! WE WON'T LET YOU THROUGH!
SURRENDER IMMEDIATELY!

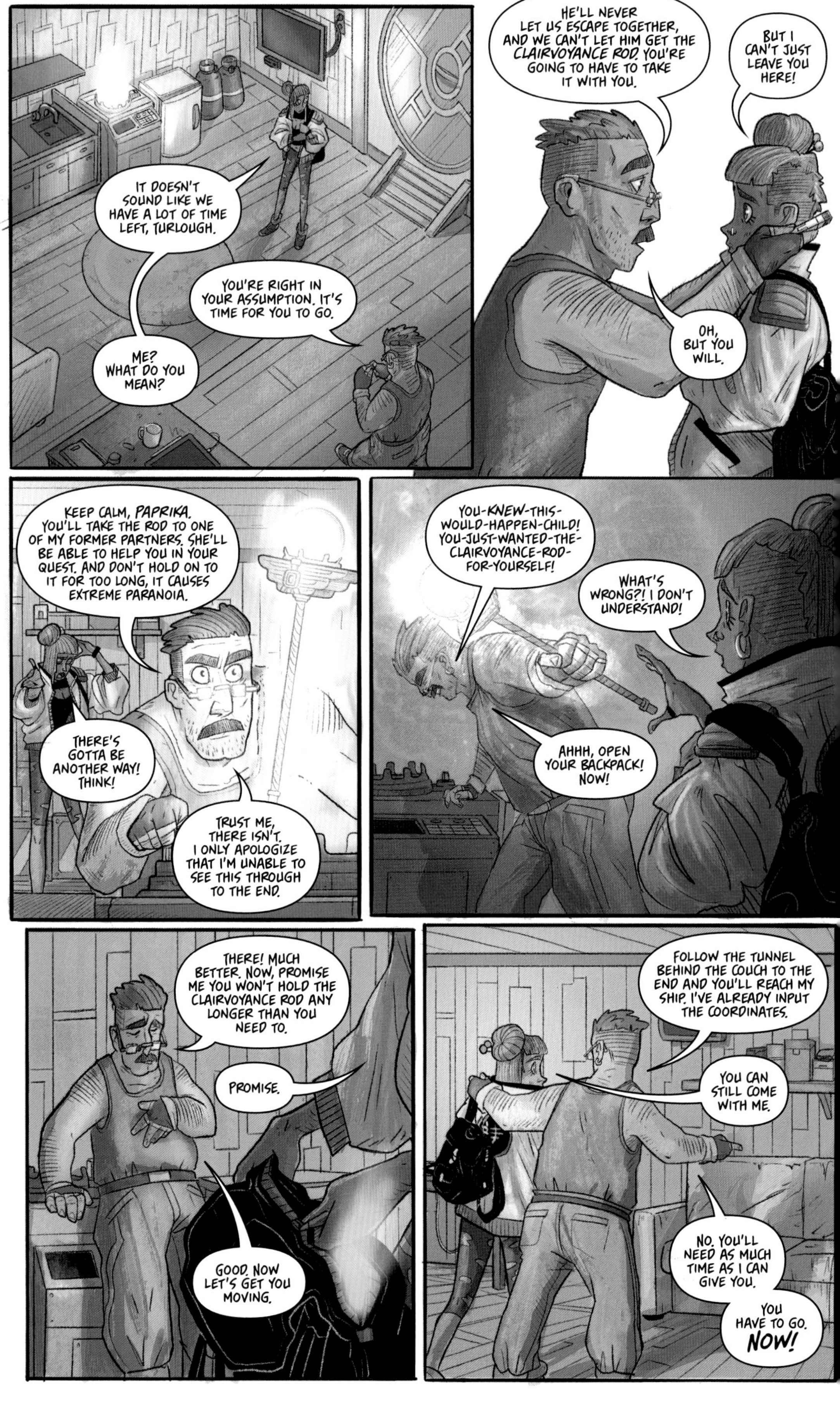
IT DOESN'T SOUND LIKE WE HAVE A LOT OF TIME LEFT, TURLOUGH.
YOU'RE RIGHT IN YOUR ASSUMPTION. IT'S TIME FOR YOU TO GO.
ME? WHAT DO YOU MEAN?
HE'LL NEVER LET US ESCAPE TOGETHER, AND WE CAN'T LET HIM GET THE CLAIRVOYANCE ROD. YOU'RE GOING TO HAVE TO TAKE IT WITH YOU.
BUT I CAN'T JUST LEAVE YOU HERE!
OH, BUT YOU WILL.
KEEP CALM, PAPRIKA. YOU'LL TAKE THE ROD TO ONE OF MY FORMER PARTNERS. SHE'LL BE ABLE TO HELP YOU IN YOUR QUEST. AND DON'T HOLD ON TO IT FOR TOO LONG, IT CAUSES EXTREME PARANOIA.
THERE'S GOTTA BE ANOTHER WAY! THINK!
TRUST ME, THERE ISN'T. I ONLY APOLOGIZE THAT I'M UNABLE TO SEE THIS THROUGH TO THE END.
YOU-KNEW-THIS-WOULD-HAPPEN-CHILD! YOU-JUST-WANTED-THE-CLAIRVOYANCE-ROD-FOR-YOURSELF!
WHAT'S WRONG?! I DON'T UNDERSTAND!
AHHH, OPEN YOUR BACKPACK! NOW!
THERE! MUCH BETTER. NOW, PROMISE ME YOU WON'T HOLD THE CLAIRVOYANCE ROD ANY LONGER THAN YOU NEED TO.
PROMISE.
GOOD. NOW LET'S GET YOU MOVING.
FOLLOW THE TUNNEL BEHIND THE COUCH TO THE END AND YOU'LL REACH MY SHIP. I'VE ALREADY INPUT THE COORDINATES.
YOU CAN STILL COME WITH ME.
NO. YOU'LL NEED AS MUCH TIME AS I CAN GIVE YOU.
YOU HAVE TO GO. NOW!

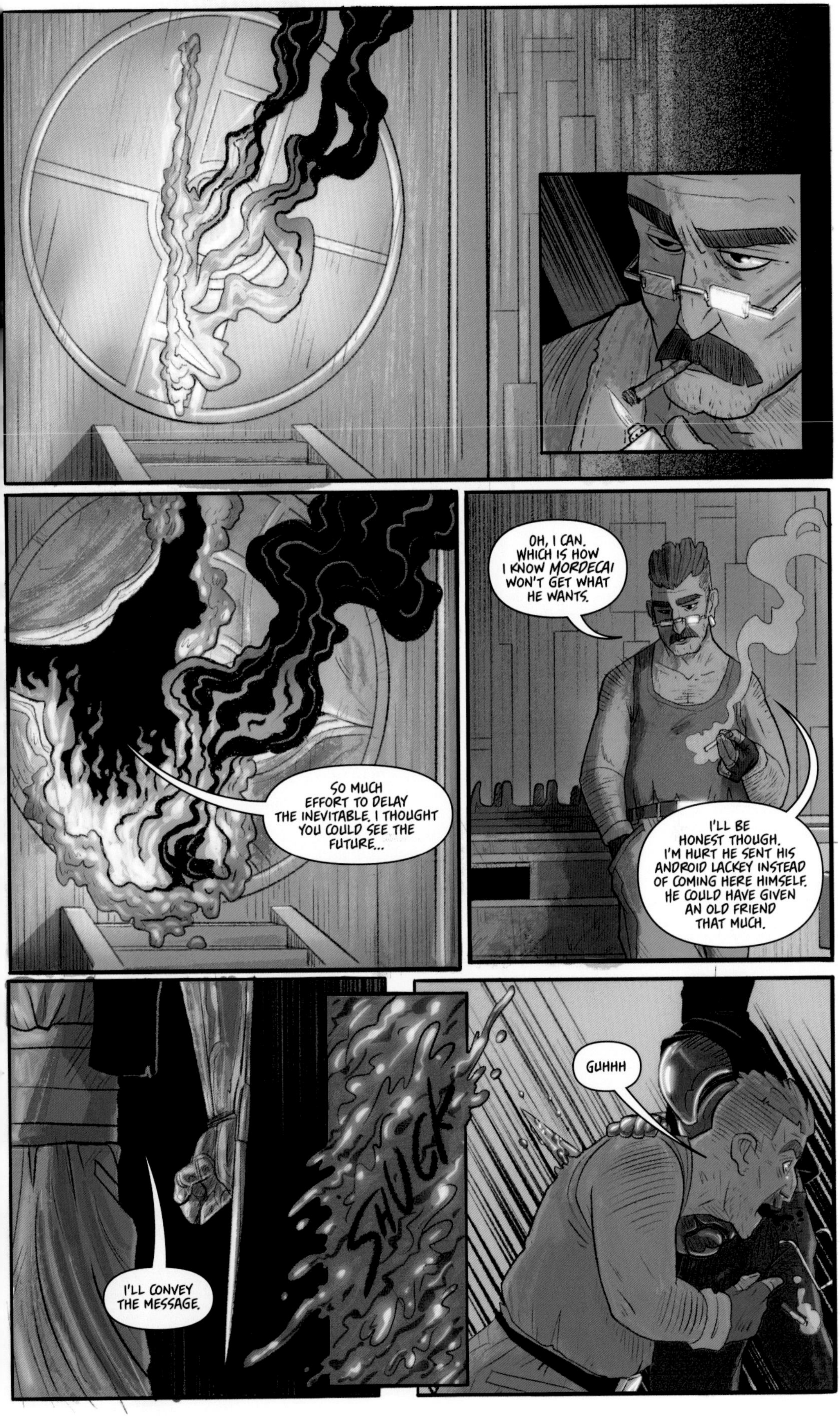

SO MUCH EFFORT TO DELAY THE INEVITABLE. I THOUGHT YOU COULD SEE THE FUTURE...
OH, I CAN. WHICH IS HOW I KNOW MORDECAI WON'T GET WHAT HE WANTS.
I'LL BE HONEST THOUGH. I'M HURT HE SENT HIS ANDROID LACKEY INSTEAD OF COMING HERE HIMSELF. HE COULD HAVE GIVEN AN OLD FRIEND THAT MUCH.
I'LL CONVEY THE MESSAGE.
SHUCK
GUHHH

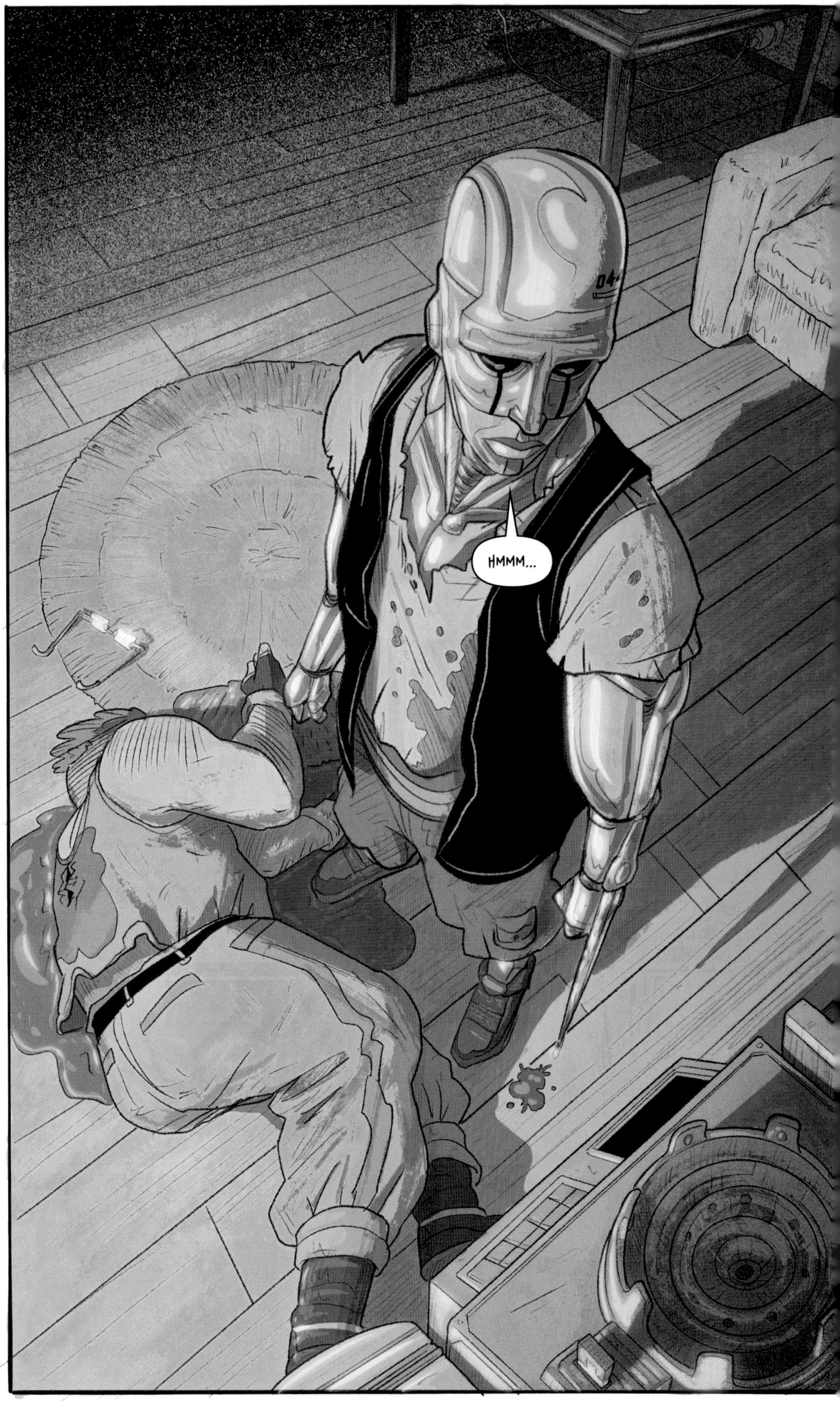
HMMM...

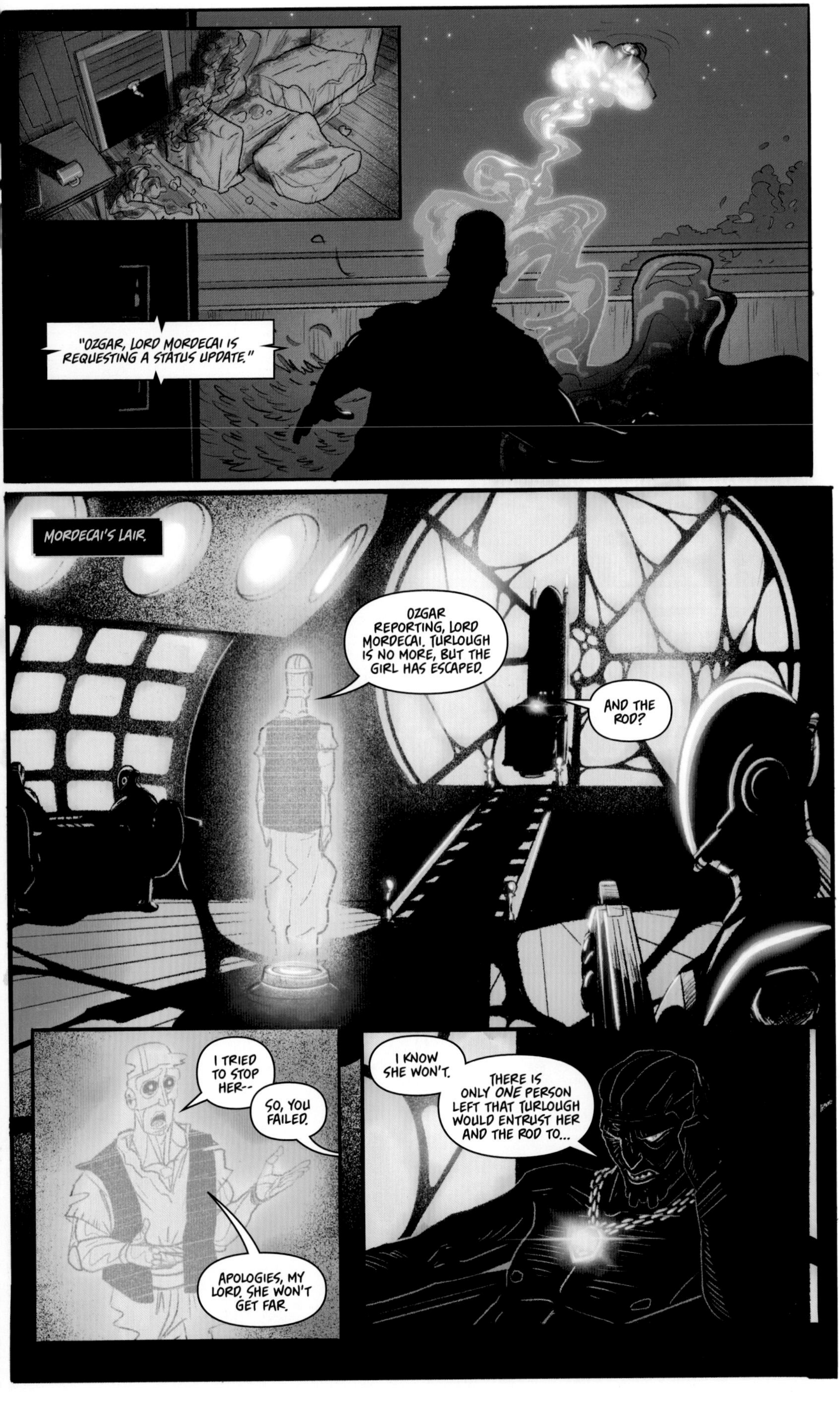
"OZGAR, LORD MORDECAI IS REQUESTING A STATUS UPDATE."
MORDECAI'S LAIR.
OZGAR REPORTING, LORD MORDECAI. TURLOUGH IS NO MORE, BUT THE GIRL HAS ESCAPED.
AND THE ROD?
I TRIED TO STOP HER--
SO, YOU FAILED.
APOLOGIES, MY LORD. SHE WON'T GET FAR.
I KNOW SHE WON'T.
THERE IS ONLY ONE PERSON LEFT THAT TURLOUGH WOULD ENTRUST HER AND THE ROD TO...

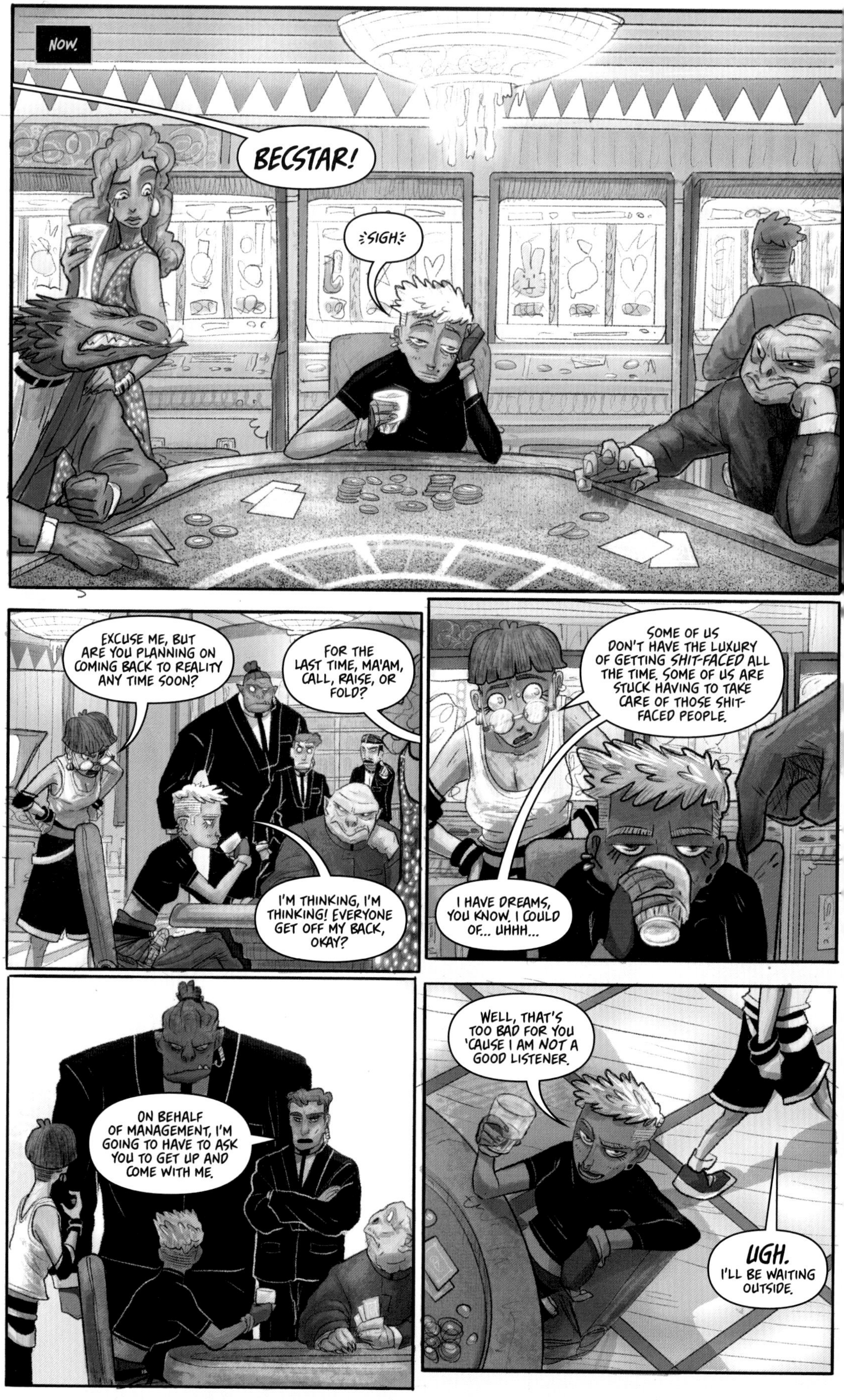
NOW.
BECSTAR!
SIGH.
EXCUSE ME, BUT ARE YOU PLANNING ON COMING BACK TO REALITY ANY TIME SOON?
FOR THE LAST TIME, MA'AM, CALL, RAISE, OR FOLD?
I'M THINKING, I'M THINKING! EVERYONE GET OFF MY BACK, OKAY?
SOME OF US DON'T HAVE THE LUXURY OF GETTING *SHIT-FACED* ALL THE TIME. SOME OF US ARE STUCK HAVING TO TAKE CARE OF THOSE SHIT-FACED PEOPLE.
I HAVE DREAMS, YOU KNOW. I COULD OF... UHHH...
ON BEHALF OF MANAGEMENT, I'M GOING TO HAVE TO ASK YOU TO GET UP AND COME WITH ME.
WELL, THAT'S TOO BAD FOR YOU 'CAUSE I AM NOT A GOOD LISTENER.
UGH.
I'LL BE WAITING OUTSIDE.

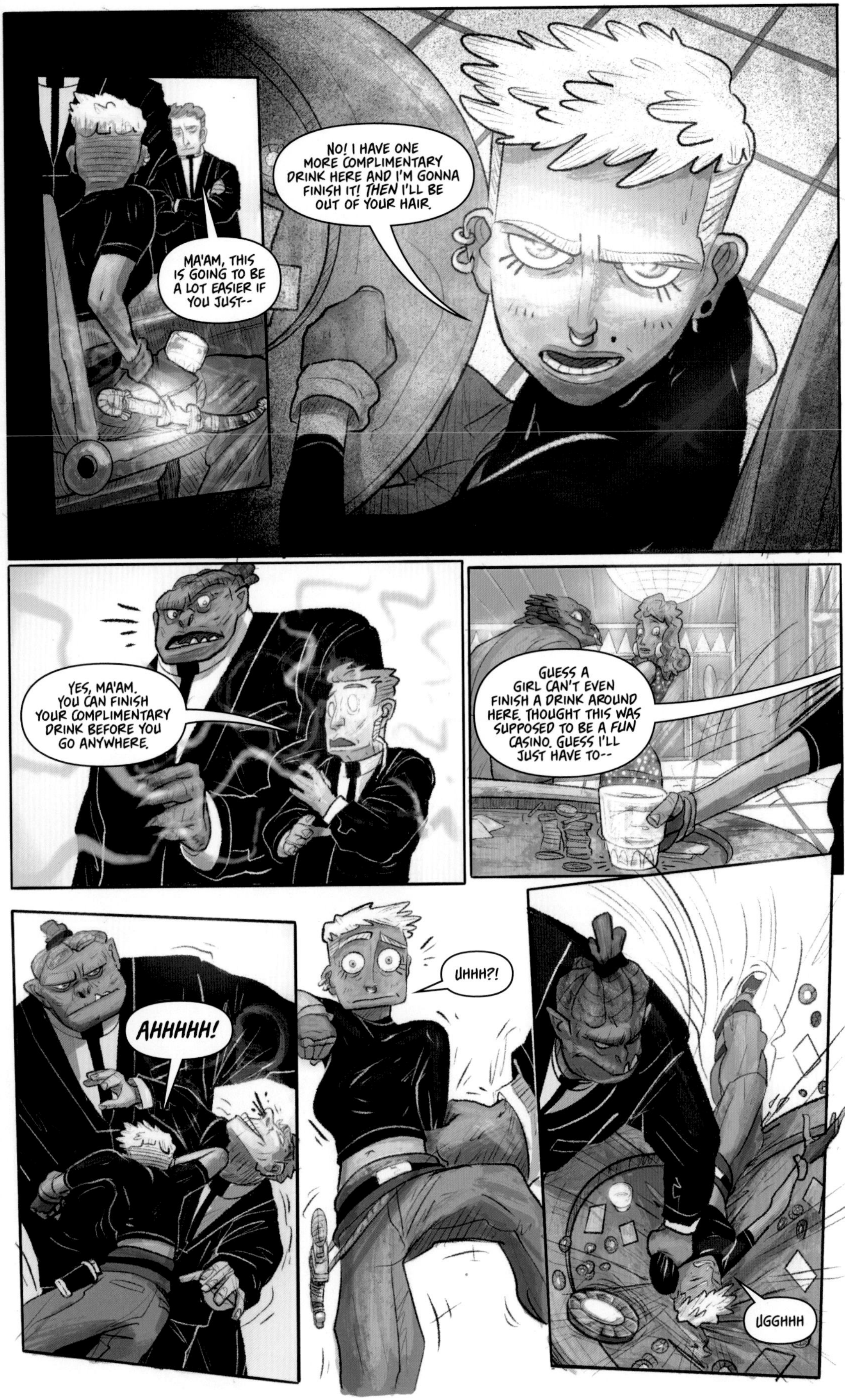

MA'AM, THIS IS GOING TO BE A LOT EASIER IF YOU JUST--
NO! I HAVE ONE MORE COMPLIMENTARY DRINK HERE AND I'M GONNA FINISH IT! *THEN* I'LL BE OUT OF YOUR HAIR.
YES, MA'AM. YOU CAN FINISH YOUR COMPLIMENTARY DRINK BEFORE YOU GO ANYWHERE.
GUESS A GIRL CAN'T EVEN FINISH A DRINK AROUND HERE. THOUGHT THIS WAS SUPPOSED TO BE A *FUN* CASINO. GUESS I'LL JUST HAVE TO--
AHHHHH!
UHHH?!
UGGHHH

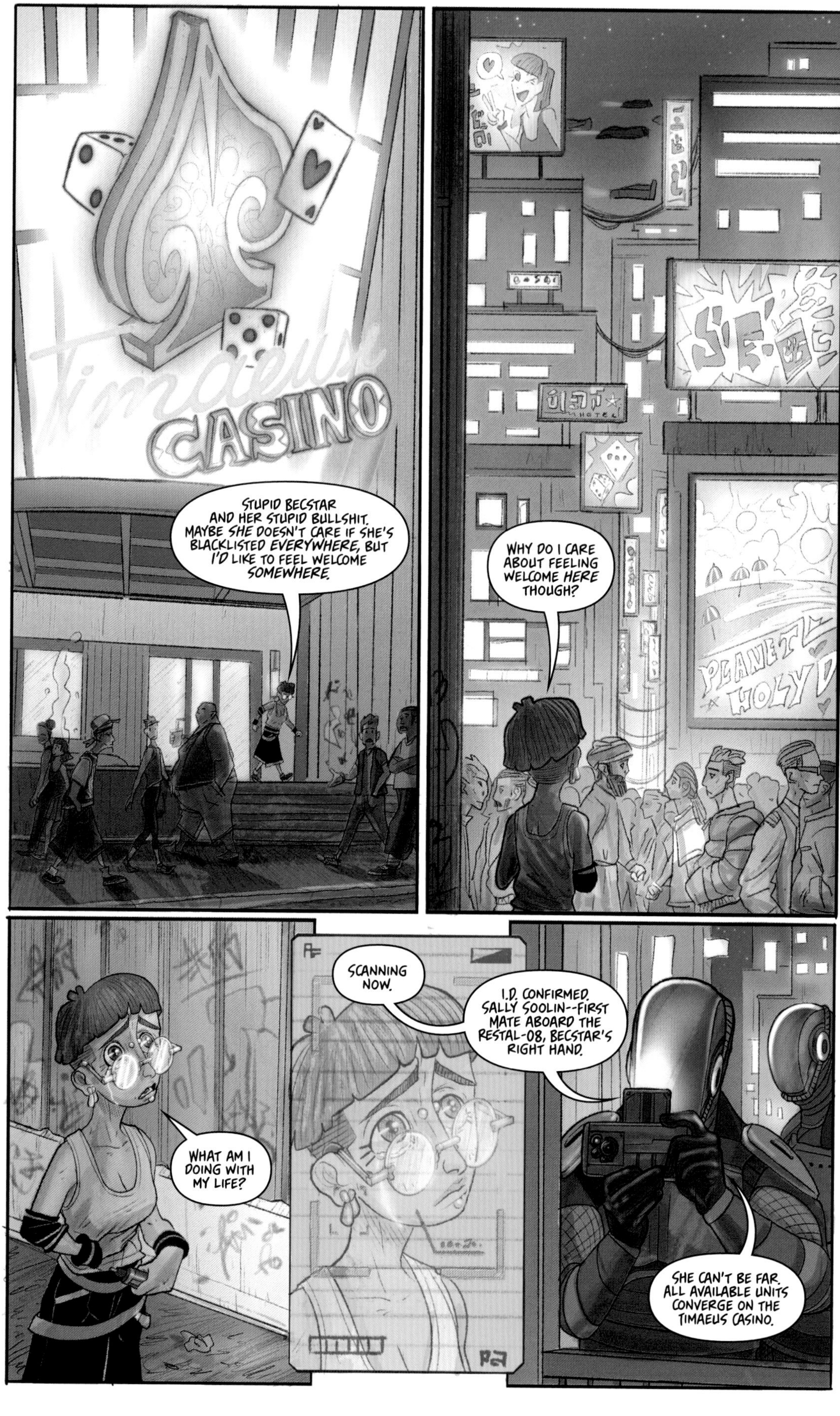

CASINO
STUPID BECSTAR AND HER STUPID BULLSHIT. MAYBE SHE DOESN'T CARE IF SHE'S BLACKLISTED EVERYWHERE, BUT I'D LIKE TO FEEL WELCOME SOMEWHERE.
WHY DO I CARE ABOUT FEELING WELCOME HERE THOUGH?
WHAT AM I DOING WITH MY LIFE?
SCANNING NOW.
I.D. CONFIRMED. SALLY SOOLIN--FIRST MATE ABOARD THE RESTAL-08, BECSTAR'S RIGHT HAND.
SHE CAN'T BE FAR. ALL AVAILABLE UNITS CONVERGE ON THE TIMAEUS CASINO.

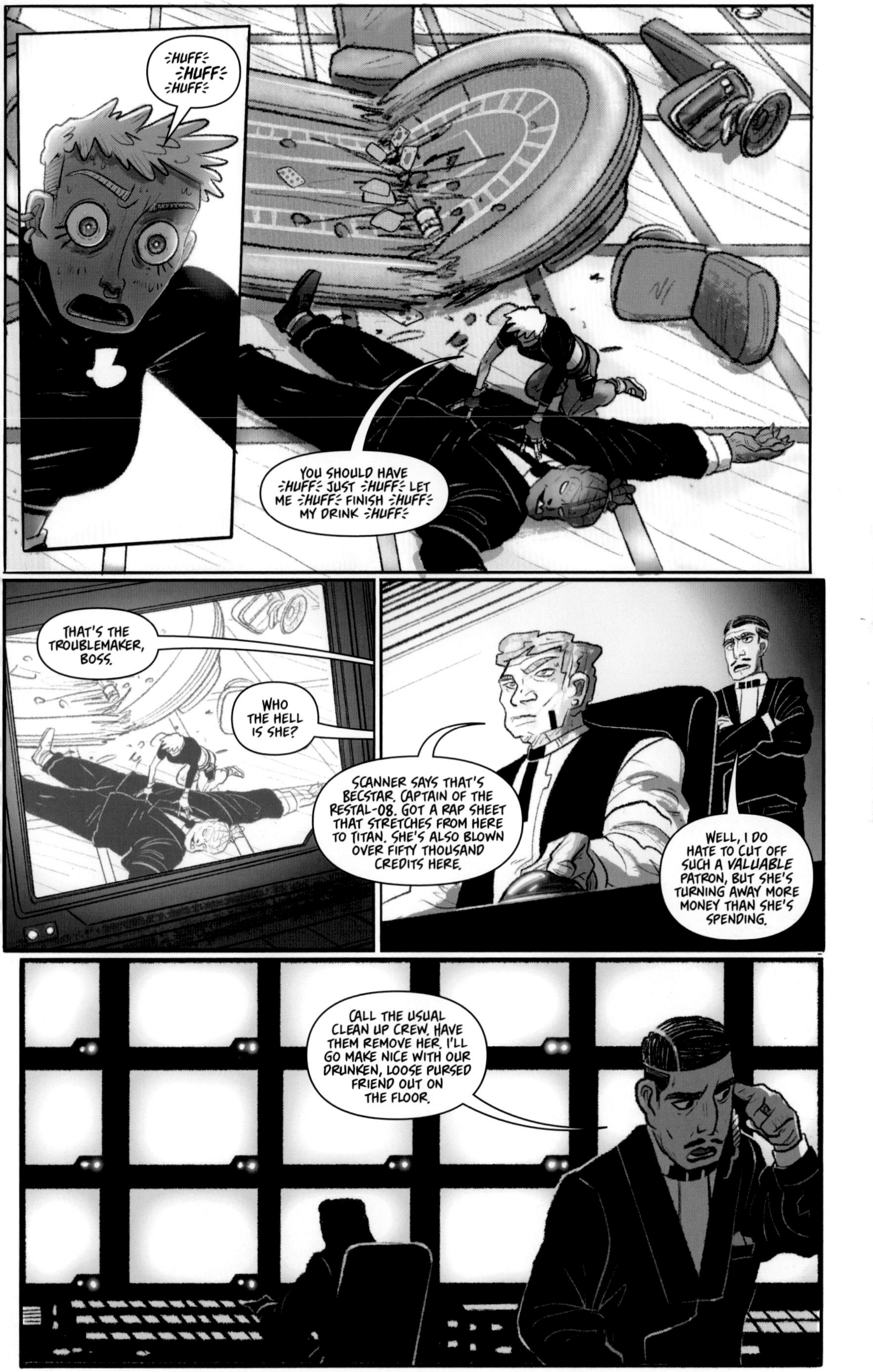

HUFF HUFF HUFF
YOU SHOULD HAVE HUFF JUST HUFF LET ME HUFF FINISH HUFF MY DRINK HUFF
THAT'S THE TROUBLEMAKER, BOSS.
WHO THE HELL IS SHE?
SCANNER SAYS THAT'S BECSTAR. CAPTAIN OF THE RESTAL-08. GOT A RAP SHEET THAT STRETCHES FROM HERE TO TITAN. SHE'S ALSO BLOWN OVER FIFTY THOUSAND CREDITS HERE.
WELL, I DO HATE TO CUT OFF SUCH A VALUABLE PATRON, BUT SHE'S TURNING AWAY MORE MONEY THAN SHE'S SPENDING.
CALL THE USUAL CLEAN UP CREW. HAVE THEM REMOVE HER. I'LL GO MAKE NICE WITH OUR DRUNKEN, LOOSE PURSED FRIEND OUT ON THE FLOOR.

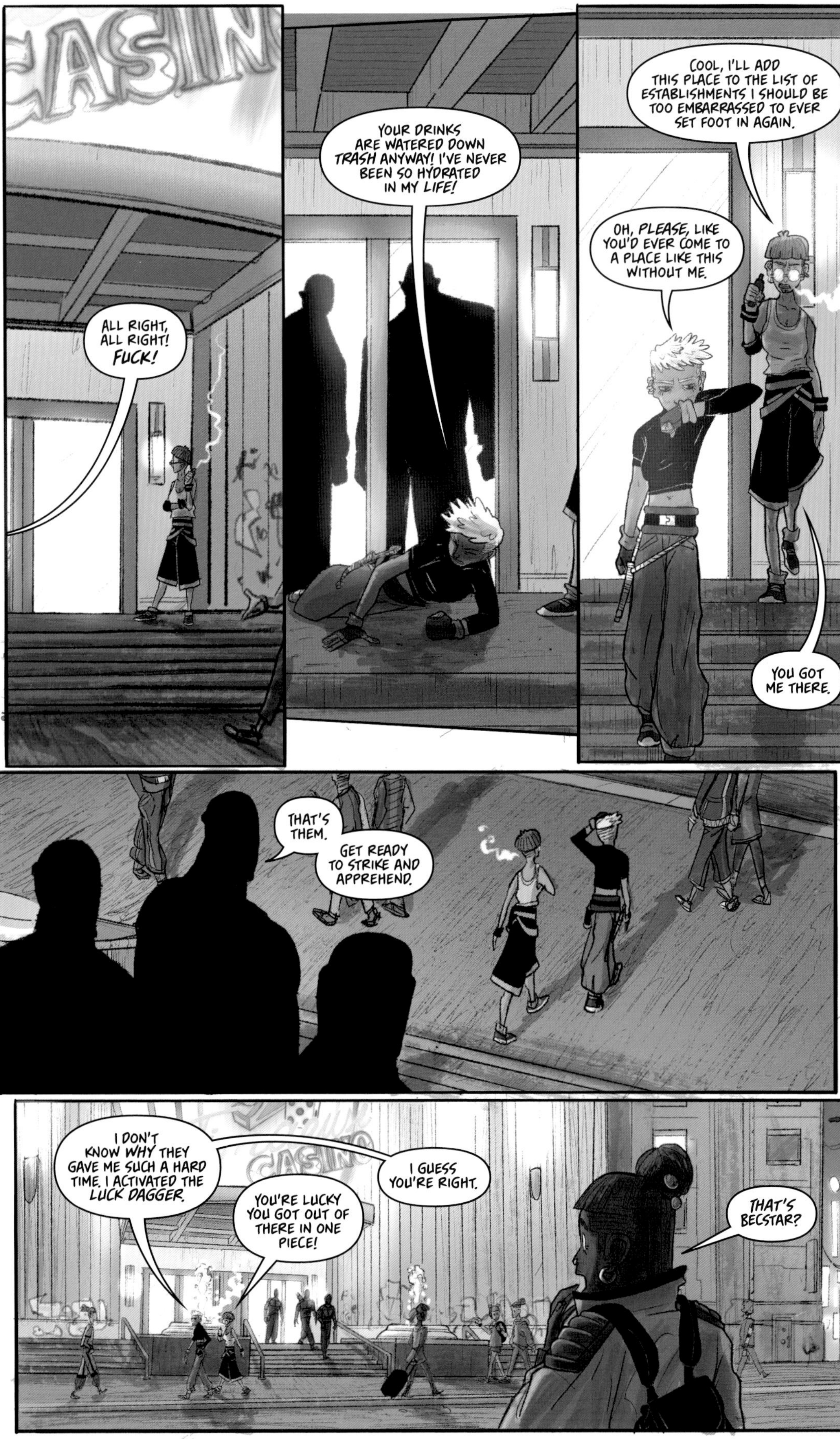
ALL RIGHT, ALL RIGHT! FUCK!
YOUR DRINKS ARE WATERED DOWN TRASH ANYWAY! I'VE NEVER BEEN SO HYDRATED IN MY LIFE!
COOL, I'LL ADD THIS PLACE TO THE LIST OF ESTABLISHMENTS I SHOULD BE TOO EMBARRASSED TO EVER SET FOOT IN AGAIN.
OH, PLEASE, LIKE YOU'D EVER COME TO A PLACE LIKE THIS WITHOUT ME.
YOU GOT ME THERE.
THAT'S THEM.
GET READY TO STRIKE AND APPREHEND.
I DON'T KNOW WHY THEY GAVE ME SUCH A HARD TIME. I ACTIVATED THE LUCK DAGGER.
YOU'RE LUCKY YOU GOT OUT OF THERE IN ONE PIECE!
I GUESS YOU'RE RIGHT.
THAT'S BECSTAR?

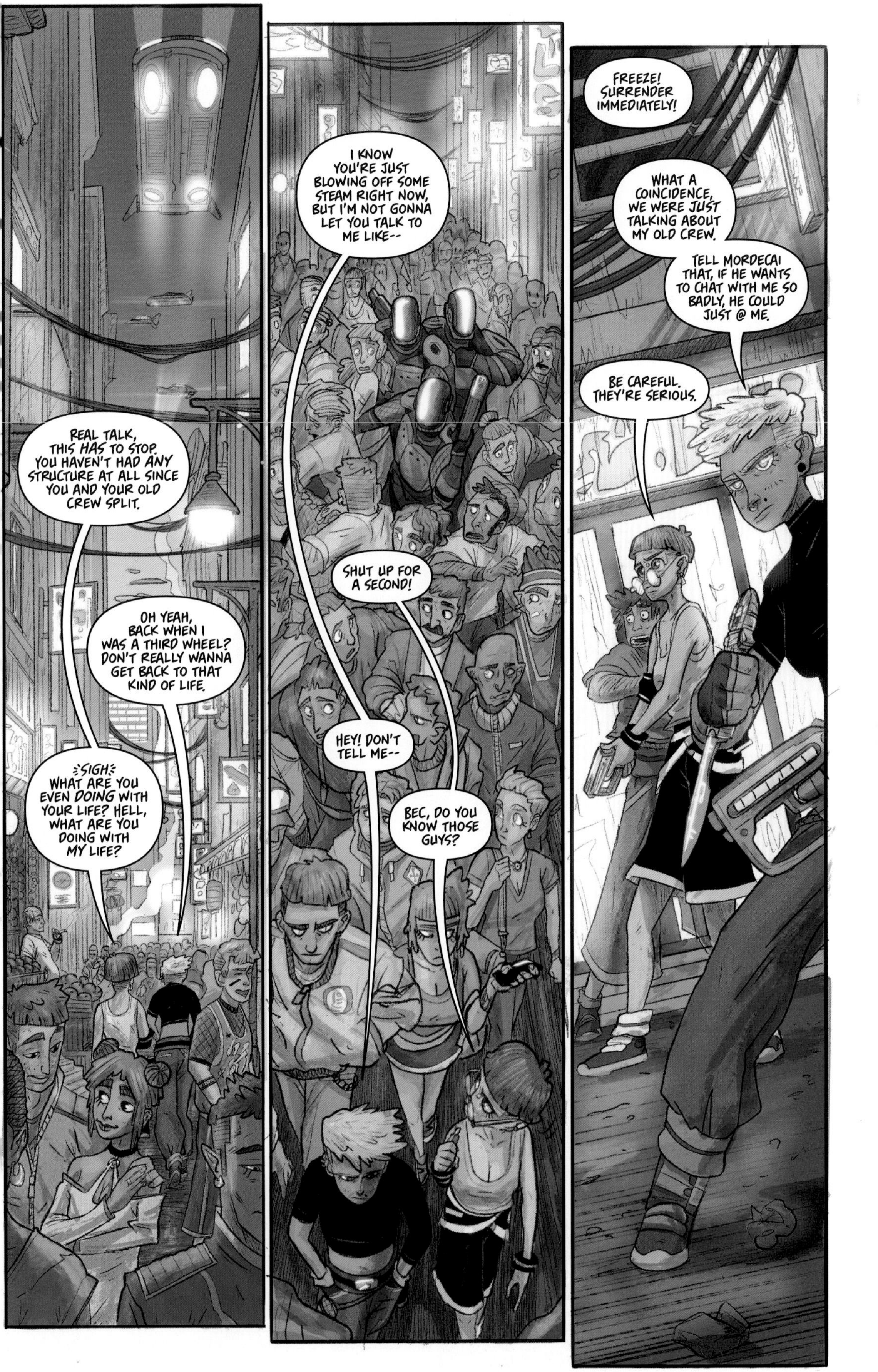
REAL TALK, THIS HAS TO STOP. YOU HAVEN'T HAD ANY STRUCTURE AT ALL SINCE YOU AND YOUR OLD CREW SPLIT.
OH YEAH, BACK WHEN I WAS A THIRD WHEEL? DON'T REALLY WANNA GET BACK TO THAT KIND OF LIFE.
SIGH
WHAT ARE YOU EVEN DOING WITH YOUR LIFE? HELL, WHAT ARE YOU DOING WITH MY LIFE?
I KNOW YOU'RE JUST BLOWING OFF SOME STEAM RIGHT NOW, BUT I'M NOT GONNA LET YOU TALK TO ME LIKE--
SHUT UP FOR A SECOND!
HEY! DON'T TELL ME--
BEC, DO YOU KNOW THOSE GUYS?
FREEZE! SURRENDER IMMEDIATELY!
WHAT A COINCIDENCE, WE WERE JUST TALKING ABOUT MY OLD CREW.
TELL MORDECAI THAT, IF HE WANTS TO CHAT WITH ME SO BADLY, HE COULD JUST @ ME.
BE CAREFUL. THEY'RE SERIOUS.

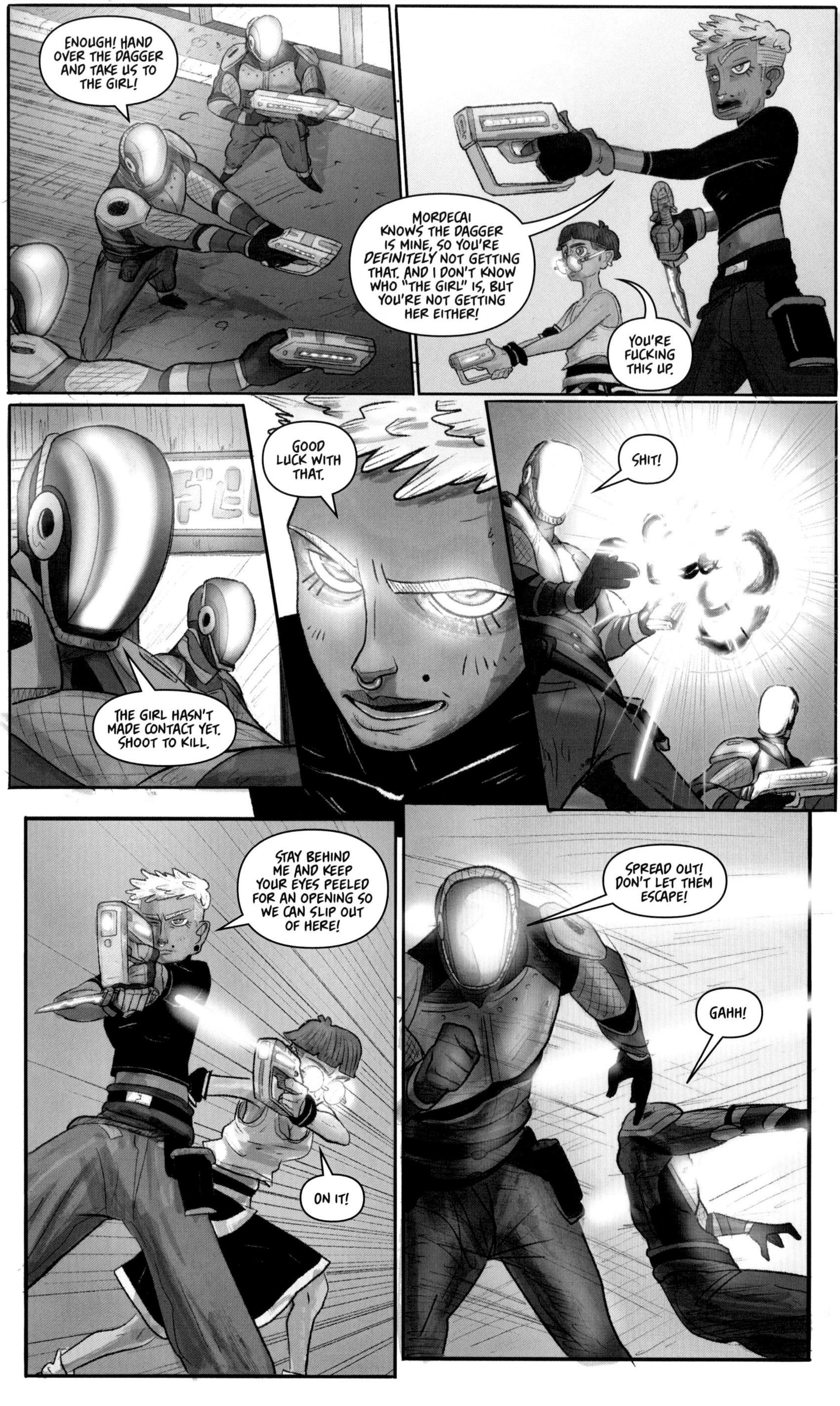
ENOUGH! HAND OVER THE DAGGER AND TAKE US TO THE GIRL!
MORDECAI KNOWS THE DAGGER IS MINE, SO YOU'RE DEFINITELY NOT GETTING THAT. AND I DON'T KNOW WHO "THE GIRL" IS, BUT YOU'RE NOT GETTING HER EITHER!
YOU'RE FUCKING THIS UP.
THE GIRL HASN'T MADE CONTACT YET. SHOOT TO KILL.
GOOD LUCK WITH THAT.
SHIT!
STAY BEHIND ME AND KEEP YOUR EYES PEELED FOR AN OPENING SO WE CAN SLIP OUT OF HERE!
ON IT!
SPREAD OUT! DON'T LET THEM ESCAPE!
GAHH!

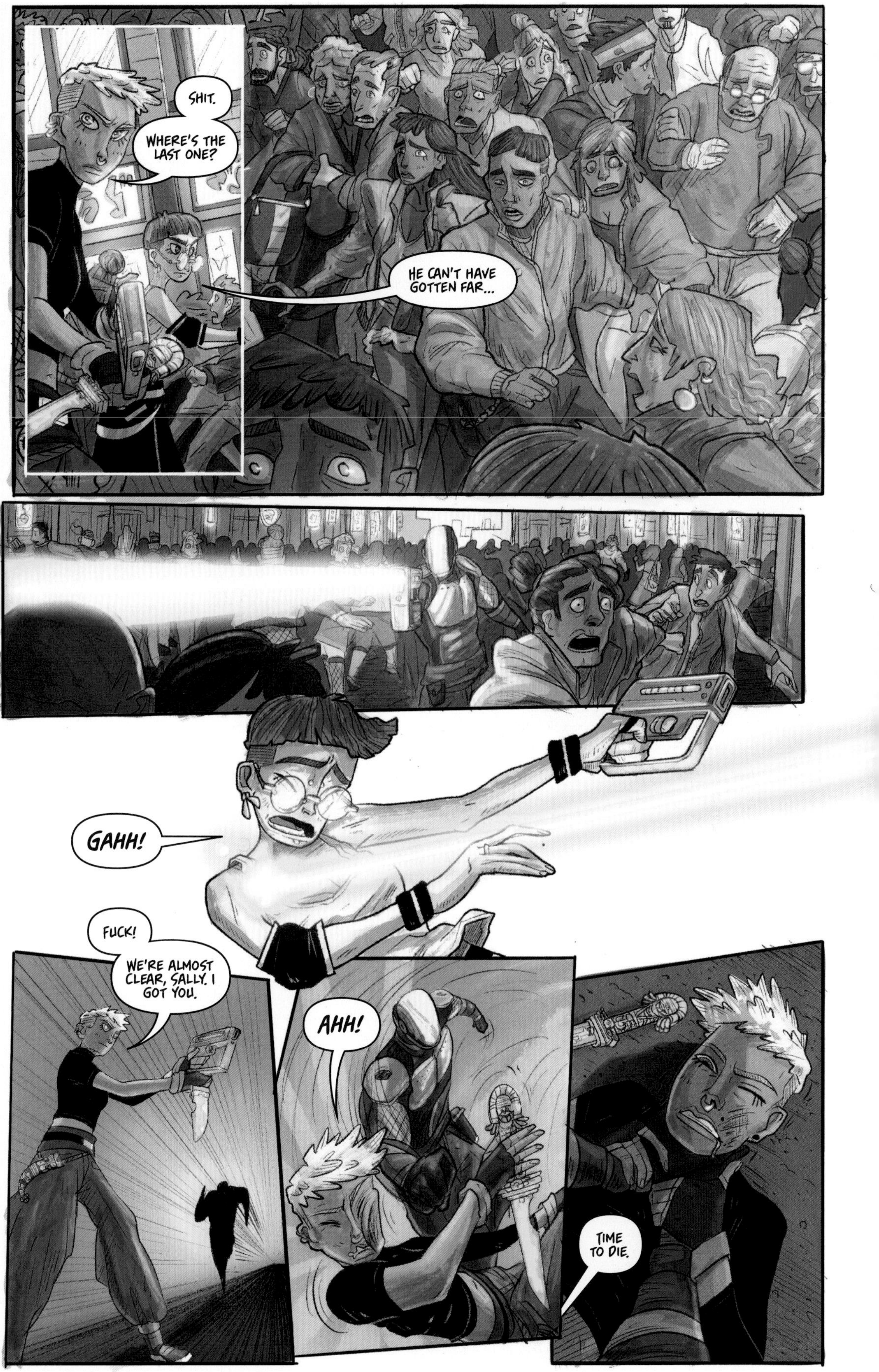
SHIT.
WHERE'S THE LAST ONE?
HE CAN'T HAVE GOTTEN FAR...
GAHH!
FUCK!
WE'RE ALMOST CLEAR, SALLY. I GOT YOU.
AHH!
TIME TO DIE.

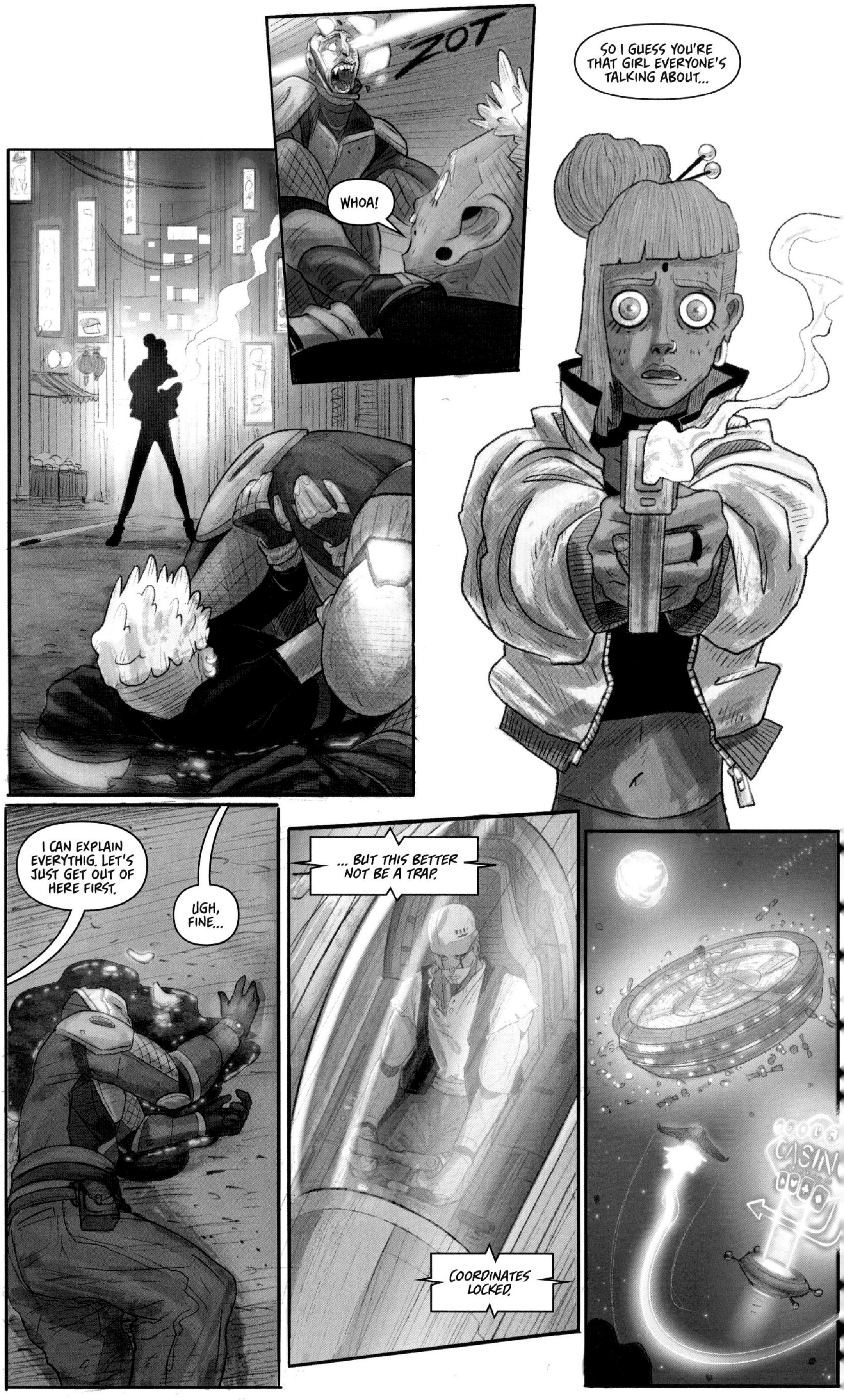
ZOT
WHOA!
SO I GUESS YOU'RE THAT GIRL EVERYONE'S TALKING ABOUT...
I CAN EXPLAIN EVERYTHIG. LET'S JUST GET OUT OF HERE FIRST.
UGH, FINE...
... BUT THIS BETTER NOT BE A TRAP.
COORDINATES LOCKED.
CASIN

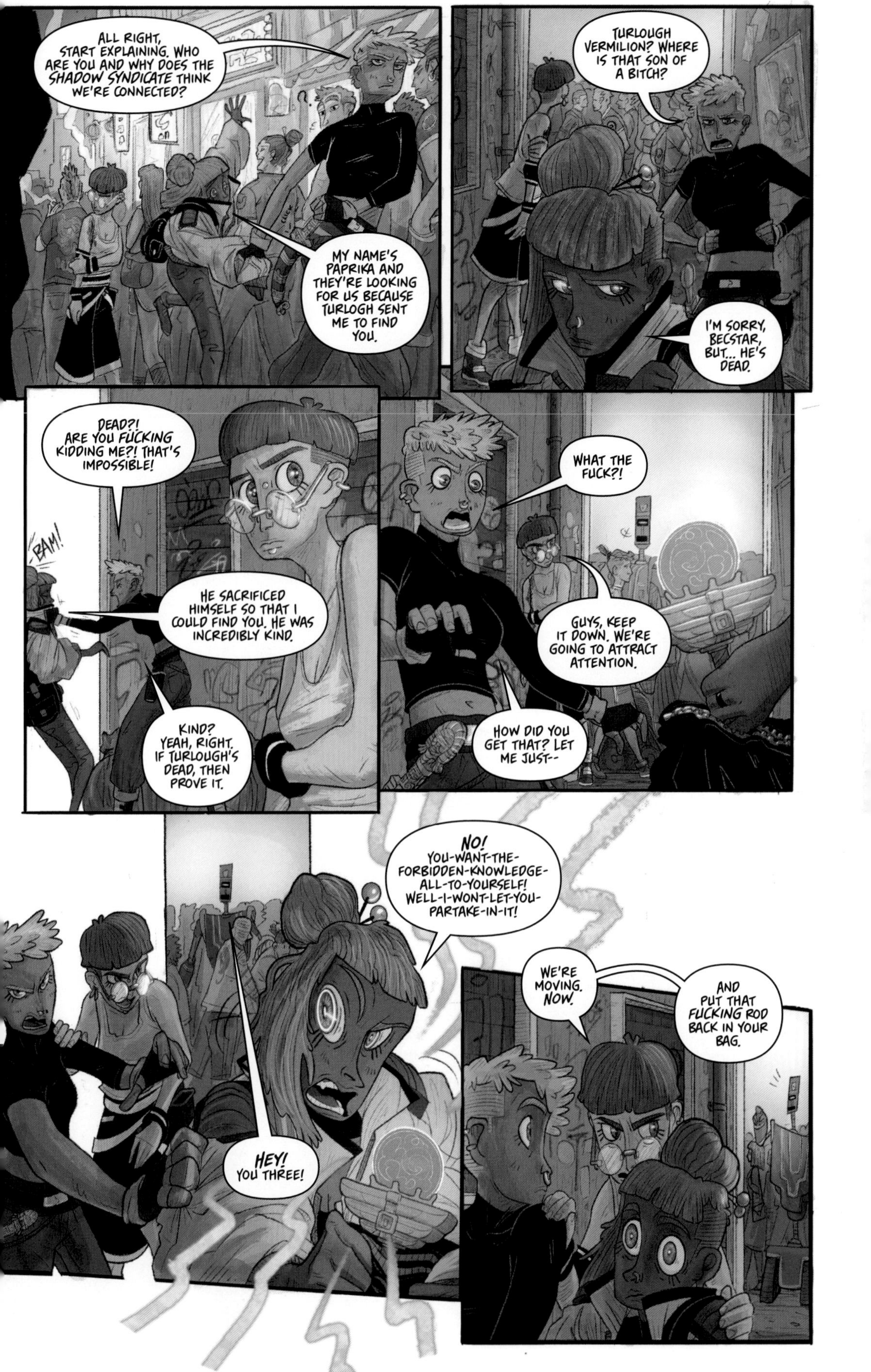
ALL RIGHT, START EXPLAINING. WHO ARE YOU AND WHY DOES THE SHADOW SYNDICATE THINK WE'RE CONNECTED?
MY NAME'S PAPRIKA AND THEY'RE LOOKING FOR US BECAUSE TURLOUGH SENT ME TO FIND YOU.
TURLOUGH VERMILION? WHERE IS THAT SON OF A BITCH?
I'M SORRY, BECSTAR, BUT... HE'S DEAD.
DEAD?! ARE YOU FUCKING KIDDING ME?! THAT'S IMPOSSIBLE!
BAM!
HE SACRIFICED HIMSELF SO THAT I COULD FIND YOU. HE WAS INCREDIBLY KIND.
KIND? YEAH, RIGHT. IF TURLOUGH'S DEAD, THEN PROVE IT.
WHAT THE FUCK?!
GUYS, KEEP IT DOWN. WE'RE GOING TO ATTRACT ATTENTION.
HOW DID YOU GET THAT? LET ME JUST--
NO! YOU-WANT-THE-FORBIDDEN-KNOWLEDGE-ALL-TO-YOURSELF! WELL-I-WONT-LET-YOU-PARTAKE-IN-IT!
HEY! YOU THREE!
WE'RE MOVING. NOW.
AND PUT THAT FUCKING ROD BACK IN YOUR BAG.

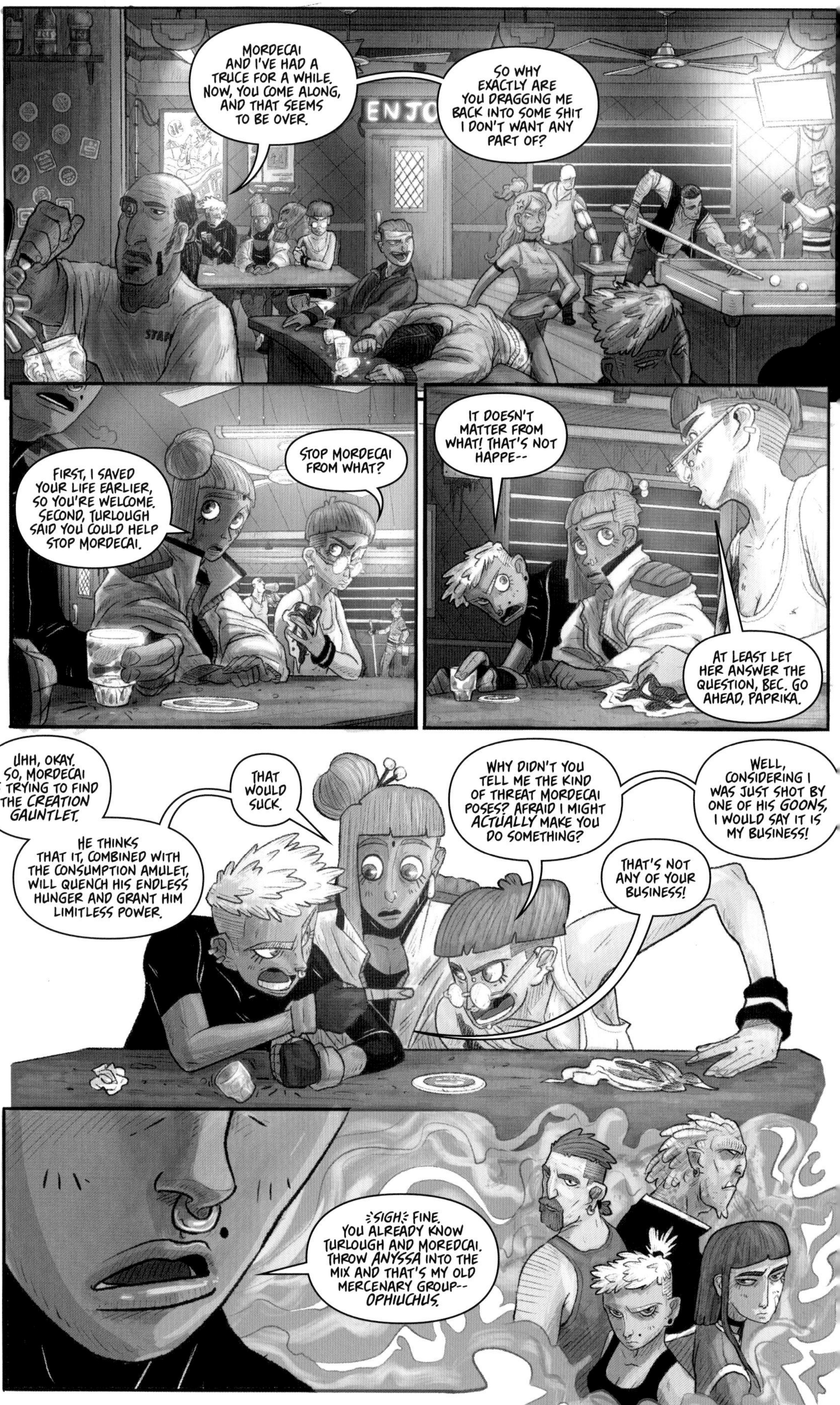
ENJO
MORDECAI AND I'VE HAD A TRUCE FOR A WHILE. NOW, YOU COME ALONG, AND THAT SEEMS TO BE OVER.
SO WHY EXACTLY ARE YOU DRAGGING ME BACK INTO SOME SHIT I DON'T WANT ANY PART OF?
STAFF
FIRST, I SAVED YOUR LIFE EARLIER, SO YOU'RE WELCOME. SECOND, TURLOUGH SAID YOU COULD HELP STOP MORDECAI.
STOP MORDECAI FROM WHAT?
IT DOESN'T MATTER FROM WHAT! THAT'S NOT HAPPE--
AT LEAST LET HER ANSWER THE QUESTION, BEC. GO AHEAD, PAPRIKA.
UHH, OKAY. SO, MORDECAI IS TRYING TO FIND THE *CREATION GAUNTLET*.
HE THINKS THAT IT, COMBINED WITH THE CONSUMPTION AMULET, WILL QUENCH HIS ENDLESS HUNGER AND GRANT HIM LIMITLESS POWER.
THAT WOULD SUCK.
WHY DIDN'T YOU TELL ME THE KIND OF THREAT MORDECAI POSES? AFRAID I MIGHT *ACTUALLY* MAKE YOU DO SOMETHING?
THAT'S NOT ANY OF YOUR BUSINESS!
WELL, CONSIDERING I WAS JUST SHOT BY ONE OF HIS *GOONS*, I WOULD SAY IT IS MY BUSINESS!
SIGH FINE. YOU ALREADY KNOW TURLOUGH AND MOREDCAI. THROW *ANYSSA* INTO THE MIX AND THAT'S MY OLD MERCENARY GROUP-- *OPHIUCHUS*.

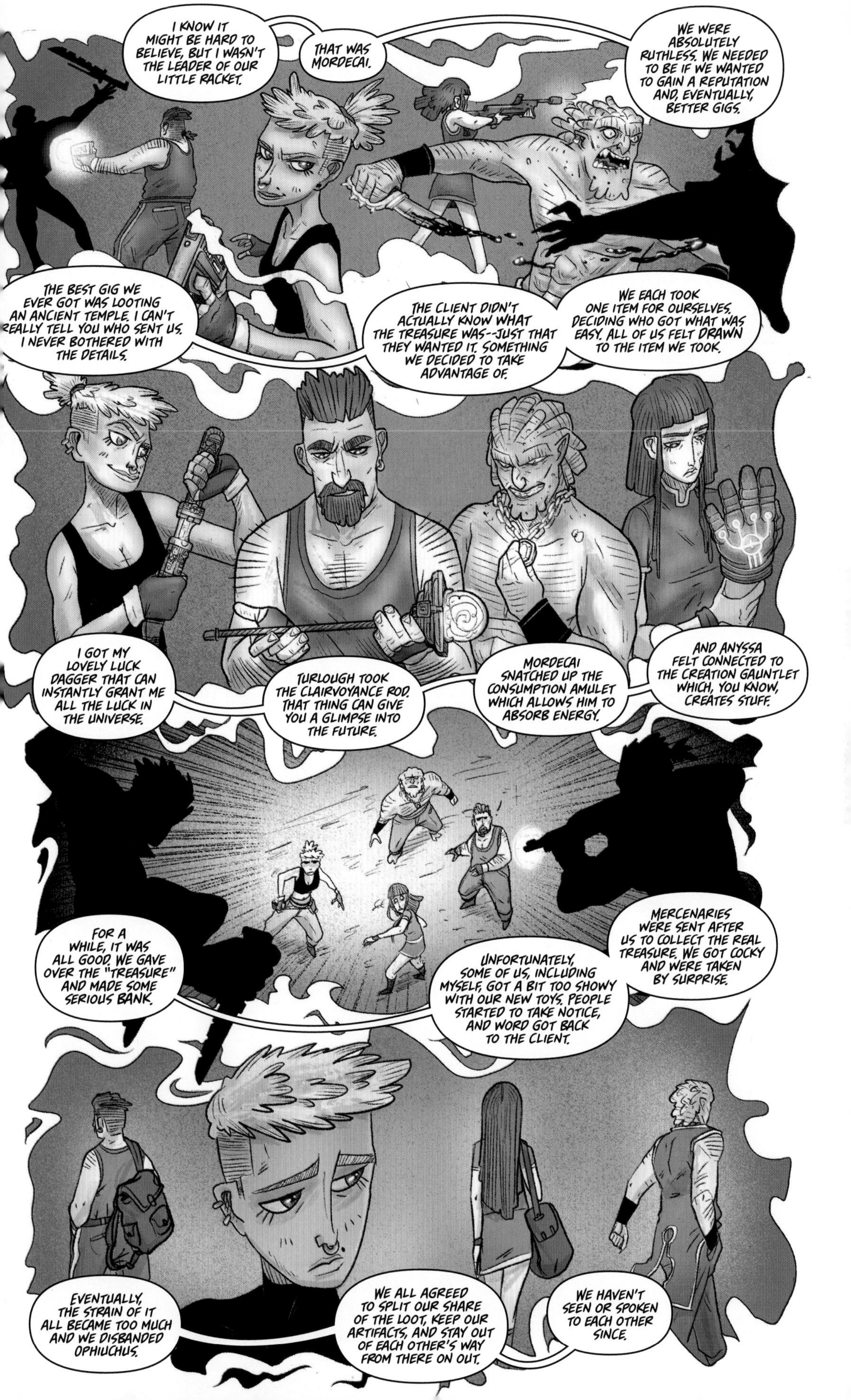
I KNOW IT MIGHT BE HARD TO BELIEVE, BUT I WASN'T THE LEADER OF OUR LITTLE RACKET.
THAT WAS MORDECAI.
WE WERE ABSOLUTELY RUTHLESS. WE NEEDED TO BE IF WE WANTED TO GAIN A REPUTATION AND, EVENTUALLY, BETTER GIGS.
THE BEST GIG WE EVER GOT WAS LOOTING AN ANCIENT TEMPLE. I CAN'T REALLY TELL YOU WHO SENT US. I NEVER BOTHERED WITH THE DETAILS.
THE CLIENT DIDN'T ACTUALLY KNOW WHAT THE TREASURE WAS--JUST THAT THEY WANTED IT. SOMETHING WE DECIDED TO TAKE ADVANTAGE OF.
WE EACH TOOK ONE ITEM FOR OURSELVES. DECIDING WHO GOT WHAT WAS EASY. ALL OF US FELT DRAWN TO THE ITEM WE TOOK.
I GOT MY LOVELY LUCK DAGGER THAT CAN INSTANTLY GRANT ME ALL THE LUCK IN THE UNIVERSE.
TURLOUGH TOOK THE CLAIRVOYANCE ROD. THAT THING CAN GIVE YOU A GLIMPSE INTO THE FUTURE.
MORDECAI SNATCHED UP THE CONSUMPTION AMULET WHICH ALLOWS HIM TO ABSORB ENERGY.
AND ANYSSA FELT CONNECTED TO THE CREATION GAUNTLET WHICH, YOU KNOW, CREATES STUFF.
FOR A WHILE, IT WAS ALL GOOD. WE GAVE OVER THE "TREASURE" AND MADE SOME SERIOUS BANK.
UNFORTUNATELY, SOME OF US, INCLUDING MYSELF, GOT A BIT TOO SHOWY WITH OUR NEW TOYS. PEOPLE STARTED TO TAKE NOTICE, AND WORD GOT BACK TO THE CLIENT.
MERCENARIES WERE SENT AFTER US TO COLLECT THE REAL TREASURE. WE GOT COCKY AND WERE TAKEN BY SURPRISE.
EVENTUALLY, THE STRAIN OF IT ALL BECAME TOO MUCH AND WE DISBANDED OPHIUCHUS.
WE ALL AGREED TO SPLIT OUR SHARE OF THE LOOT, KEEP OUR ARTIFACTS, AND STAY OUT OF EACH OTHER'S WAY FROM THERE ON OUT.
WE HAVEN'T SEEN OR SPOKEN TO EACH OTHER SINCE.

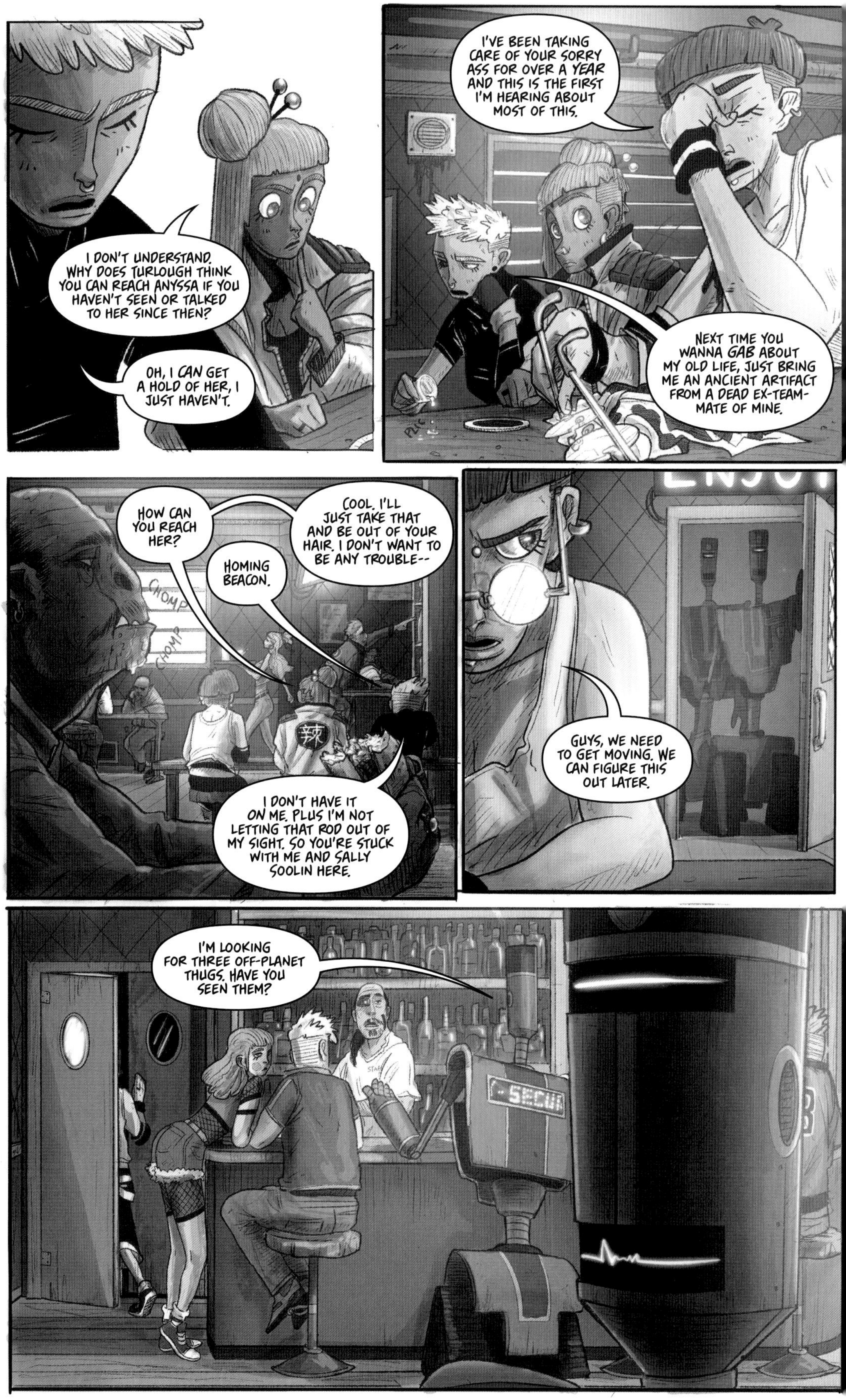
I DON'T UNDERSTAND. WHY DOES TURLOUGH THINK YOU CAN REACH ANYSSA IF YOU HAVEN'T SEEN OR TALKED TO HER SINCE THEN?
OH, I CAN GET A HOLD OF HER, I JUST HAVEN'T.
I'VE BEEN TAKING CARE OF YOUR SORRY ASS FOR OVER A YEAR AND THIS IS THE FIRST I'M HEARING ABOUT MOST OF THIS.
NEXT TIME YOU WANNA GAB ABOUT MY OLD LIFE, JUST BRING ME AN ANCIENT ARTIFACT FROM A DEAD EX-TEAM-MATE OF MINE.
PLIC
HOW CAN YOU REACH HER?
COOL. I'LL JUST TAKE THAT AND BE OUT OF YOUR HAIR. I DON'T WANT TO BE ANY TROUBLE--
HOMING BEACON.
CHOMP
CHOMP
I DON'T HAVE IT ON ME. PLUS I'M NOT LETTING THAT ROD OUT OF MY SIGHT. SO YOU'RE STUCK WITH ME AND SALLY SOOLIN HERE.
GUYS, WE NEED TO GET MOVING. WE CAN FIGURE THIS OUT LATER.
I'M LOOKING FOR THREE OFF-PLANET THUGS. HAVE YOU SEEN THEM?
SECU

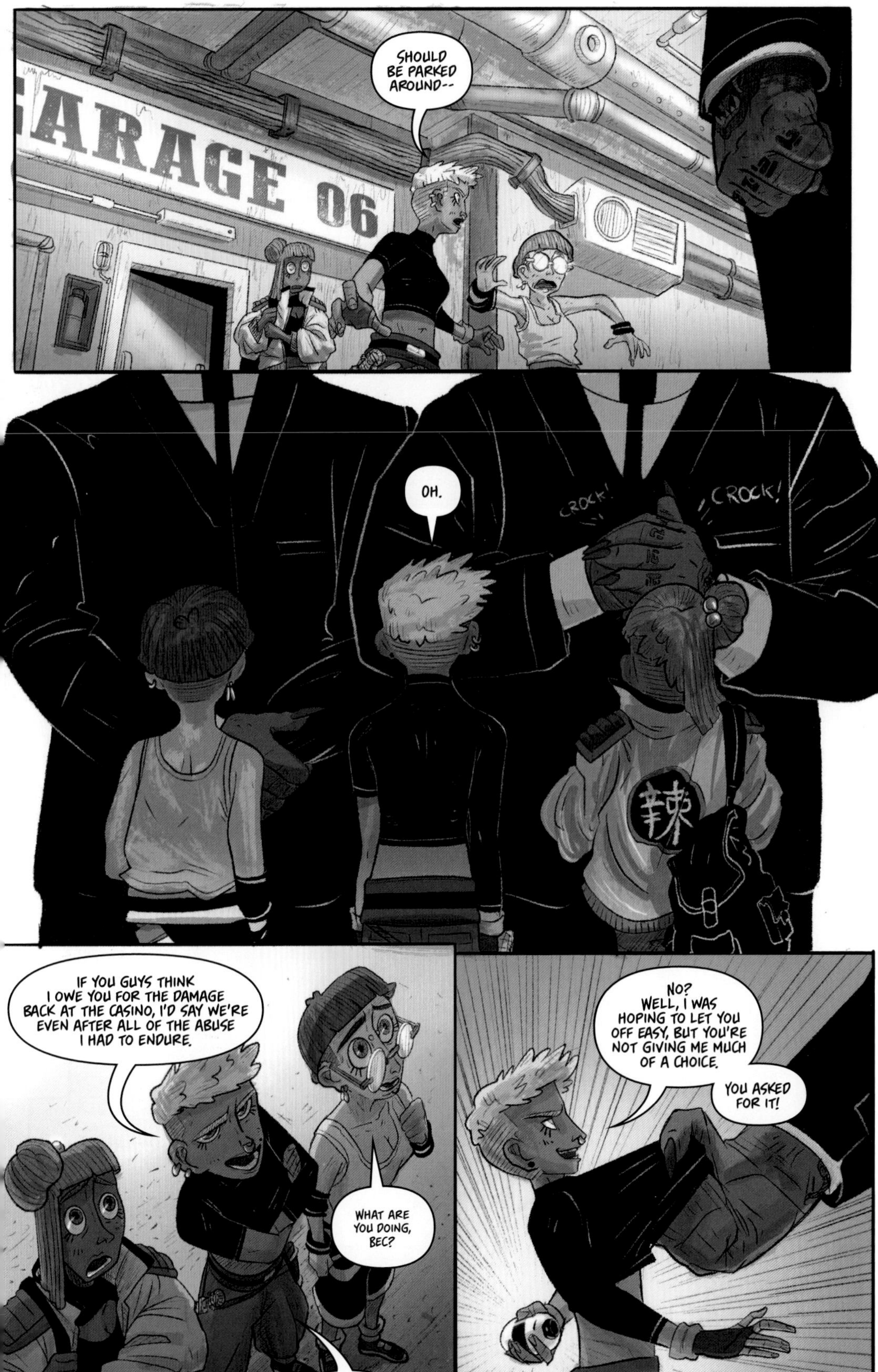
GARAGE 06
SHOULD BE PARKED AROUND--
OH.
CROCK!
CROCK!
IF YOU GUYS THINK I OWE YOU FOR THE DAMAGE BACK AT THE CASINO, I'D SAY WE'RE EVEN AFTER ALL OF THE ABUSE I HAD TO ENDURE.
WHAT ARE YOU DOING, BEC?
TRUST ME.
NO? WELL, I WAS HOPING TO LET YOU OFF EASY, BUT YOU'RE NOT GIVING ME MUCH OF A CHOICE.
YOU ASKED FOR IT!

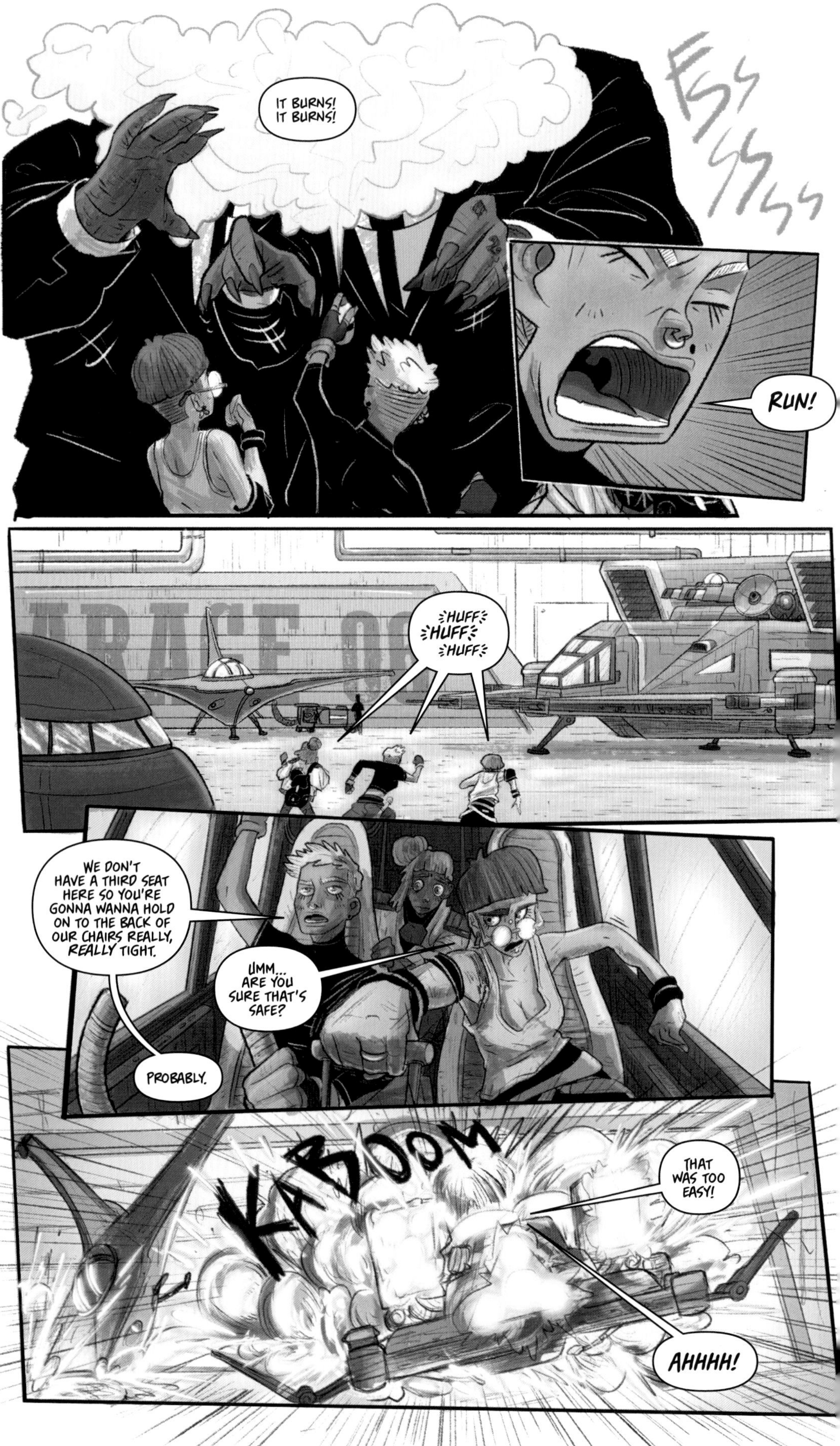
IT BURNS! IT BURNS!
RUN!
HUFF HUFF HUFF
WE DON'T HAVE A THIRD SEAT HERE SO YOU'RE GONNA WANNA HOLD ON TO THE BACK OF OUR CHAIRS REALLY, REALLY TIGHT.
UMM... ARE YOU SURE THAT'S SAFE?
PROBABLY.
KABOOM
THAT WAS TOO EASY!
AHHHH!

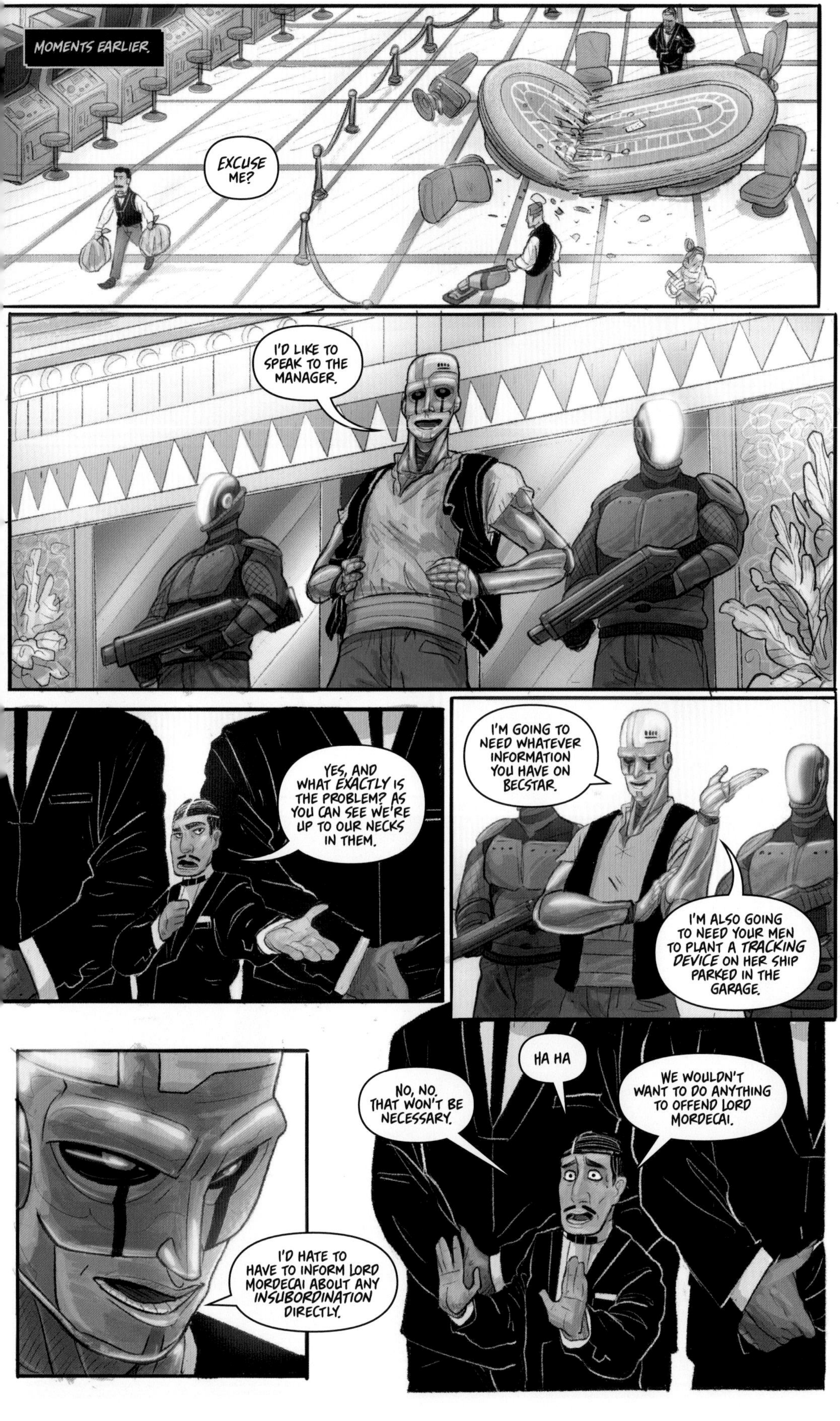
MOMENTS EARLIER.
EXCUSE ME?
I'D LIKE TO SPEAK TO THE MANAGER.
YES, AND WHAT EXACTLY IS THE PROBLEM? AS YOU CAN SEE WE'RE UP TO OUR NECKS IN THEM.
I'M GOING TO NEED WHATEVER INFORMATION YOU HAVE ON BECSTAR.
I'M ALSO GOING TO NEED YOUR MEN TO PLANT A TRACKING DEVICE ON HER SHIP PARKED IN THE GARAGE.
I'D HATE TO HAVE TO INFORM LORD MORDECAI ABOUT ANY INSUBORDINATION DIRECTLY.
NO, NO. THAT WON'T BE NECESSARY.
HA HA
WE WOULDN'T WANT TO DO ANYTHING TO OFFEND LORD MORDECAI.

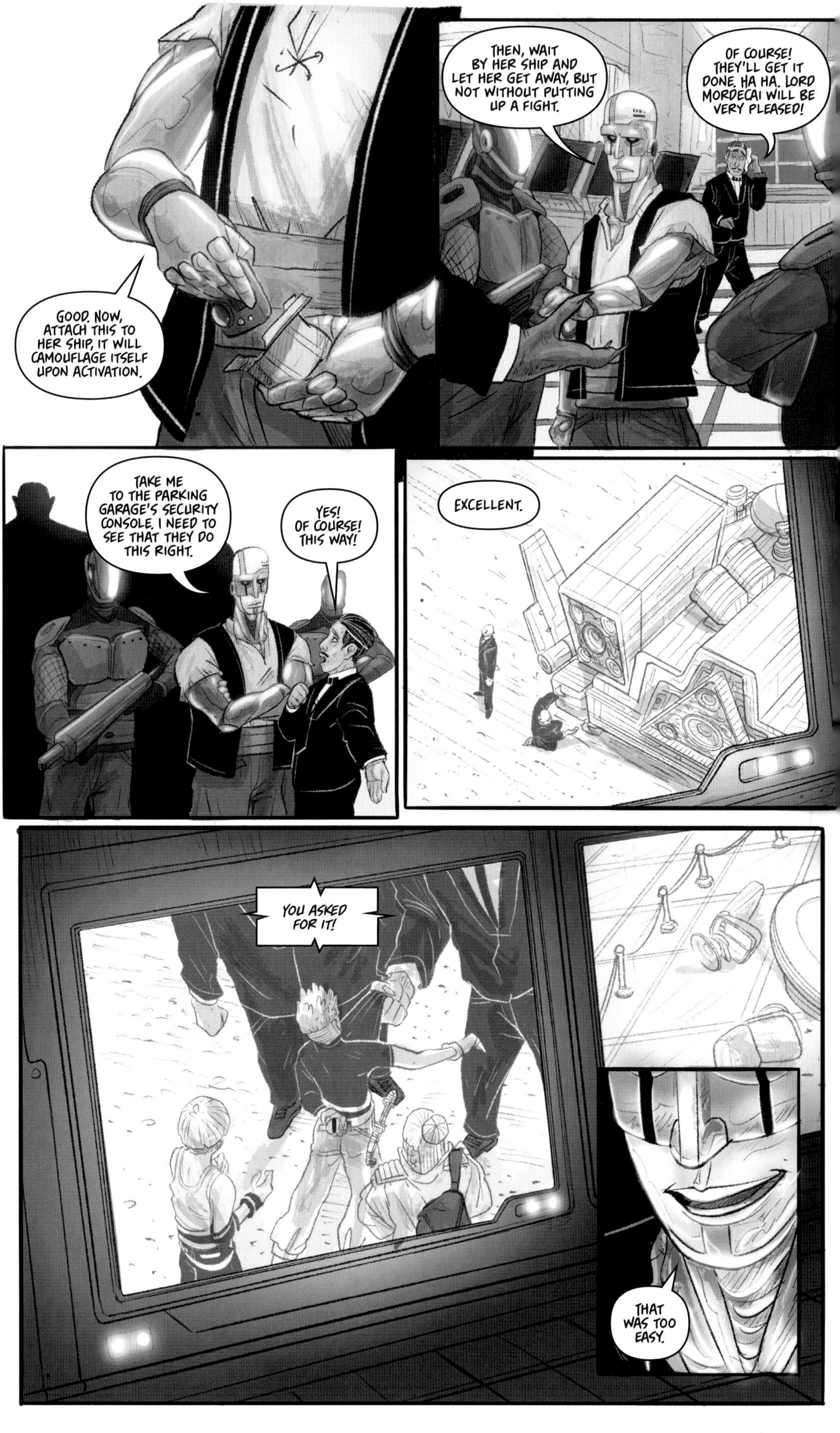
GOOD. NOW, ATTACH THIS TO HER SHIP, IT WILL CAMOUFLAGE ITSELF UPON ACTIVATION.
THEN, WAIT BY HER SHIP AND LET HER GET AWAY, BUT NOT WITHOUT PUTTING UP A FIGHT.
OF COURSE! THEY'LL GET IT DONE. HA HA. LORD MORDECAI WILL BE VERY PLEASED!
TAKE ME TO THE PARKING GARAGE'S SECURITY CONSOLE. I NEED TO SEE THAT THEY DO THIS RIGHT.
YES! OF COURSE! THIS WAY!
EXCELLENT.
YOU ASKED FOR IT!
THAT WAS TOO EASY.

PART 02

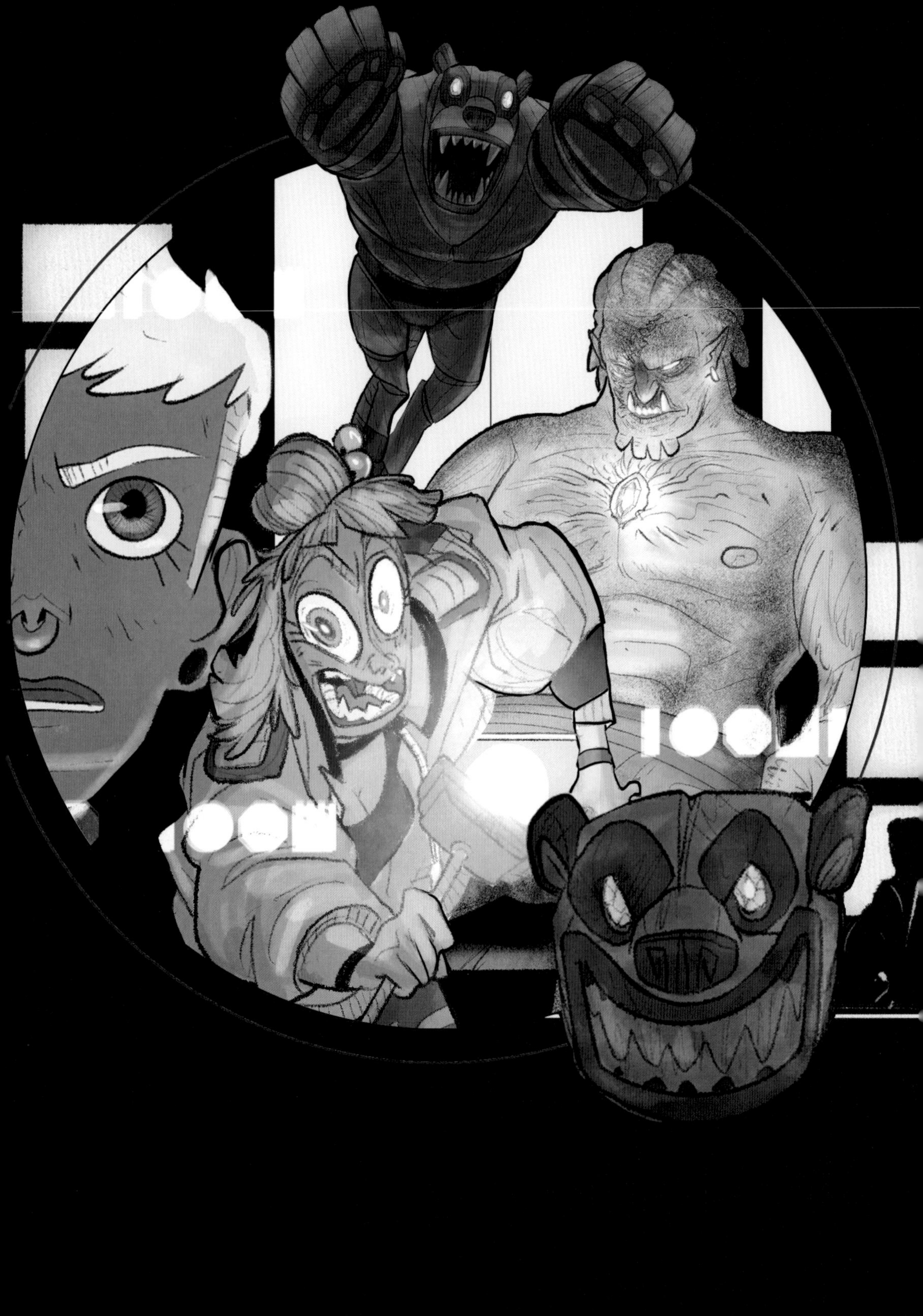

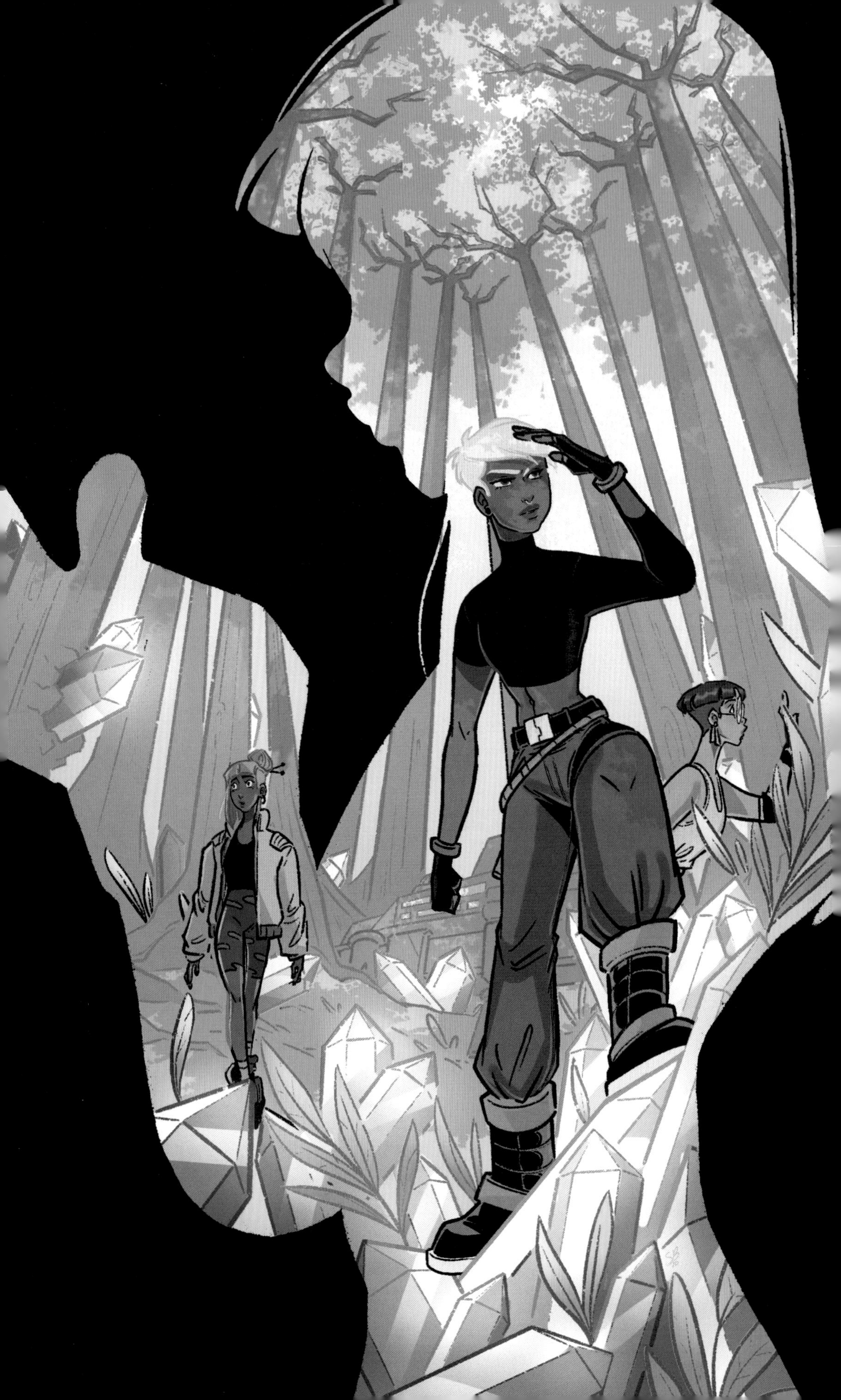

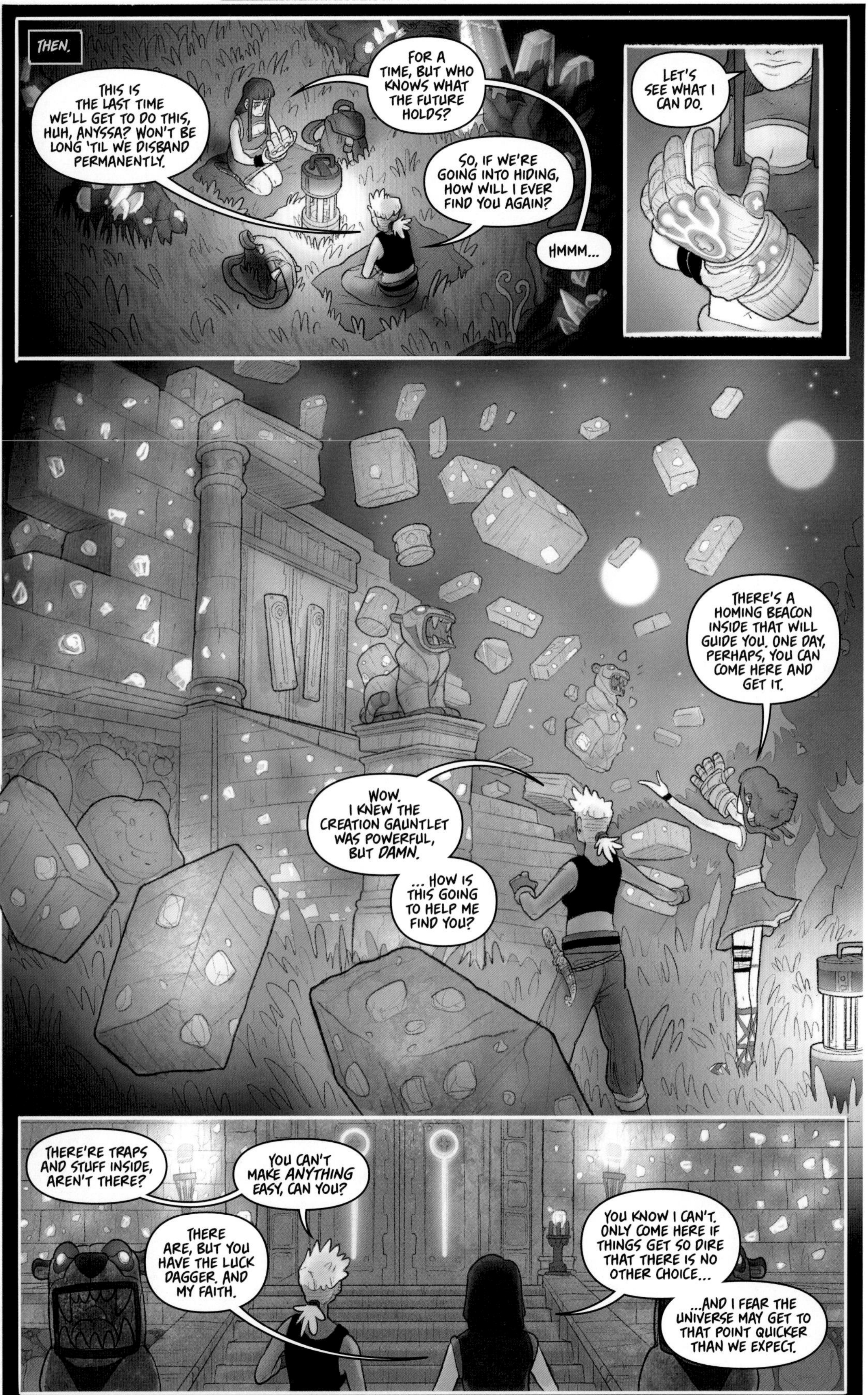
THEN.
THIS IS THE LAST TIME WE'LL GET TO DO THIS, HUH, ANYSSA? WON'T BE LONG 'TIL WE DISBAND PERMANENTLY.
FOR A TIME, BUT WHO KNOWS WHAT THE FUTURE HOLDS?
SO, IF WE'RE GOING INTO HIDING, HOW WILL I EVER FIND YOU AGAIN?
HMMM...
LET'S SEE WHAT I CAN DO.
THERE'S A HOMING BEACON INSIDE THAT WILL GUIDE YOU. ONE DAY, PERHAPS, YOU CAN COME HERE AND GET IT.
WOW. I KNEW THE CREATION GAUNTLET WAS POWERFUL, BUT *DAMN*.
... HOW IS THIS GOING TO HELP ME FIND YOU?
THERE'RE TRAPS AND STUFF INSIDE, AREN'T THERE?
THERE ARE, BUT YOU HAVE THE LUCK DAGGER. AND MY FAITH.
YOU CAN'T MAKE *ANYTHING* EASY, CAN YOU?
YOU KNOW I CAN'T. ONLY COME HERE IF THINGS GET SO DIRE THAT THERE IS NO OTHER CHOICE...
...AND I FEAR THE UNIVERSE MAY GET TO THAT POINT QUICKER THAN WE EXPECT.

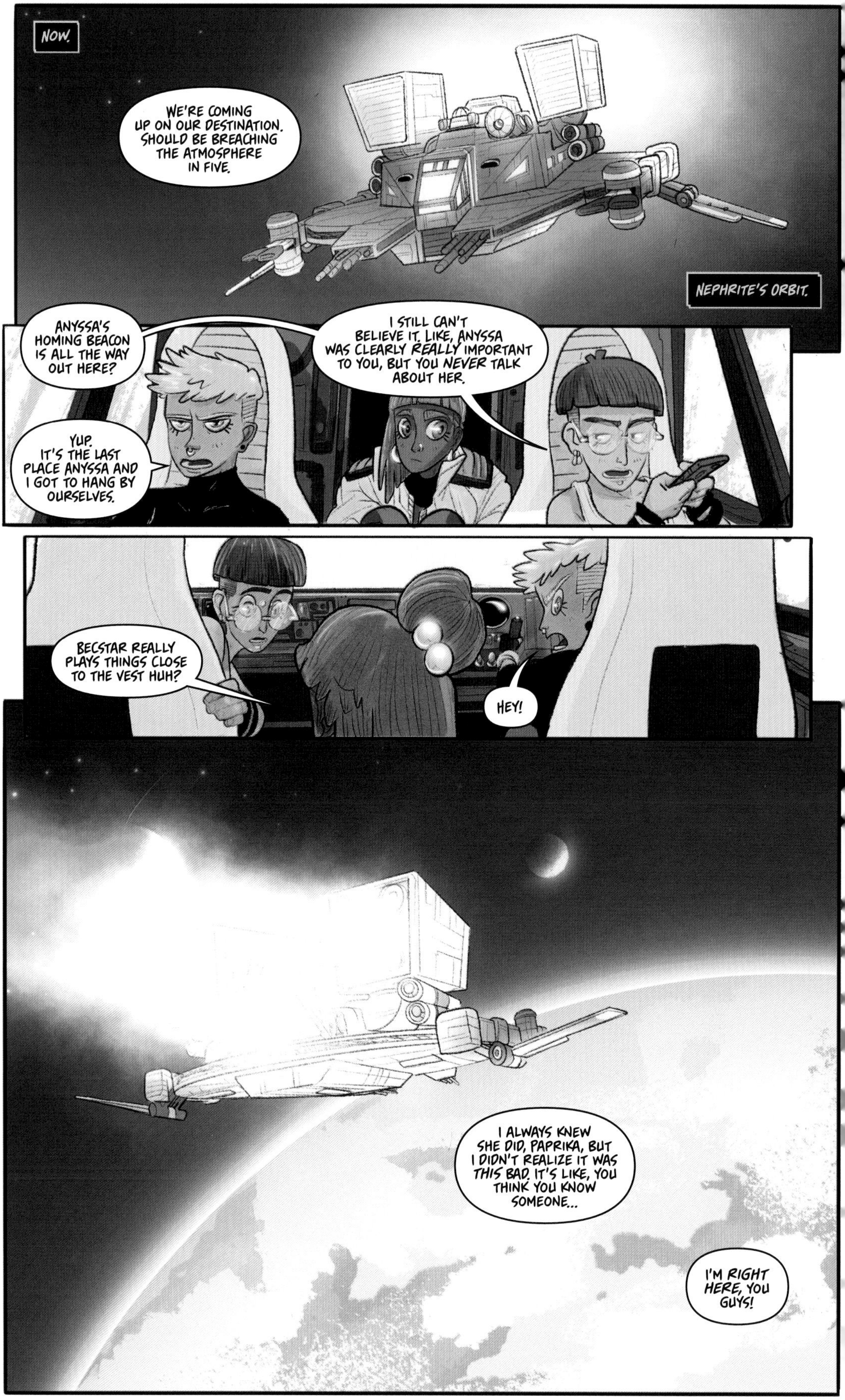
NOW.
WE'RE COMING UP ON OUR DESTINATION. SHOULD BE BREACHING THE ATMOSPHERE IN FIVE.
NEPHRITE'S ORBIT.
ANYSSA'S HOMING BEACON IS ALL THE WAY OUT HERE?
YUP. IT'S THE LAST PLACE ANYSSA AND I GOT TO HANG BY OURSELVES.
I STILL CAN'T BELIEVE IT. LIKE, ANYSSA WAS CLEARLY REALLY IMPORTANT TO YOU, BUT YOU NEVER TALK ABOUT HER.
BECSTAR REALLY PLAYS THINGS CLOSE TO THE VEST HUH?
HEY!
I ALWAYS KNEW SHE DID, PAPRIKA, BUT I DIDN'T REALIZE IT WAS THIS BAD. IT'S LIKE, YOU THINK YOU KNOW SOMEONE...
I'M RIGHT HERE, YOU GUYS!

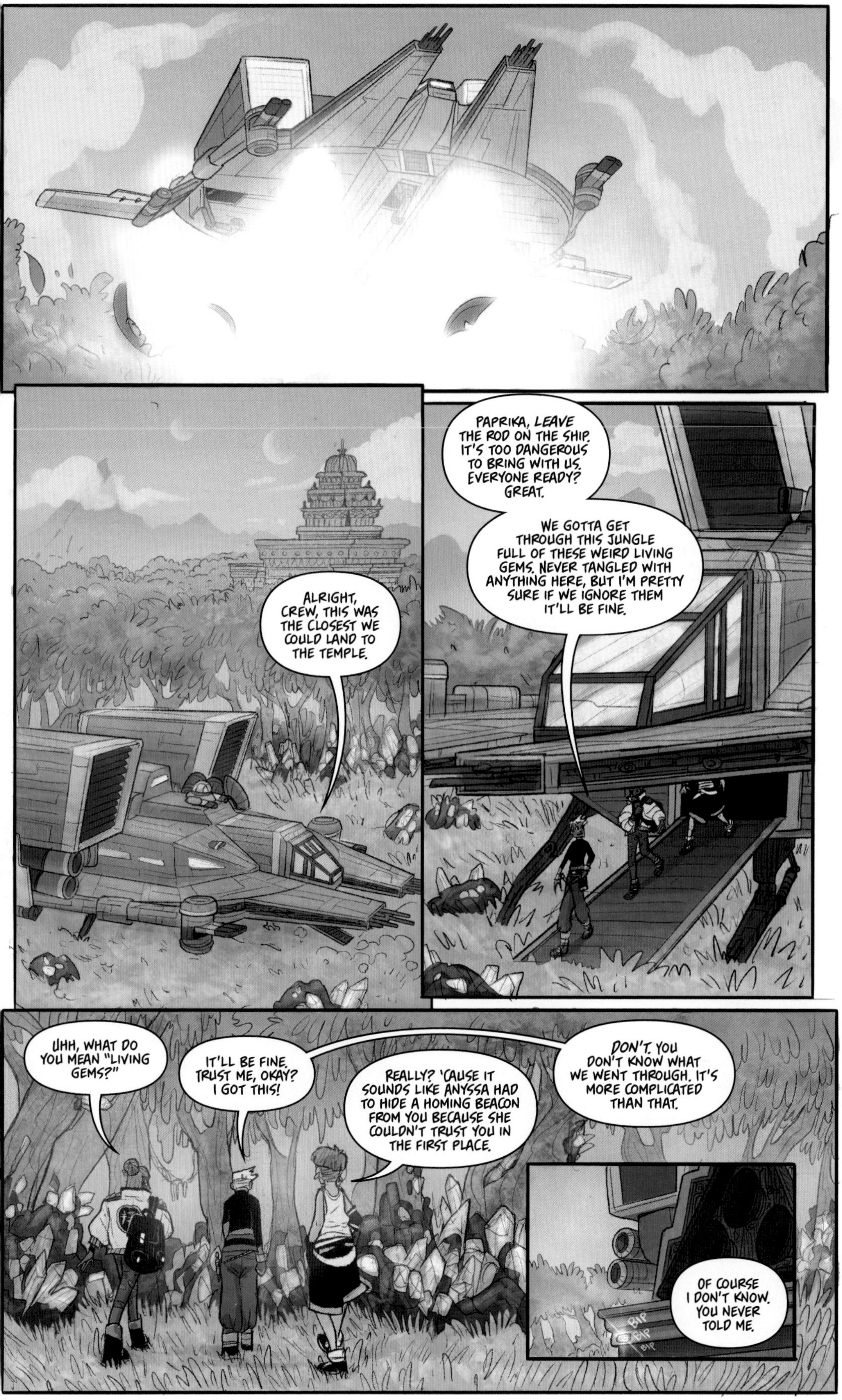
ALRIGHT, CREW, THIS WAS THE CLOSEST WE COULD LAND TO THE TEMPLE.
PAPRIKA, LEAVE THE ROD ON THE SHIP. IT'S TOO DANGEROUS TO BRING WITH US. EVERYONE READY? GREAT.
WE GOTTA GET THROUGH THIS JUNGLE FULL OF THESE WEIRD LIVING GEMS. NEVER TANGLED WITH ANYTHING HERE, BUT I'M PRETTY SURE IF WE IGNORE THEM IT'LL BE FINE.
UHH, WHAT DO YOU MEAN "LIVING GEMS?"
IT'LL BE FINE. TRUST ME, OKAY? I GOT THIS!
REALLY? 'CAUSE IT SOUNDS LIKE ANYSSA HAD TO HIDE A HOMING BEACON FROM YOU BECAUSE SHE COULDN'T TRUST YOU IN THE FIRST PLACE.
DON'T. YOU DON'T KNOW WHAT WE WENT THROUGH. IT'S MORE COMPLICATED THAN THAT.
BIP BIP BIP
OF COURSE I DON'T KNOW. YOU NEVER TOLD ME.

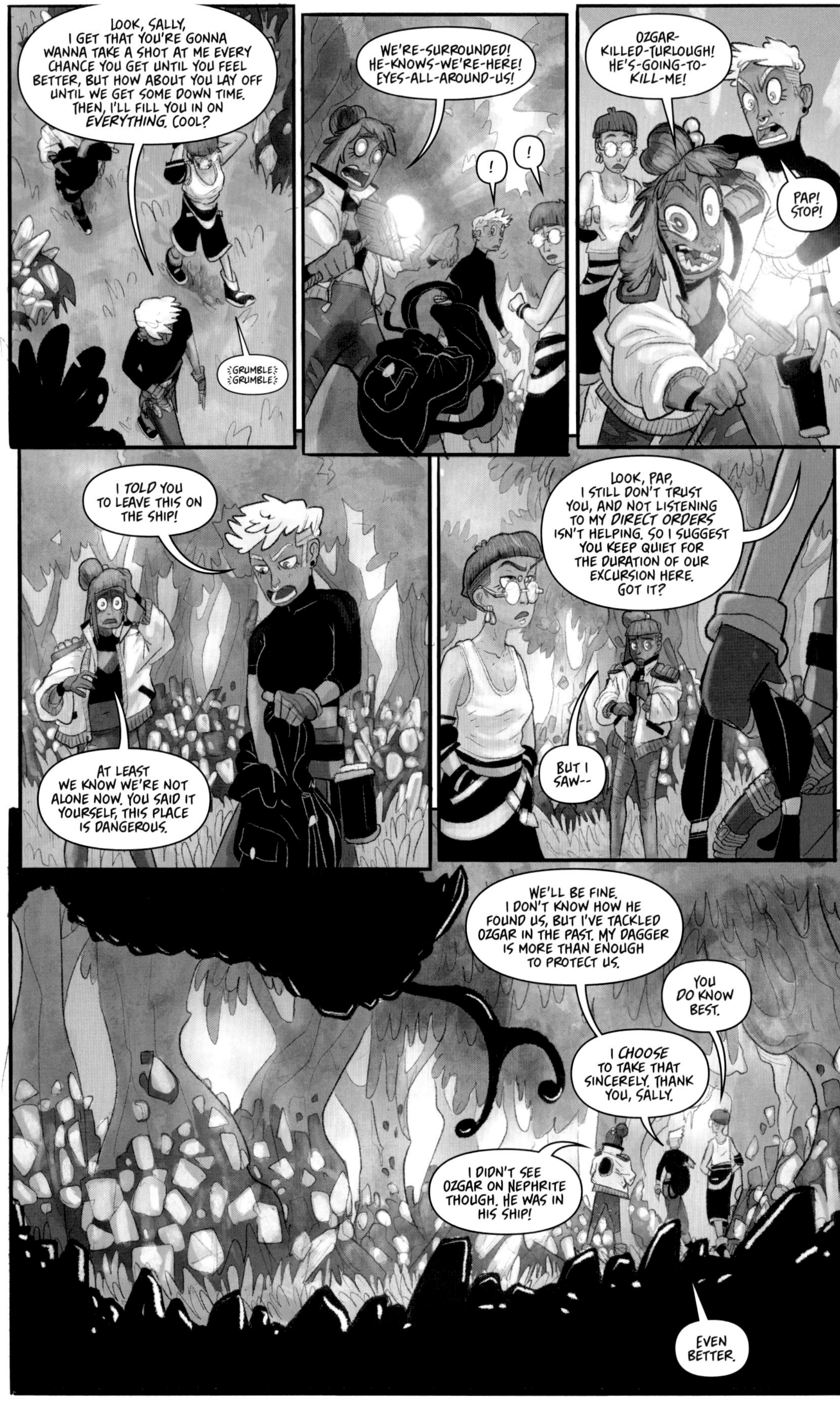
LOOK, SALLY, I GET THAT YOU'RE GONNA WANNA TAKE A SHOT AT ME EVERY CHANCE YOU GET UNTIL YOU FEEL BETTER, BUT HOW ABOUT YOU LAY OFF UNTIL WE GET SOME DOWN TIME. THEN, I'LL FILL YOU IN ON *EVERYTHING*. COOL?
GRUMBLE GRUMBLE
WE'RE-SURROUNDED! HE-KNOWS-WE'RE-HERE! EYES-ALL-AROUND-US!
!
!
OZGAR-KILLED-TURLOUGH! HE'S-GOING-TO-KILL-ME!
PAP! STOP!
I *TOLD* YOU TO LEAVE THIS ON THE SHIP!
AT LEAST WE KNOW WE'RE NOT ALONE NOW. YOU SAID IT YOURSELF, THIS PLACE IS DANGEROUS.
LOOK, PAP, I STILL DON'T TRUST YOU, AND NOT LISTENING TO MY *DIRECT ORDERS* ISN'T HELPING. SO I SUGGEST YOU KEEP QUIET FOR THE DURATION OF OUR EXCURSION HERE. GOT IT?
BUT I SAW--
WE'LL BE FINE. I DON'T KNOW HOW HE FOUND US, BUT I'VE TACKLED OZGAR IN THE PAST. MY DAGGER IS MORE THAN ENOUGH TO PROTECT US.
YOU DO KNOW BEST.
I *CHOOSE* TO TAKE THAT SINCERELY. THANK YOU, SALLY.
I DIDN'T SEE OZGAR ON NEPHRITE THOUGH. HE WAS IN HIS SHIP!
EVEN BETTER.

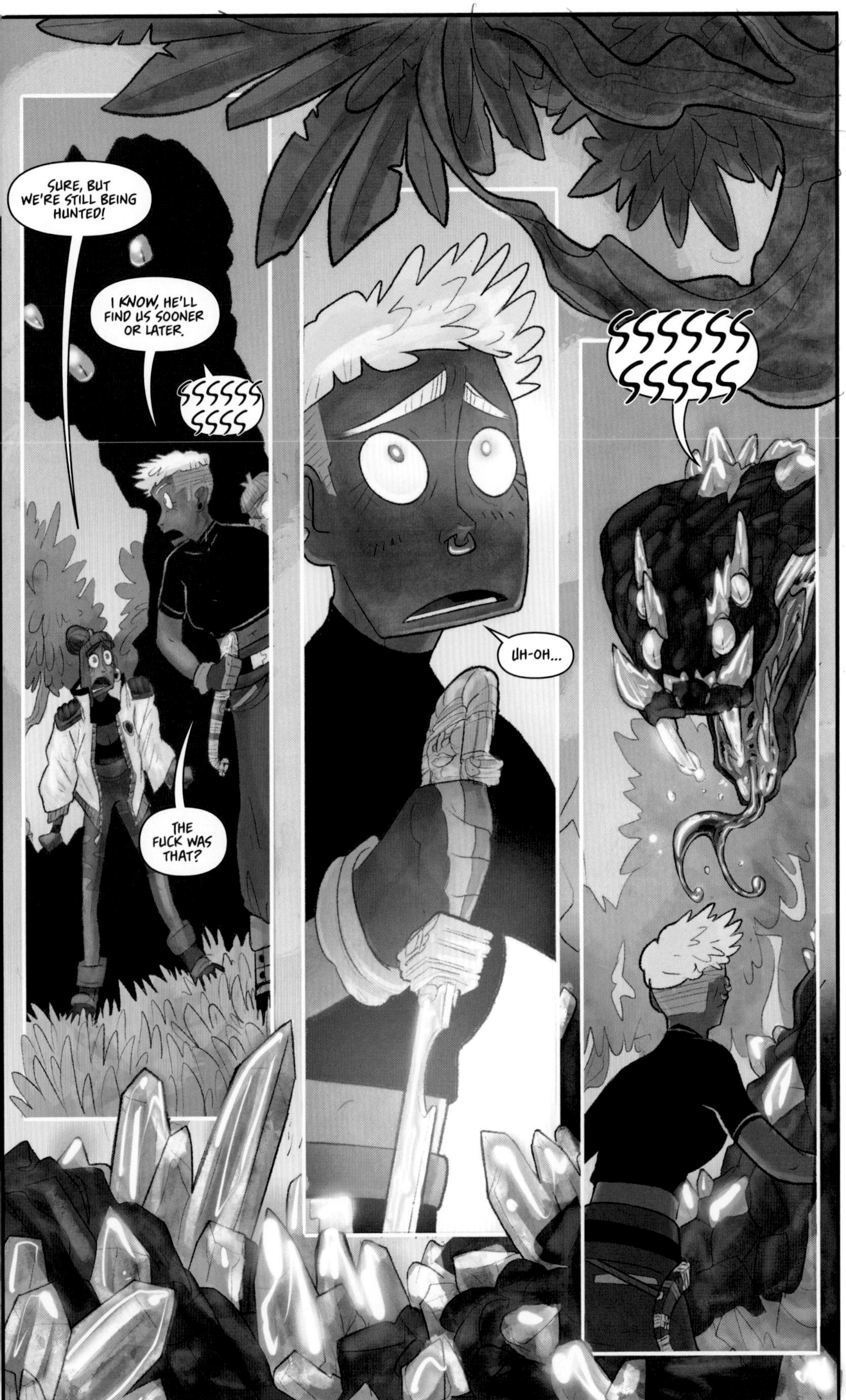
SURE, BUT WE'RE STILL BEING HUNTED!
I KNOW, HE'LL FIND US SOONER OR LATER.
SSSSSS SSSS
THE FUCK WAS THAT?
UH-OH...
SSSSSS SSSSS

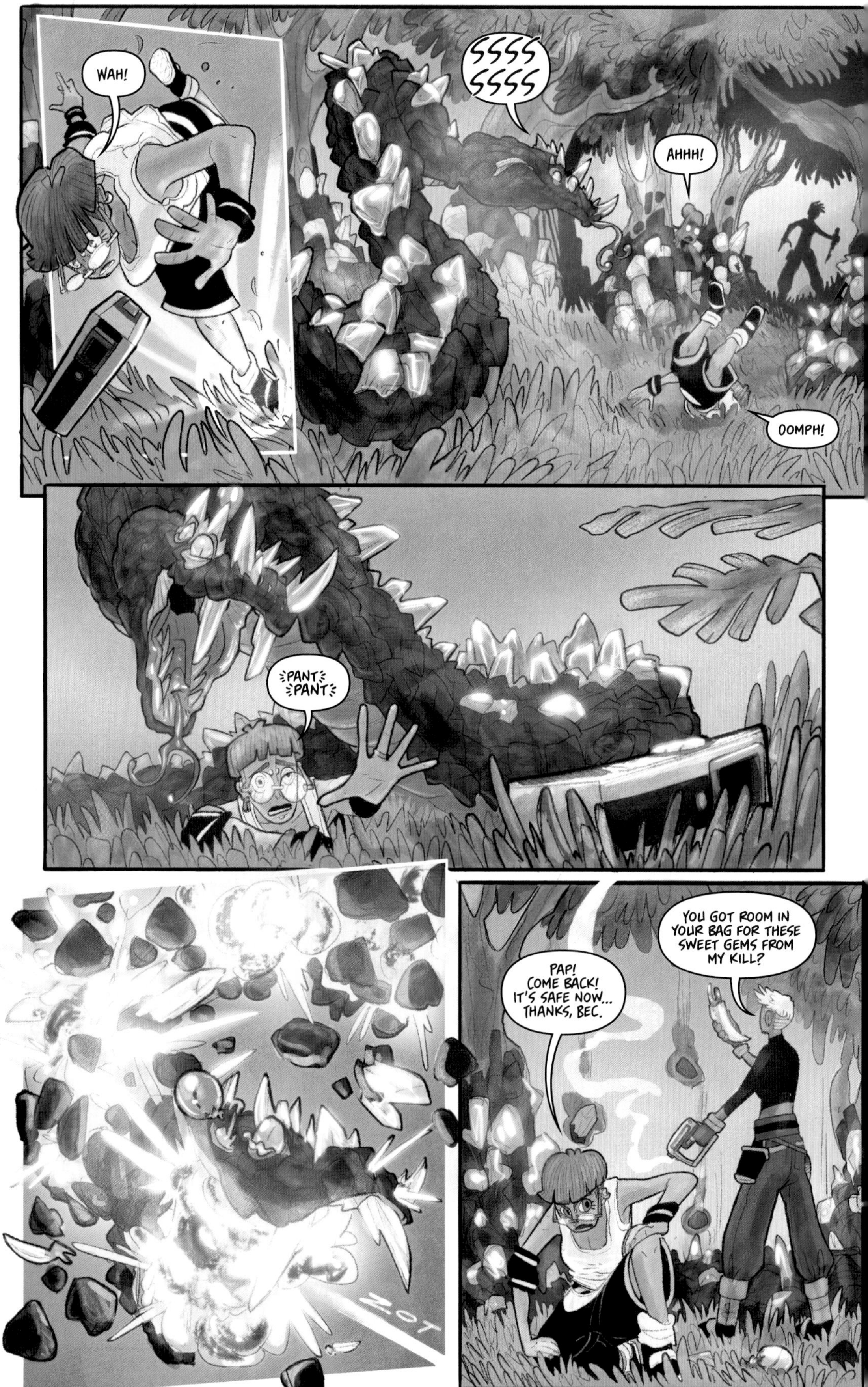
WAH!
SSSS SSSS
AHHH!
OOMPH!
PANT PANT
ZOT
PAP! COME BACK! IT'S SAFE NOW... THANKS, BEC.
YOU GOT ROOM IN YOUR BAG FOR THESE SWEET GEMS FROM MY KILL?

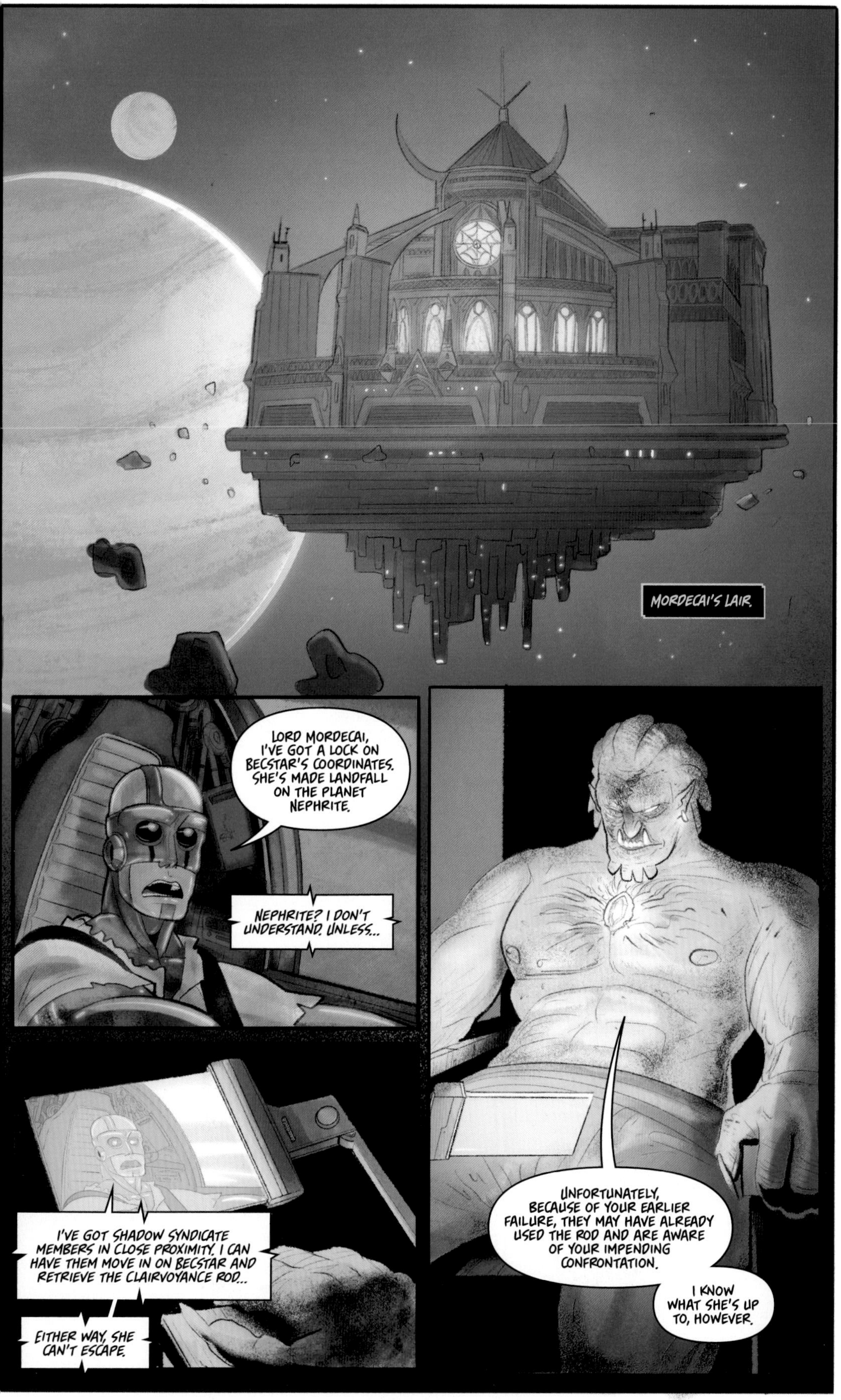
MORDECAI'S LAIR.
LORD MORDECAI, I'VE GOT A LOCK ON BECSTAR'S COORDINATES. SHE'S MADE LANDFALL ON THE PLANET NEPHRITE.
NEPHRITE? I DON'T UNDERSTAND. UNLESS...
UNFORTUNATELY, BECAUSE OF YOUR EARLIER FAILURE, THEY MAY HAVE ALREADY USED THE ROD AND ARE AWARE OF YOUR IMPENDING CONFRONTATION.
I KNOW WHAT SHE'S UP TO, HOWEVER.
I'VE GOT SHADOW SYNDICATE MEMBERS IN CLOSE PROXIMITY. I CAN HAVE THEM MOVE IN ON BECSTAR AND RETRIEVE THE CLAIRVOYANCE ROD...
EITHER WAY, SHE CAN'T ESCAPE.

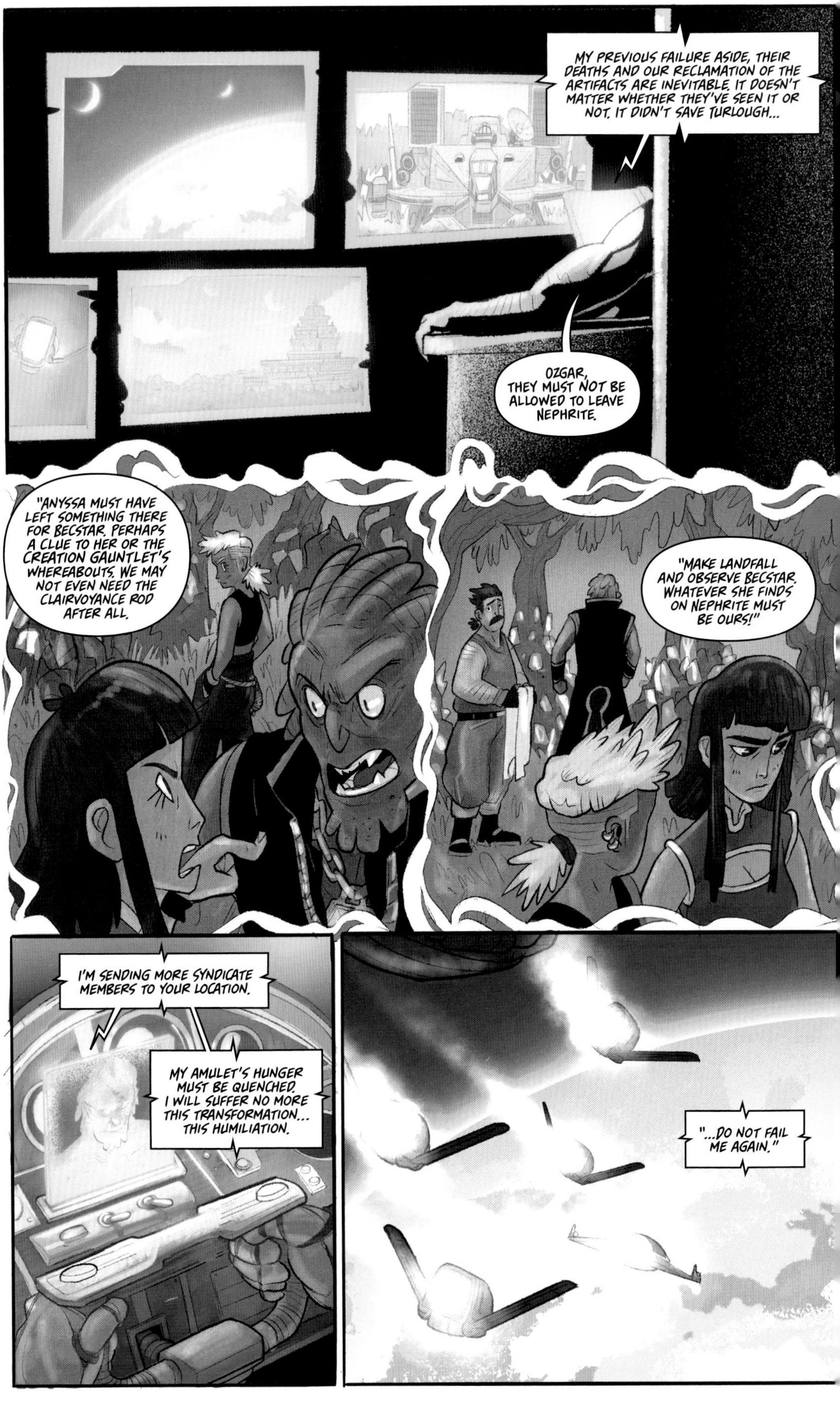

MY PREVIOUS FAILURE ASIDE, THEIR DEATHS AND OUR RECLAMATION OF THE ARTIFACTS ARE INEVITABLE. IT DOESN'T MATTER WHETHER THEY'VE SEEN IT OR NOT. IT DIDN'T SAVE TURLOUGH...
OZGAR, THEY MUST NOT BE ALLOWED TO LEAVE NEPHRITE.
"ANYSSA MUST HAVE LEFT SOMETHING THERE FOR BECSTAR. PERHAPS A CLUE TO HER OR THE CREATION GAUNTLET'S WHEREABOUTS. WE MAY NOT EVEN NEED THE CLAIRVOYANCE ROD AFTER ALL.
"MAKE LANDFALL AND OBSERVE BECSTAR. WHATEVER SHE FINDS ON NEPHRITE MUST BE OURS!"
I'M SENDING MORE SYNDICATE MEMBERS TO YOUR LOCATION.
MY AMULET'S HUNGER MUST BE QUENCHED. I WILL SUFFER NO MORE THIS TRANSFORMATION... THIS HUMILIATION.
"...DO NOT FAIL ME AGAIN."

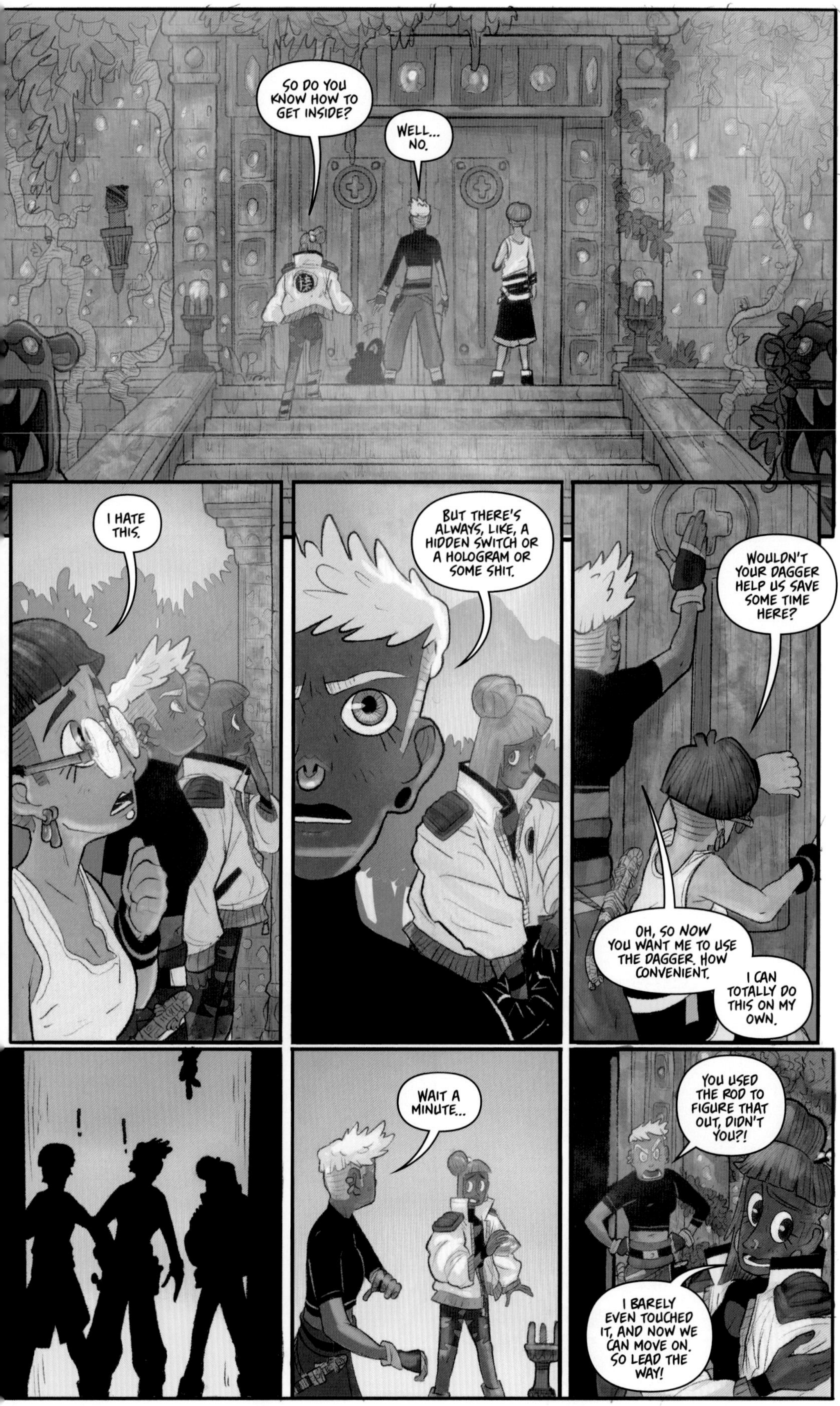
SO DO YOU KNOW HOW TO GET INSIDE?
WELL... NO.
I HATE THIS.
BUT THERE'S ALWAYS, LIKE, A HIDDEN SWITCH OR A HOLOGRAM OR SOME SHIT.
WOULDN'T YOUR DAGGER HELP US SAVE SOME TIME HERE?
OH, SO NOW YOU WANT ME TO USE THE DAGGER. HOW CONVENIENT.
I CAN TOTALLY DO THIS ON MY OWN.
!
!
WAIT A MINUTE...
YOU USED THE ROD TO FIGURE THAT OUT, DIDN'T YOU?!
I BARELY EVEN TOUCHED IT, AND NOW WE CAN MOVE ON. SO LEAD THE WAY!

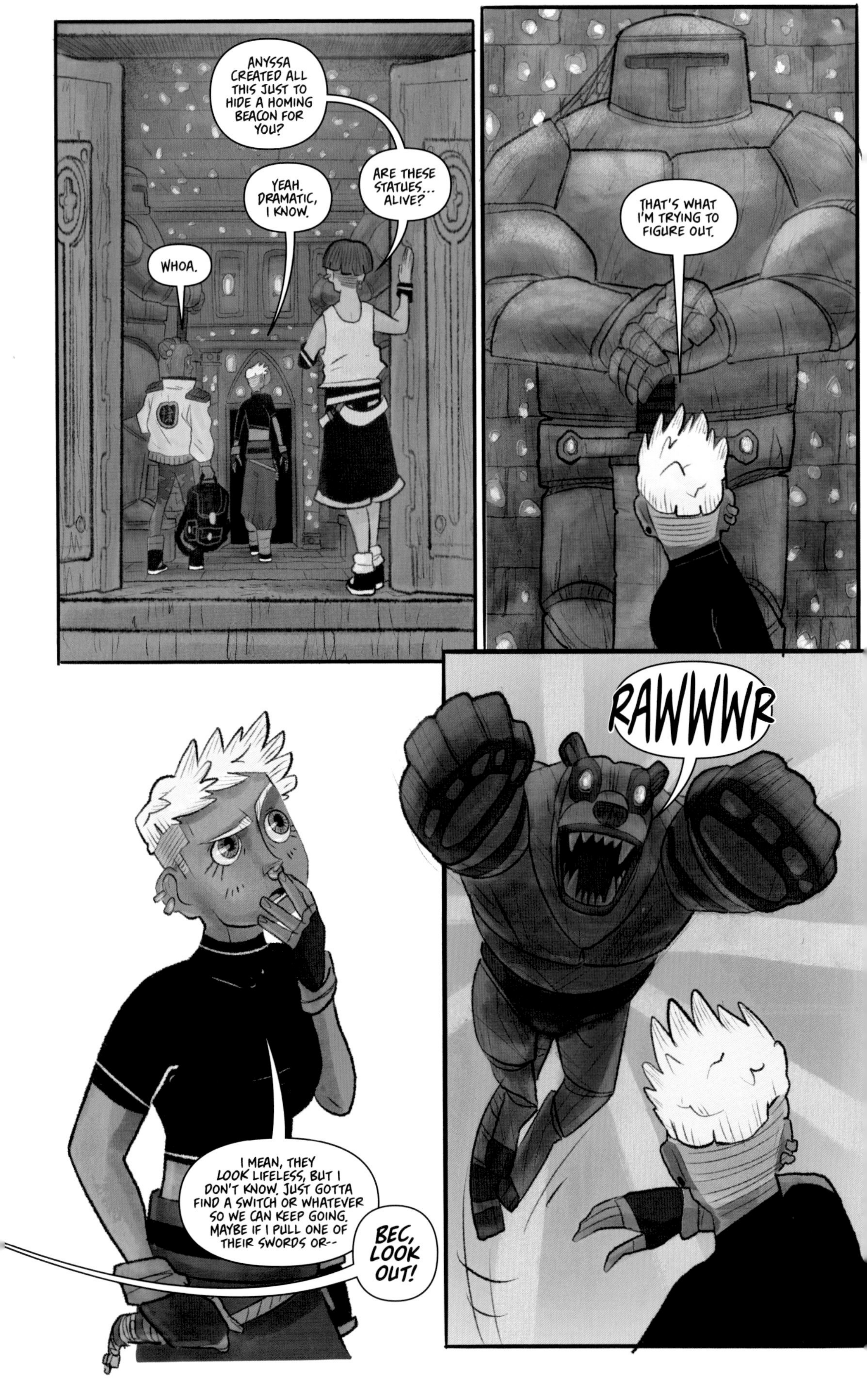
ANYSSA CREATED ALL THIS JUST TO HIDE A HOMING BEACON FOR YOU?
YEAH. DRAMATIC, I KNOW.
ARE THESE STATUES... ALIVE?
WHOA.
THAT'S WHAT I'M TRYING TO FIGURE OUT.
I MEAN, THEY LOOK LIFELESS, BUT I DON'T KNOW. JUST GOTTA FIND A SWITCH OR WHATEVER SO WE CAN KEEP GOING. MAYBE IF I PULL ONE OF THEIR SWORDS OR--
BEC, LOOK OUT!
RAWWWR

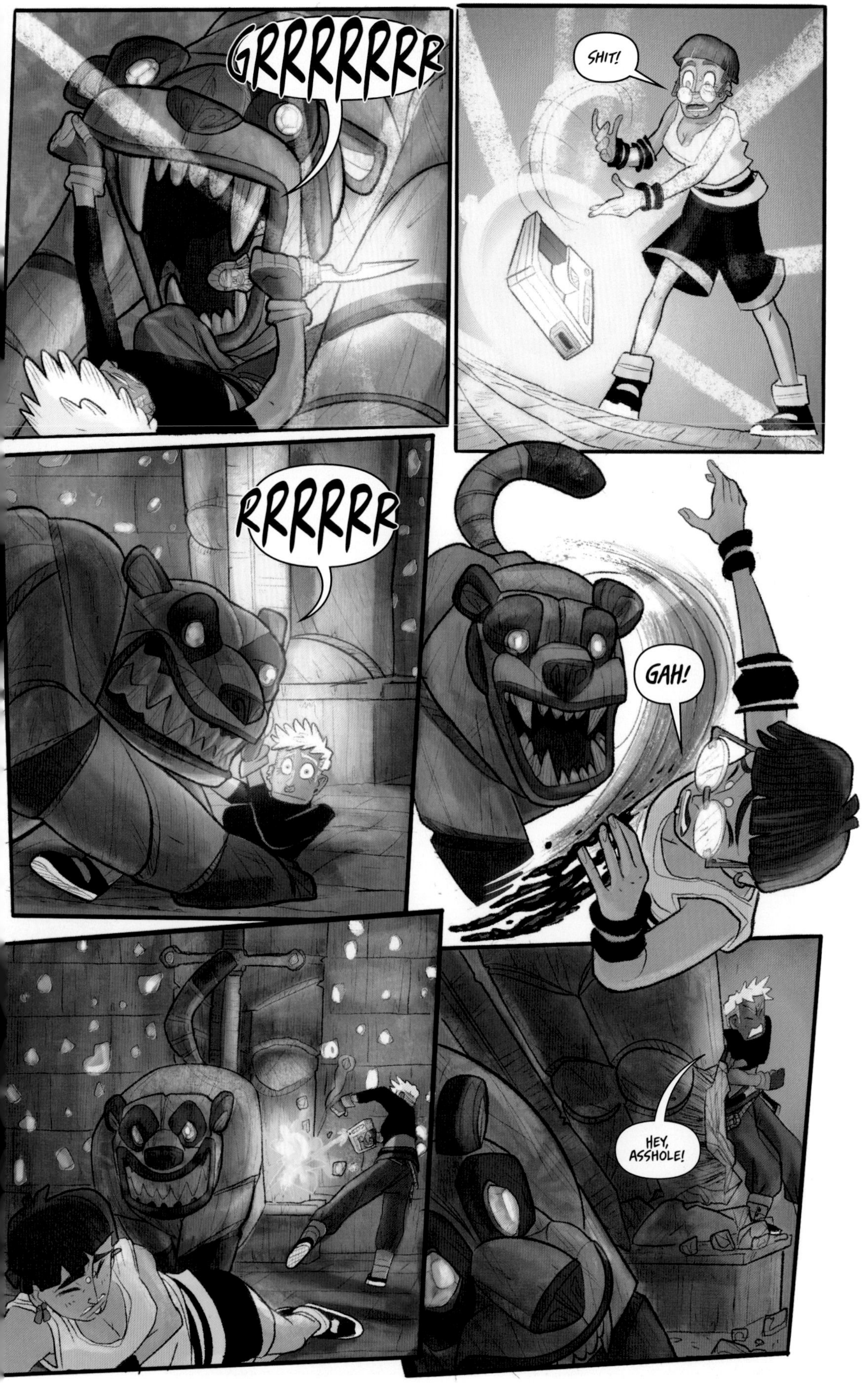
GRRRRRRR
SHIT!
RRRRRR
GAH!
HEY, ASSHOLE!

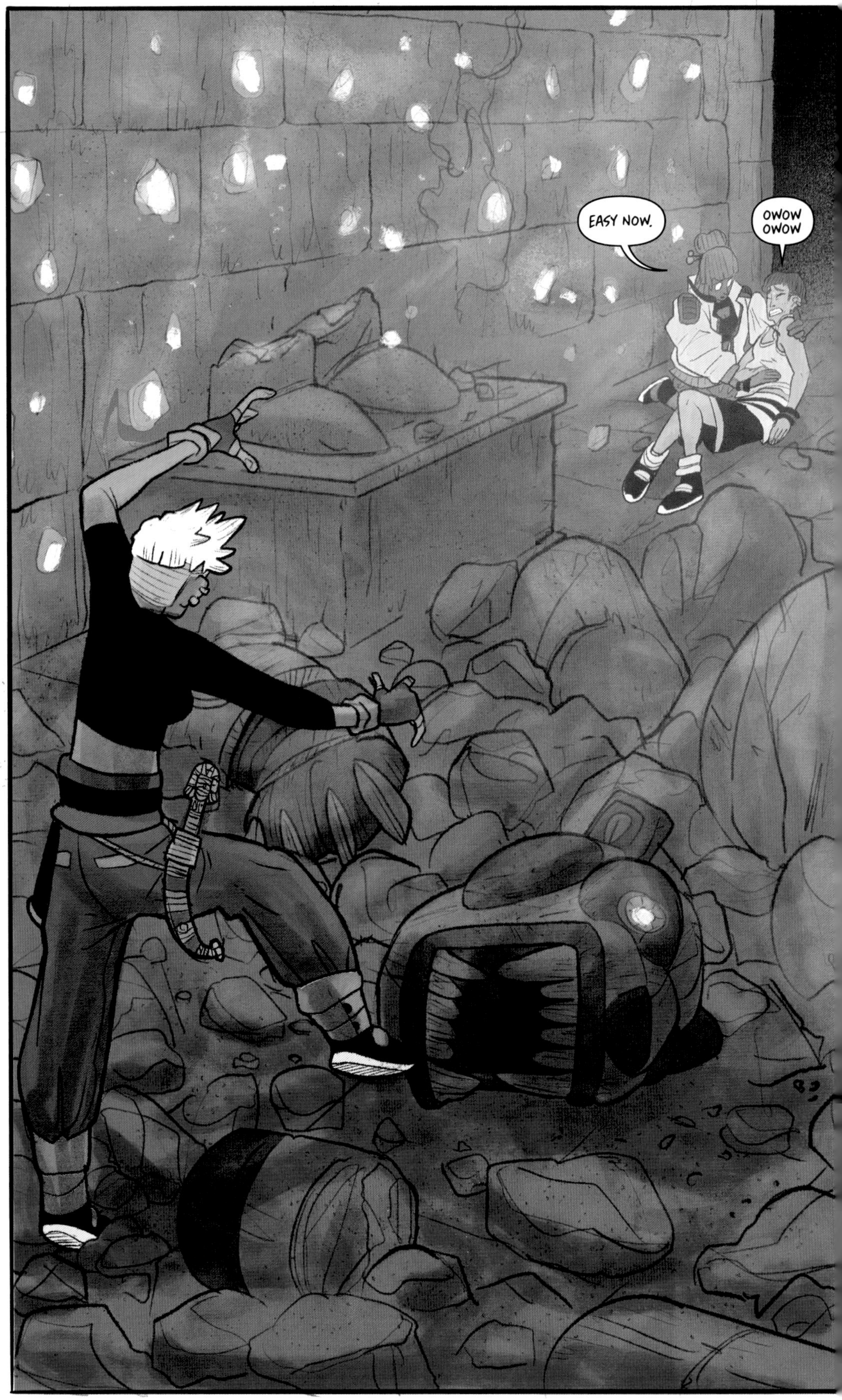
EASY NOW.
OWOW OWOW

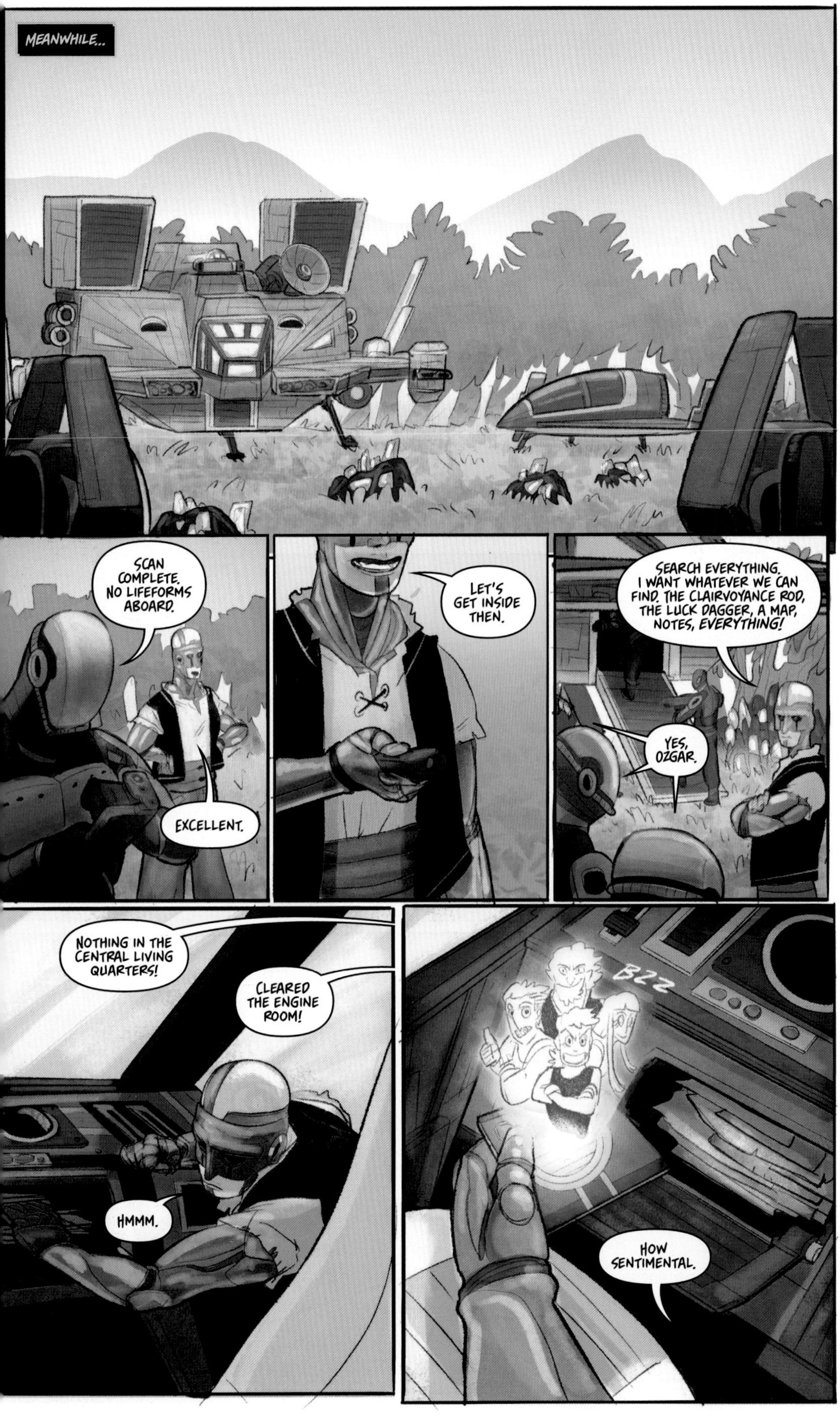
MEANWHILE...
SCAN COMPLETE. NO LIFEFORMS ABOARD.
EXCELLENT.
LET'S GET INSIDE THEN.
SEARCH EVERYTHING. I WANT WHATEVER WE CAN FIND, THE CLAIRVOYANCE ROD, THE LUCK DAGGER, A MAP, NOTES, EVERYTHING!
YES, OZGAR.
NOTHING IN THE CENTRAL LIVING QUARTERS!
CLEARED THE ENGINE ROOM!
HMMM.
BZZ
HOW SENTIMENTAL.

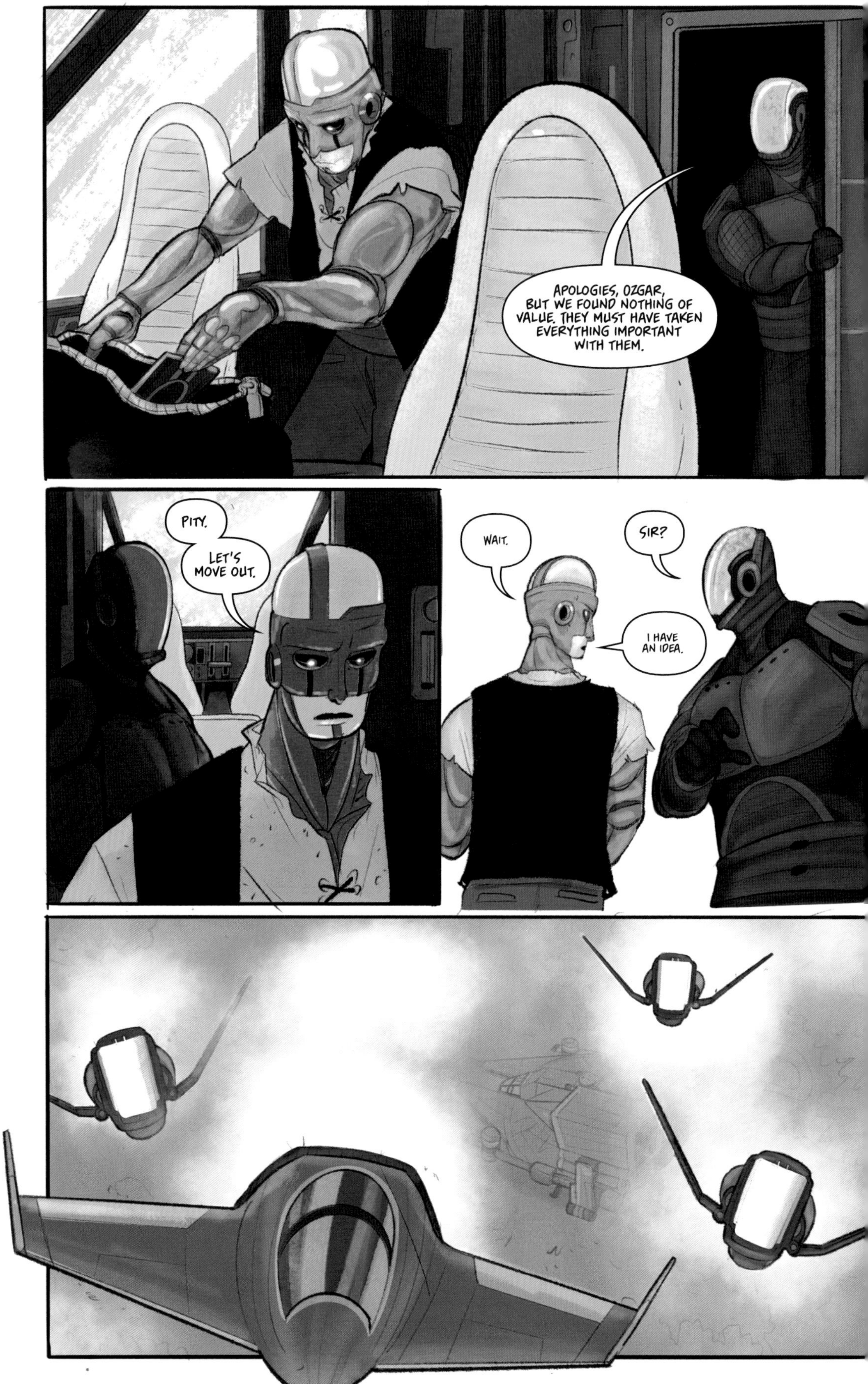
APOLOGIES, OZGAR, BUT WE FOUND NOTHING OF VALUE. THEY MUST HAVE TAKEN EVERYTHING IMPORTANT WITH THEM.
PITY.
LET'S MOVE OUT.
WAIT.
SIR?
I HAVE AN IDEA.

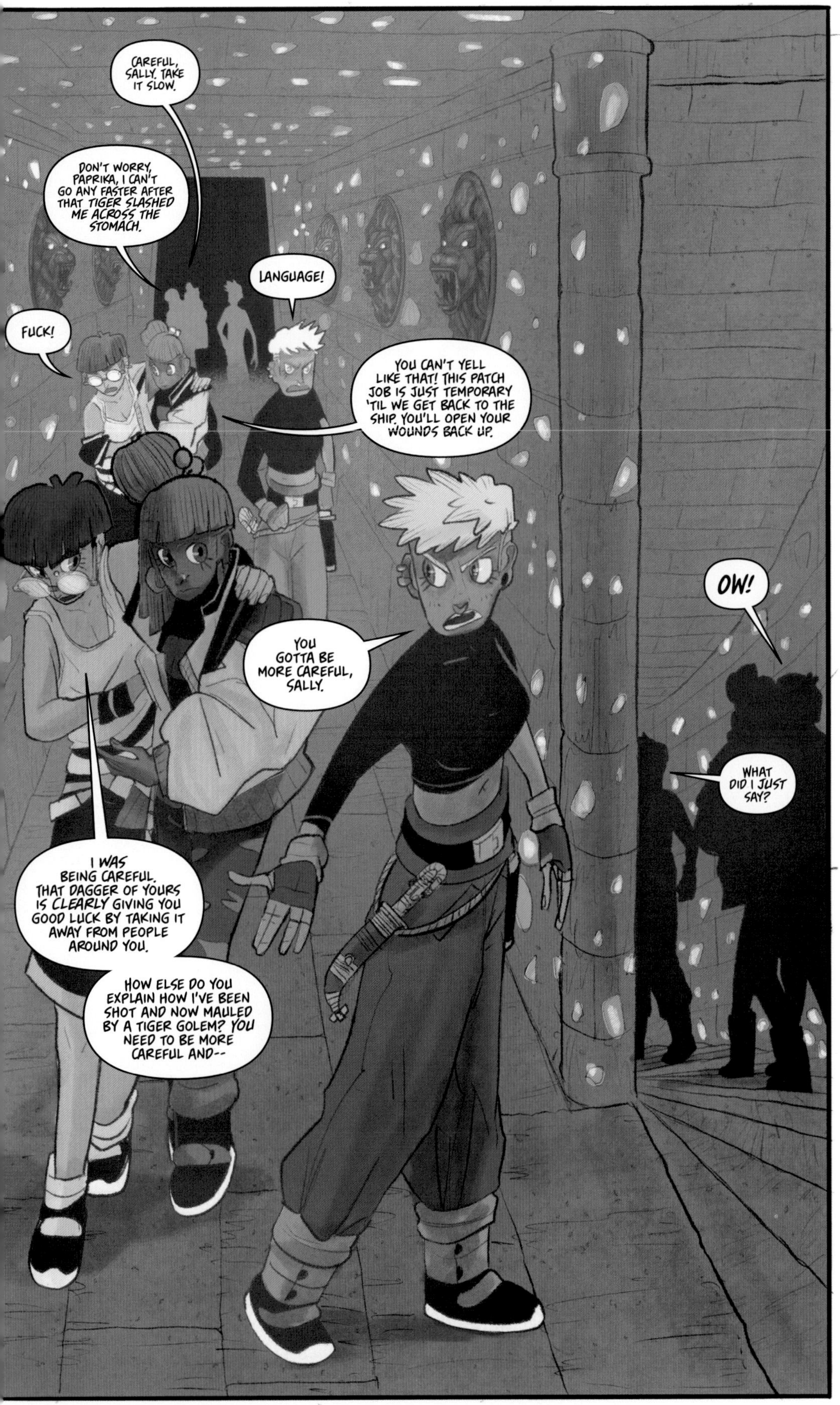
CAREFUL, SALLY. TAKE IT SLOW.
DON'T WORRY, PAPRIKA, I CAN'T GO ANY FASTER AFTER THAT TIGER SLASHED ME ACROSS THE STOMACH.
LANGUAGE!
FUCK!
YOU CAN'T YELL LIKE THAT! THIS PATCH JOB IS JUST TEMPORARY 'TIL WE GET BACK TO THE SHIP. YOU'LL OPEN YOUR WOUNDS BACK UP.
OW!
YOU GOTTA BE MORE CAREFUL, SALLY.
WHAT DID I JUST SAY?
I WAS BEING CAREFUL. THAT DAGGER OF YOURS IS CLEARLY GIVING YOU GOOD LUCK BY TAKING IT AWAY FROM PEOPLE AROUND YOU.
HOW ELSE DO YOU EXPLAIN HOW I'VE BEEN SHOT AND NOW MAULED BY A TIGER GOLEM? YOU NEED TO BE MORE CAREFUL AND--

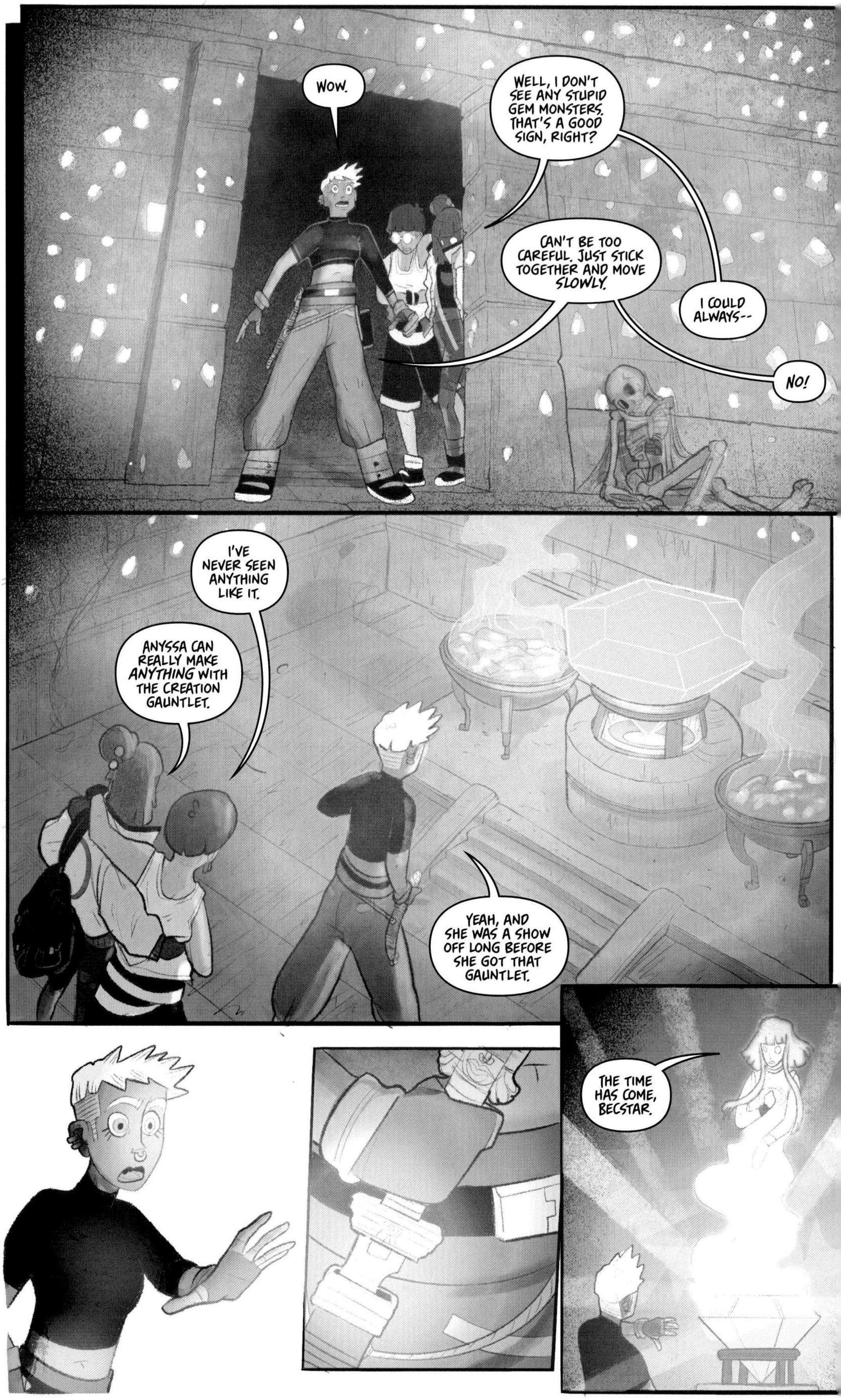
WOW.
WELL, I DON'T SEE ANY STUPID GEM MONSTERS. THAT'S A GOOD SIGN, RIGHT?
CAN'T BE TOO CAREFUL. JUST STICK TOGETHER AND MOVE SLOWLY.
I COULD ALWAYS--
NO!
I'VE NEVER SEEN ANYTHING LIKE IT.
ANYSSA CAN REALLY MAKE ANYTHING WITH THE CREATION GAUNTLET.
YEAH, AND SHE WAS A SHOW OFF LONG BEFORE SHE GOT THAT GAUNTLET.
THE TIME HAS COME, BECSTAR.

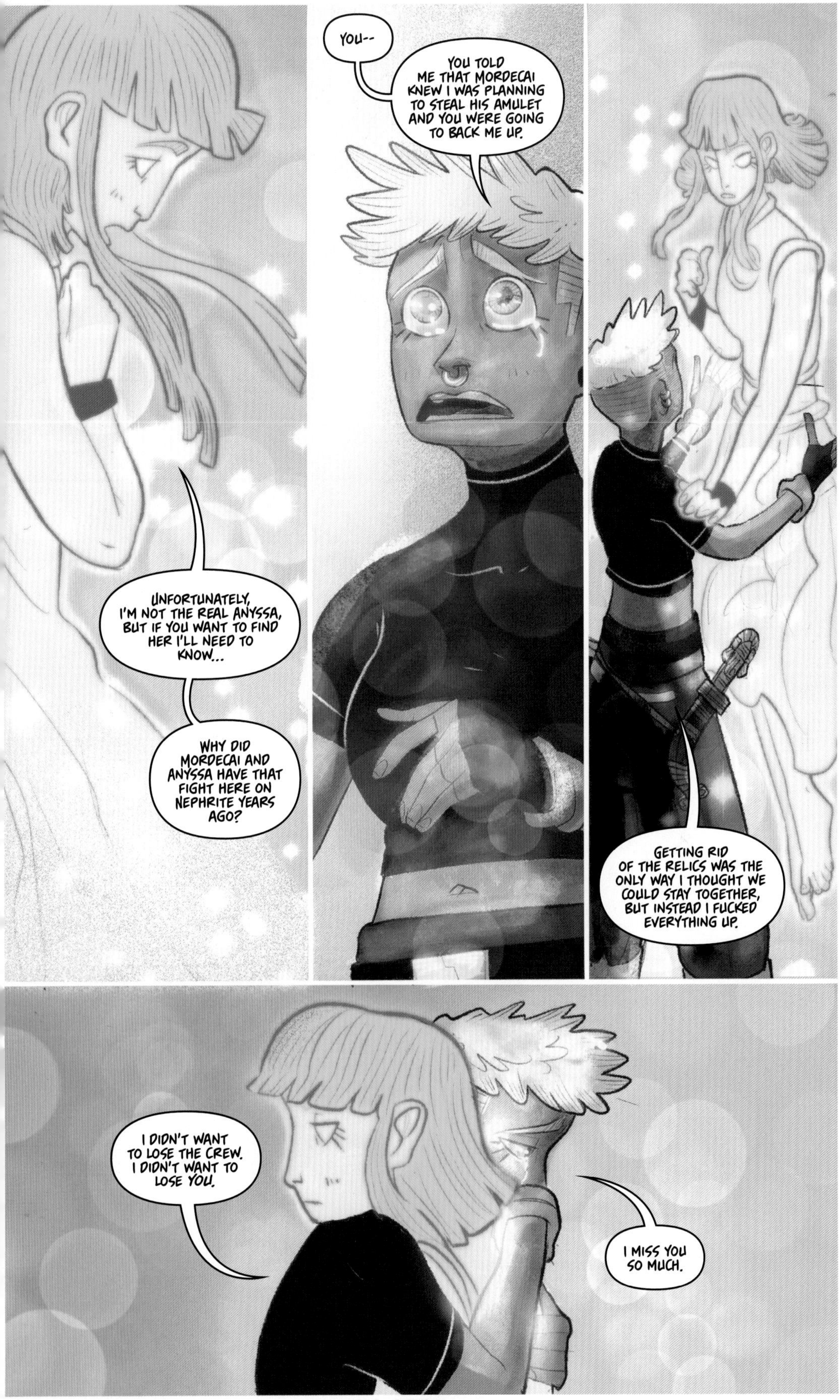
YOU--
YOU TOLD ME THAT MORDECAI KNEW I WAS PLANNING TO STEAL HIS AMULET AND YOU WERE GOING TO BACK ME UP.
UNFORTUNATELY, I'M NOT THE REAL ANYSSA, BUT IF YOU WANT TO FIND HER I'LL NEED TO KNOW...
WHY DID MORDECAI AND ANYSSA HAVE THAT FIGHT HERE ON NEPHRITE YEARS AGO?
GETTING RID OF THE RELICS WAS THE ONLY WAY I THOUGHT WE COULD STAY TOGETHER, BUT INSTEAD I FUCKED EVERYTHING UP.
I DIDN'T WANT TO LOSE THE CREW. I DIDN'T WANT TO LOSE YOU.
I MISS YOU SO MUCH.

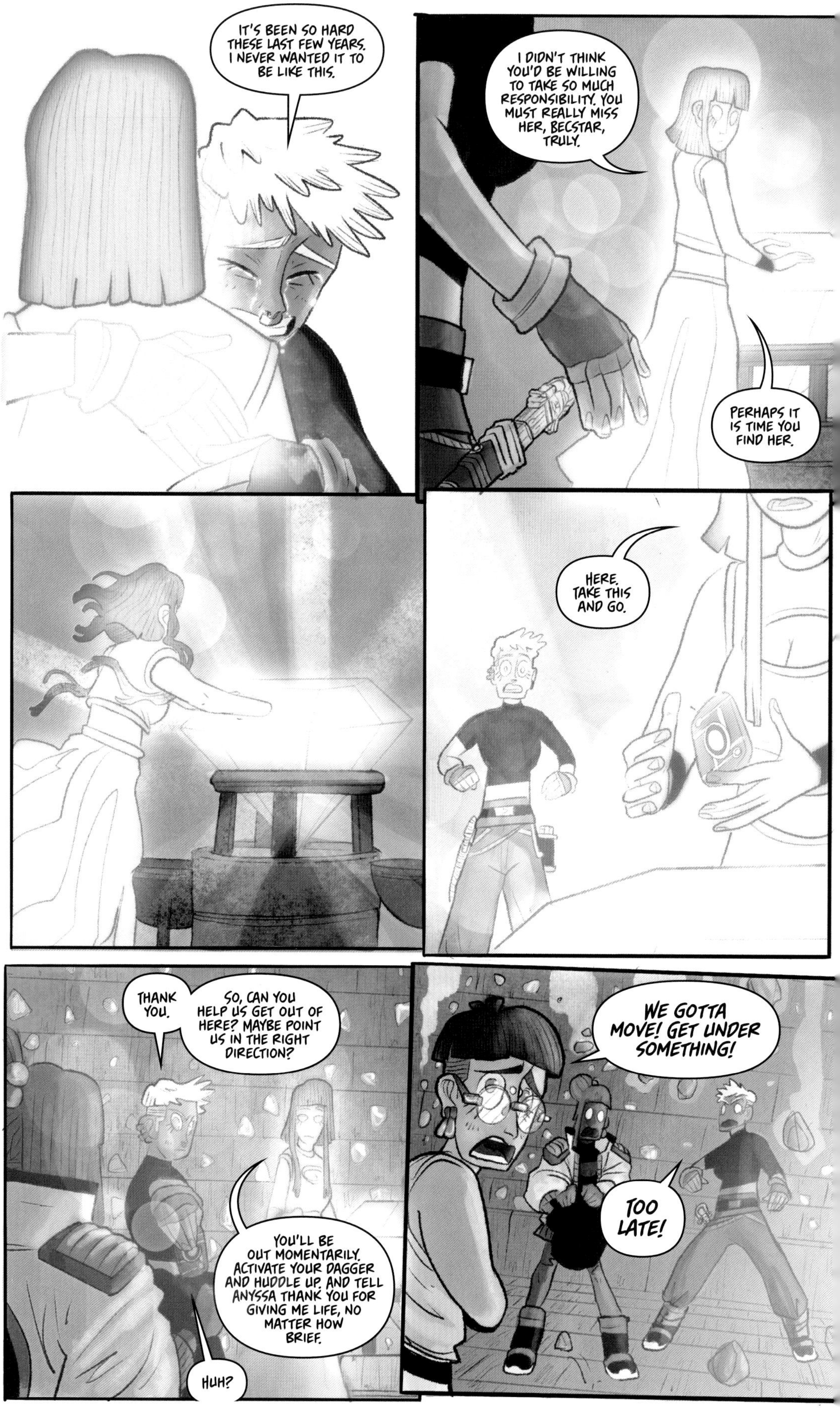
IT'S BEEN SO HARD THESE LAST FEW YEARS. I NEVER WANTED IT TO BE LIKE THIS.
I DIDN'T THINK YOU'D BE WILLING TO TAKE SO MUCH RESPONSIBILITY. YOU MUST REALLY MISS HER, BECSTAR, TRULY.
PERHAPS IT IS TIME YOU FIND HER.
HERE. TAKE THIS AND GO.
THANK YOU.
SO, CAN YOU HELP US GET OUT OF HERE? MAYBE POINT US IN THE RIGHT DIRECTION?
YOU'LL BE OUT MOMENTARILY. ACTIVATE YOUR DAGGER AND HUDDLE UP. AND TELL ANYSSA THANK YOU FOR GIVING ME LIFE, NO MATTER HOW BRIEF.
HUH?
WE GOTTA MOVE! GET UNDER SOMETHING!
TOO LATE!

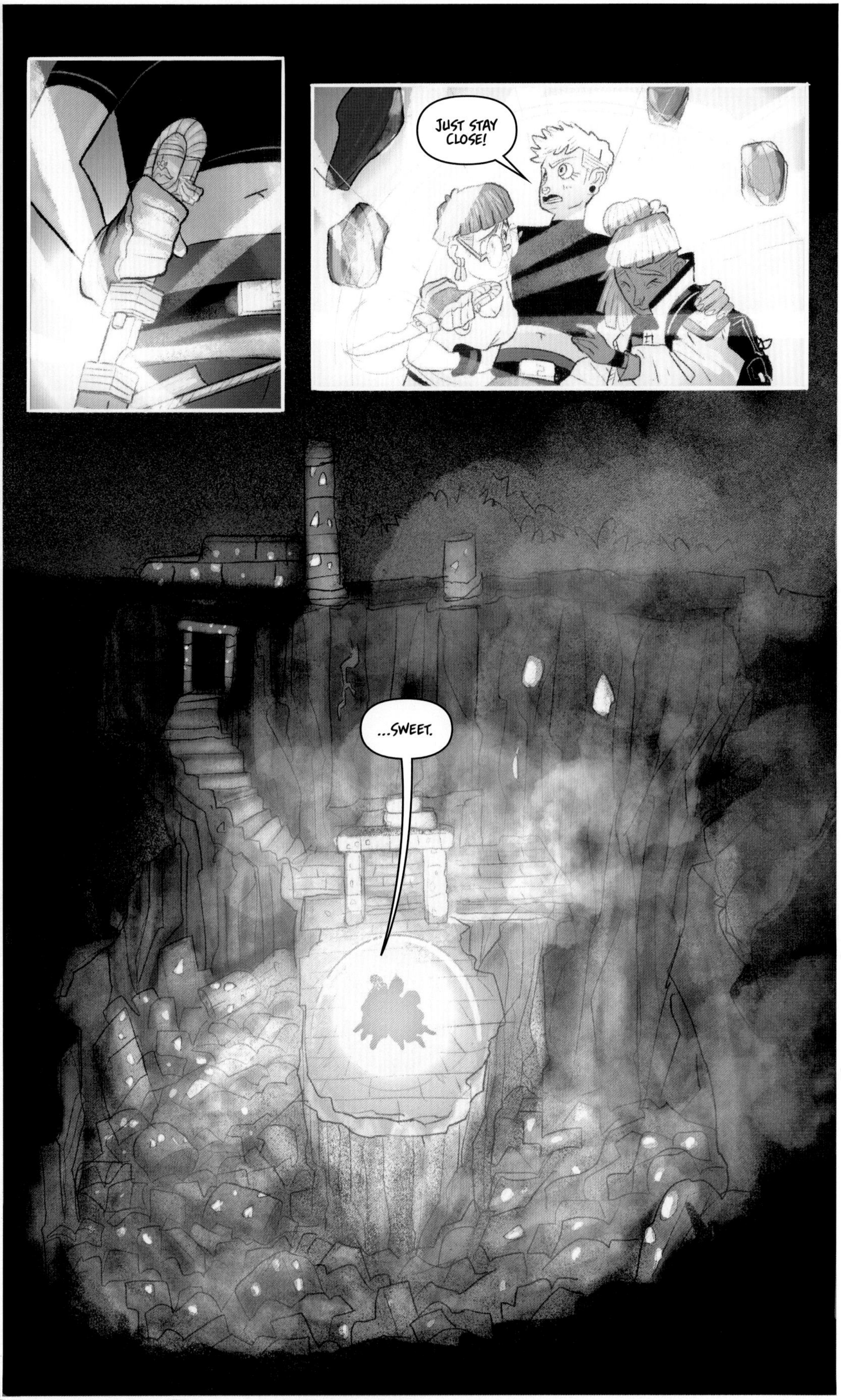
JUST STAY CLOSE!
...SWEET.

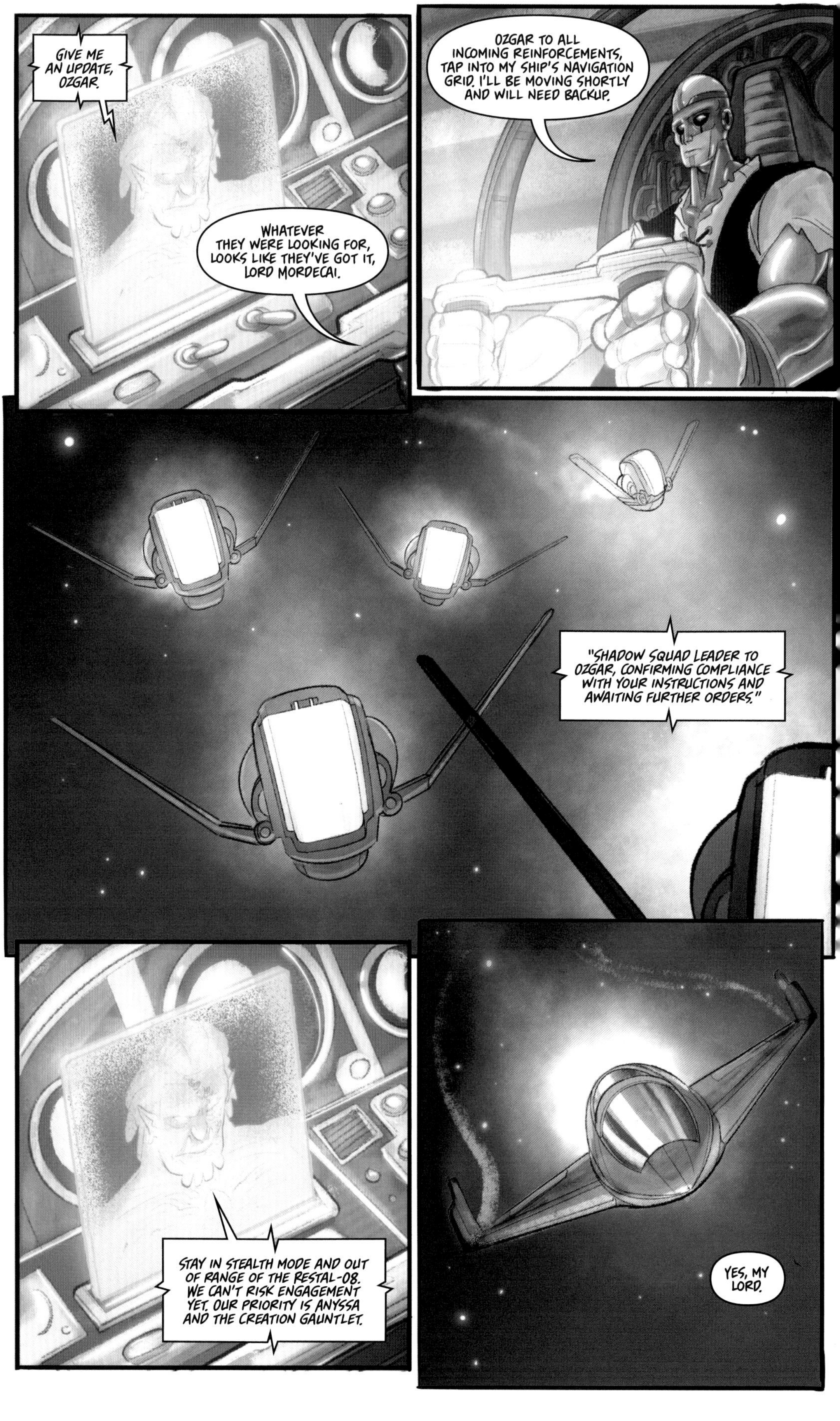
GIVE ME AN UPDATE, OZGAR.
WHATEVER THEY WERE LOOKING FOR, LOOKS LIKE THEY'VE GOT IT, LORD MORDECAI.
OZGAR TO ALL INCOMING REINFORCEMENTS, TAP INTO MY SHIP'S NAVIGATION GRID. I'LL BE MOVING SHORTLY AND WILL NEED BACKUP.
"SHADOW SQUAD LEADER TO OZGAR, CONFIRMING COMPLIANCE WITH YOUR INSTRUCTIONS AND AWAITING FURTHER ORDERS."
STAY IN STEALTH MODE AND OUT OF RANGE OF THE RESTAL-08. WE CAN'T RISK ENGAGEMENT YET. OUR PRIORITY IS ANYSSA AND THE CREATION GAUNTLET.
YES, MY LORD.

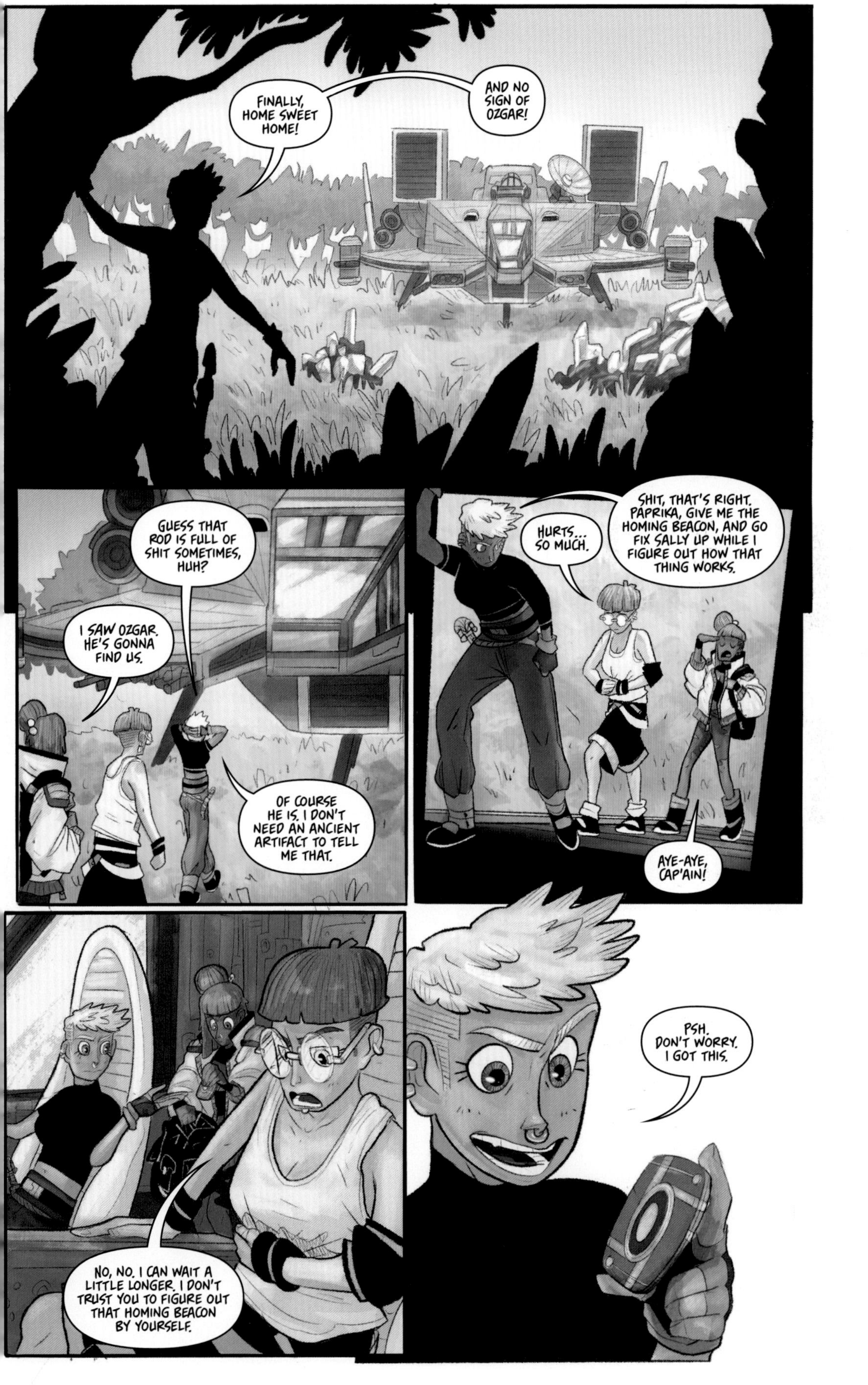
FINALLY, HOME SWEET HOME!
AND NO SIGN OF OZGAR!
GUESS THAT ROD IS FULL OF SHIT SOMETIMES, HUH?
I SAW OZGAR. HE'S GONNA FIND US.
OF COURSE HE IS. I DON'T NEED AN ANCIENT ARTIFACT TO TELL ME THAT.
HURTS... SO MUCH.
SHIT, THAT'S RIGHT. PAPRIKA, GIVE ME THE HOMING BEACON, AND GO FIX SALLY UP WHILE I FIGURE OUT HOW THAT THING WORKS.
AYE-AYE, CAP'AIN!
NO, NO. I CAN WAIT A LITTLE LONGER. I DON'T TRUST YOU TO FIGURE OUT THAT HOMING BEACON BY YOURSELF.
PSH. DON'T WORRY. I GOT THIS.

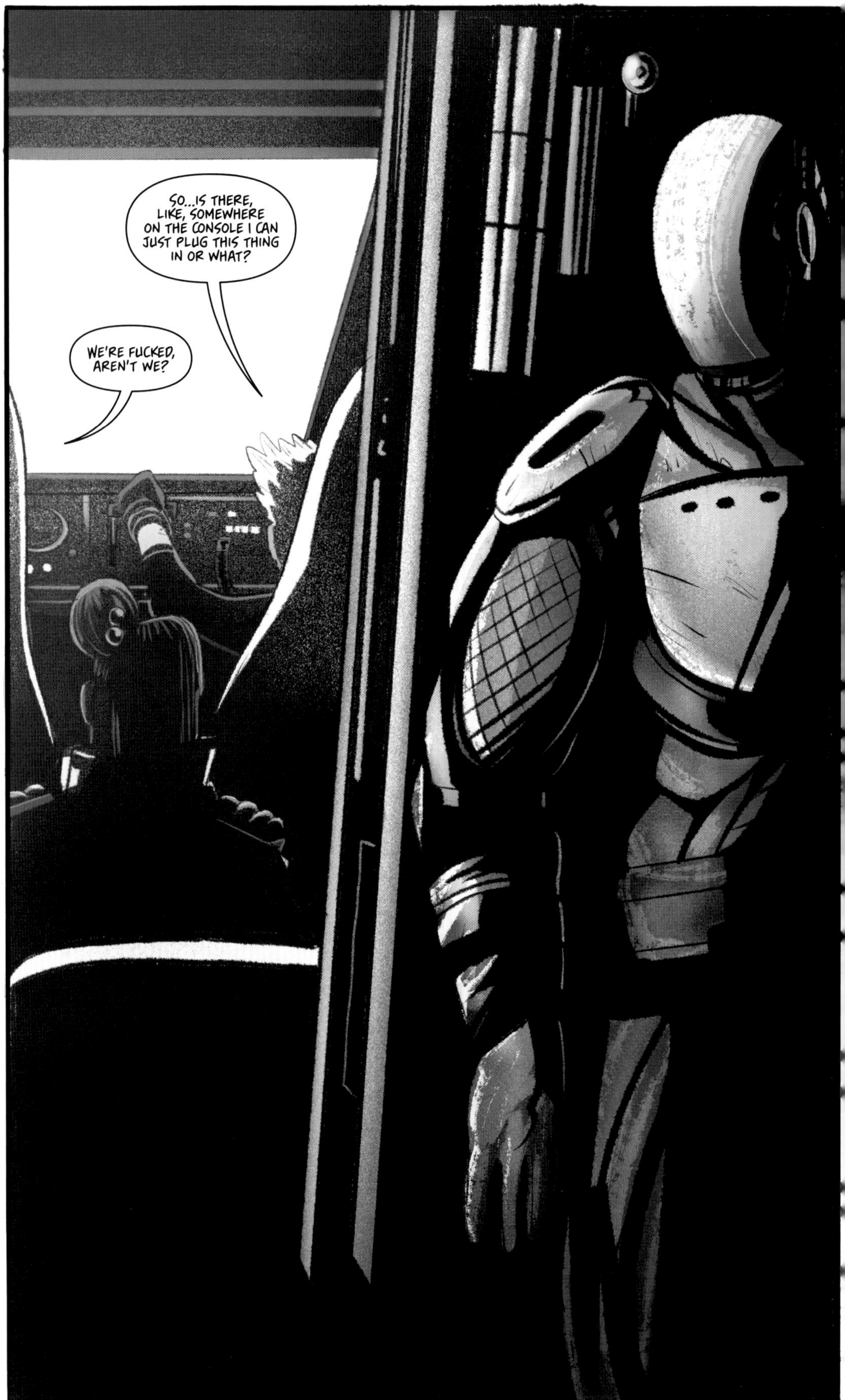
SO...IS THERE, LIKE, SOMEWHERE ON THE CONSOLE I CAN JUST PLUG THIS THING IN OR WHAT?
WE'RE FUCKED, AREN'T WE?

PART 03

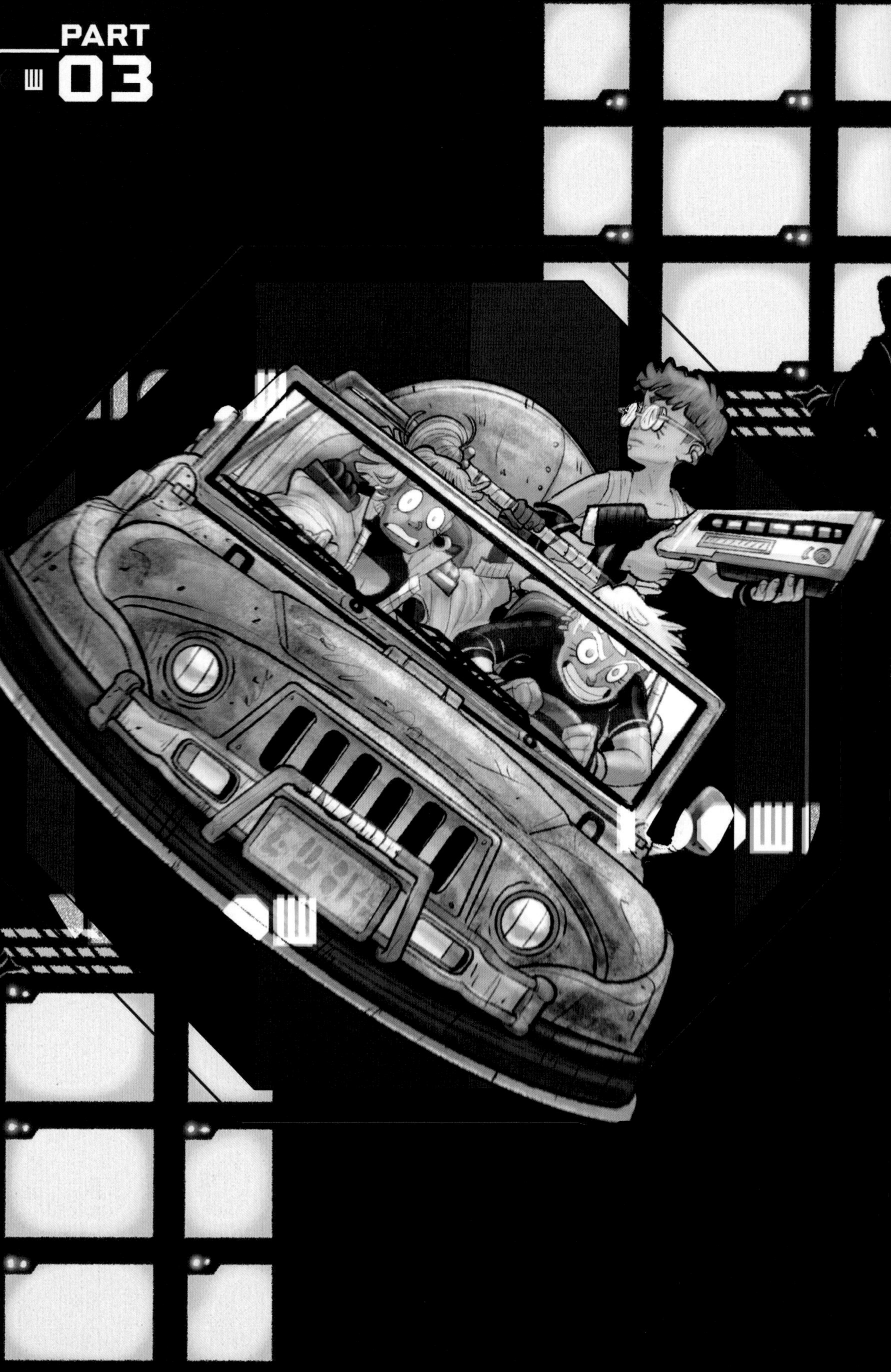

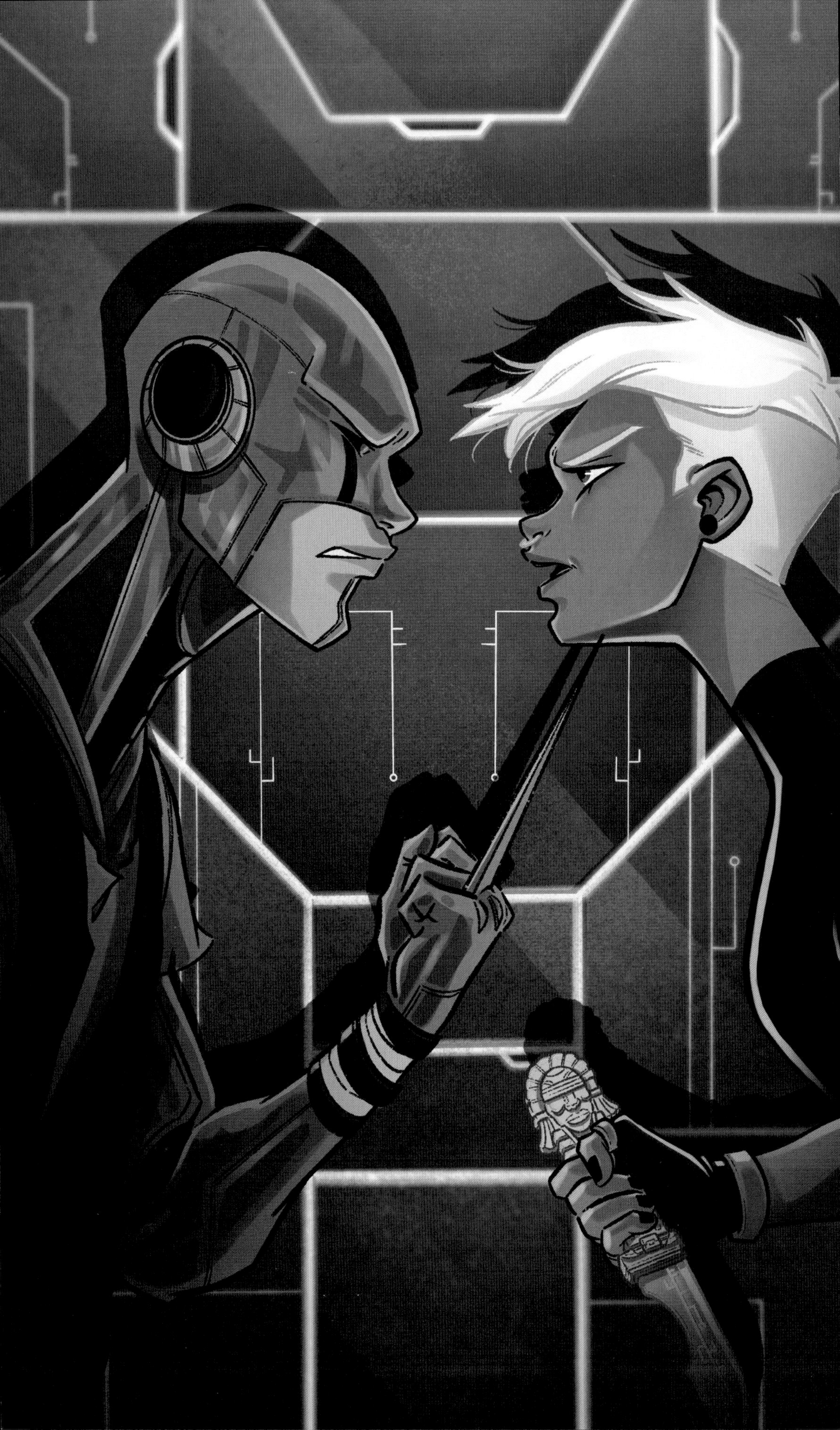

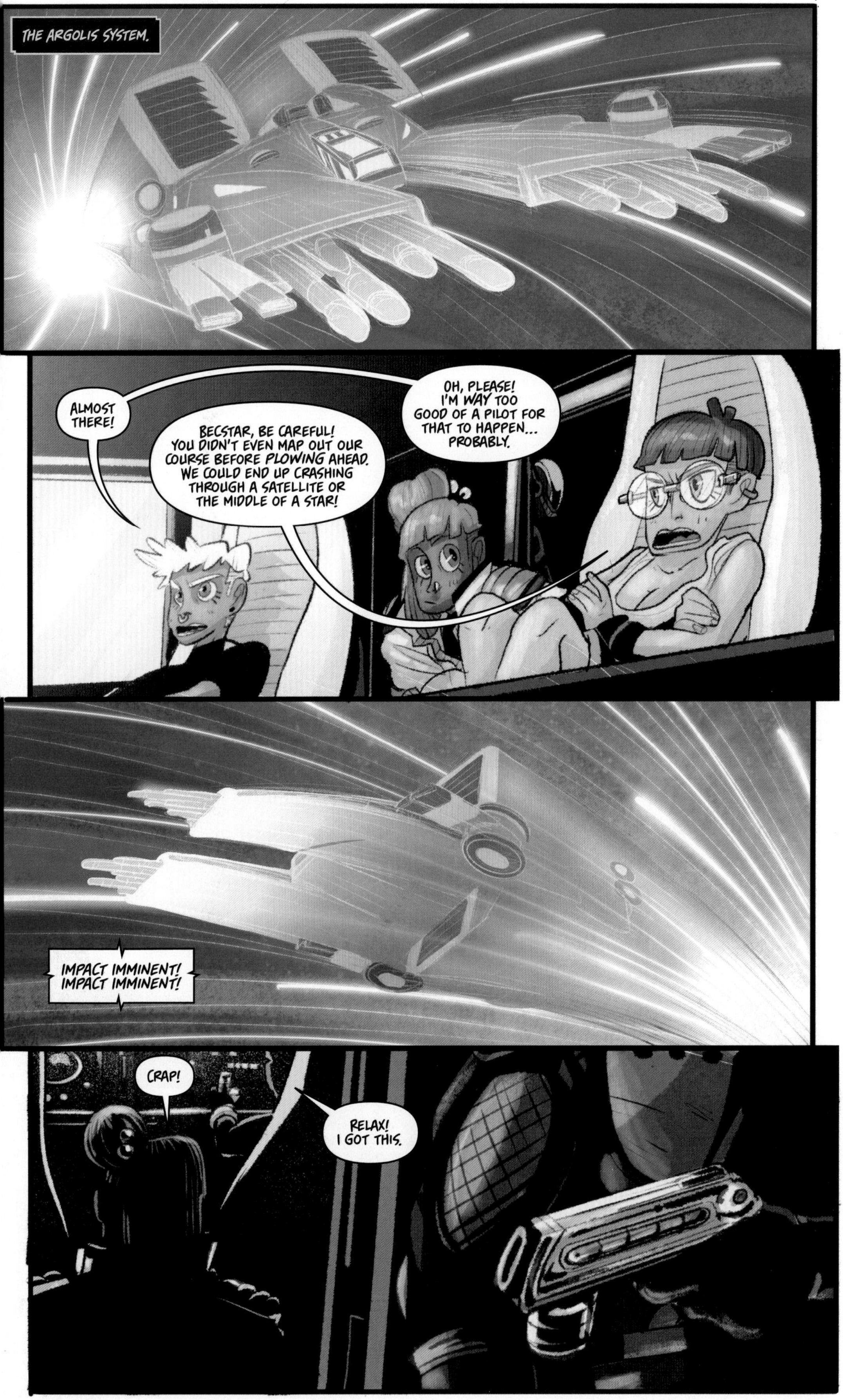
THE ARGOLIS SYSTEM.
ALMOST THERE!
BECSTAR, BE CAREFUL! YOU DIDN'T EVEN MAP OUT OUR COURSE BEFORE PLOWING AHEAD. WE COULD END UP CRASHING THROUGH A SATELLITE OR THE MIDDLE OF A STAR!
OH, PLEASE! I'M WAY TOO GOOD OF A PILOT FOR THAT TO HAPPEN... PROBABLY.
IMPACT IMMINENT! IMPACT IMMINENT!
CRAP!
RELAX! I GOT THIS.

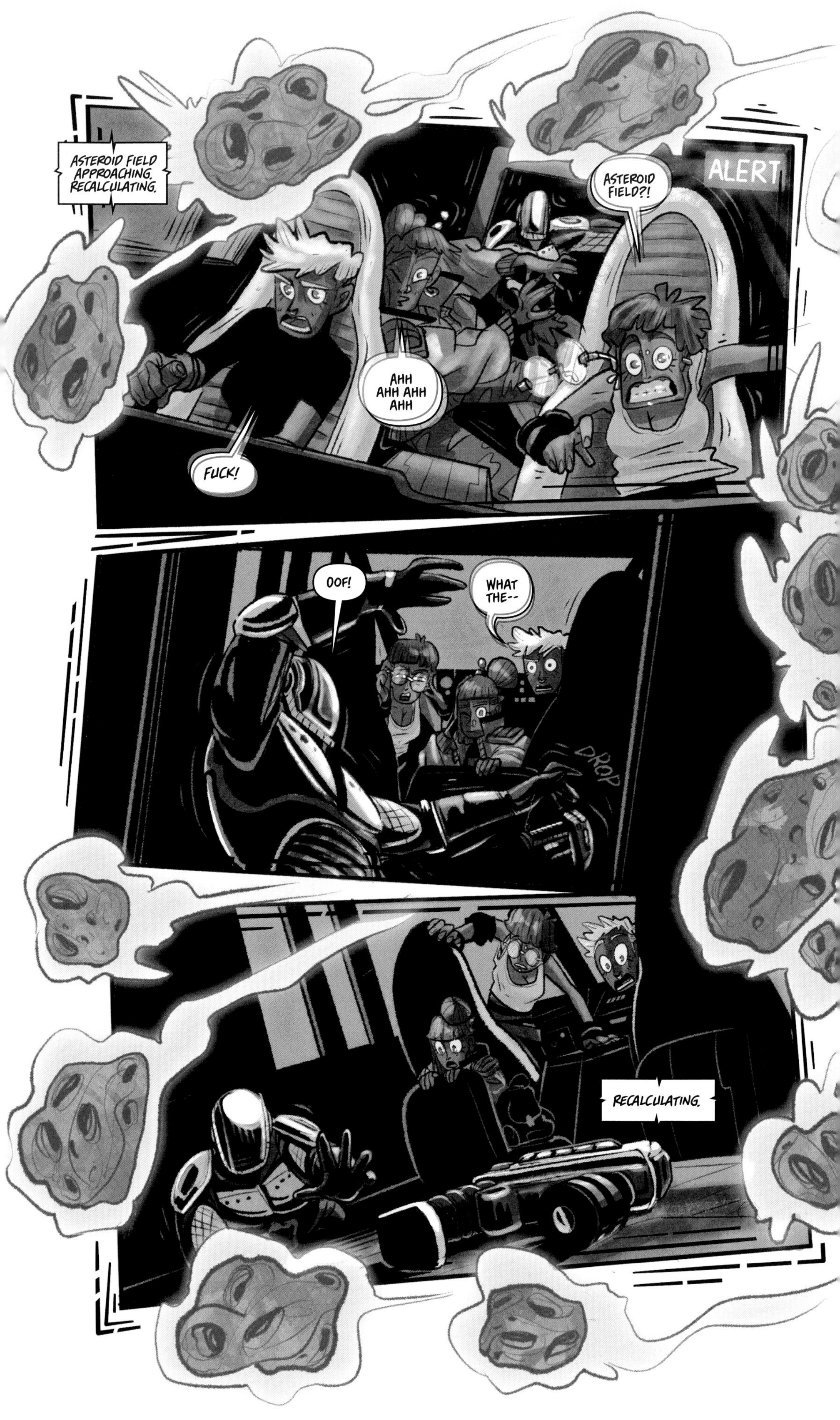
ASTEROID FIELD APPROACHING. RECALCULATING.
ALERT
ASTEROID FIELD?!
AHH AHH AHH AHH
FUCK!
OOF!
WHAT THE--
DROP
RECALCULATING.

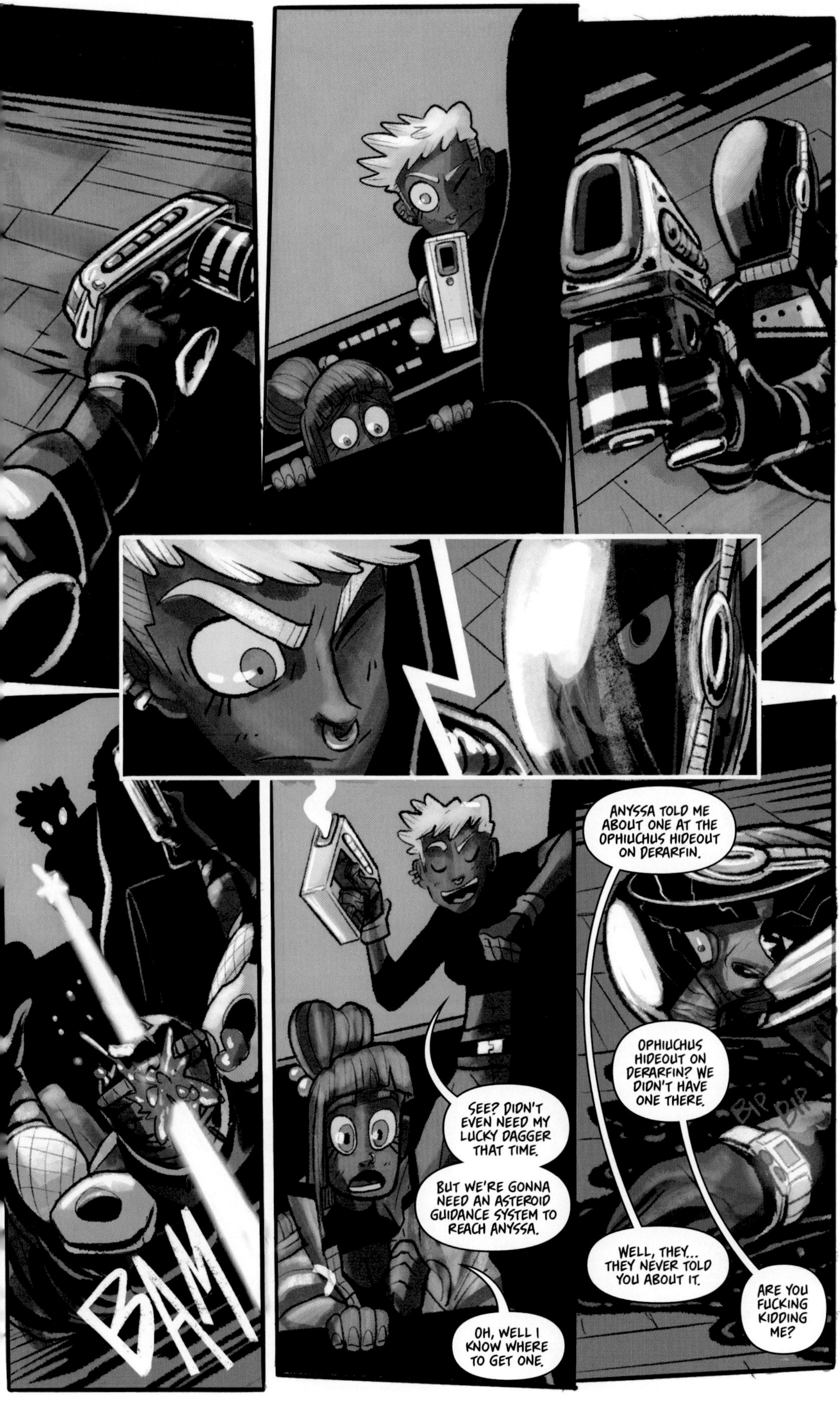
BAM
SEE? DIDN'T EVEN NEED MY LUCKY DAGGER THAT TIME.
BUT WE'RE GONNA NEED AN ASTEROID GUIDANCE SYSTEM TO REACH ANYSSA.
OH, WELL I KNOW WHERE TO GET ONE.
ANYSSA TOLD ME ABOUT ONE AT THE OPHIUCHUS HIDEOUT ON DERARFIN.
OPHIUCHUS HIDEOUT ON DERARFIN? WE DIDN'T HAVE ONE THERE.
BIP BIP
WELL, THEY... THEY NEVER TOLD YOU ABOUT IT.
ARE YOU FUCKING KIDDING ME?

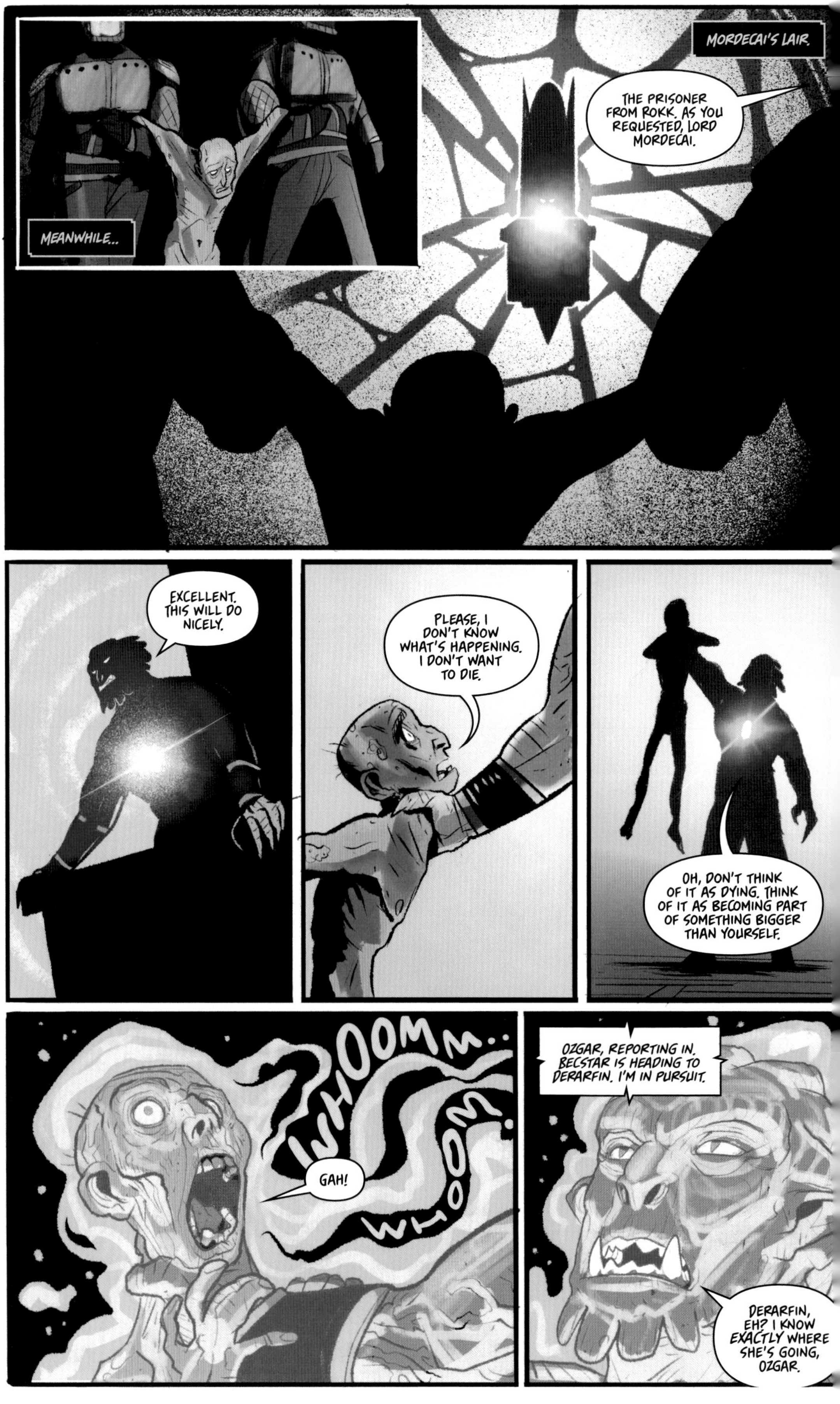
MEANWHILE...
MORDECAI'S LAIR.
THE PRISONER FROM ROKK. AS YOU REQUESTED, LORD MORDECAI.
EXCELLENT. THIS WILL DO NICELY.
PLEASE, I DON'T KNOW WHAT'S HAPPENING. I DON'T WANT TO DIE.
OH, DON'T THINK OF IT AS DYING. THINK OF IT AS BECOMING PART OF SOMETHING BIGGER THAN YOURSELF.
WHOOMM...
WHOOM
WHOOM
GAH!
OZGAR, REPORTING IN. BECSTAR IS HEADING TO DERARFIN. I'M IN PURSUIT.
DERARFIN, EH? I KNOW EXACTLY WHERE SHE'S GOING, OZGAR.

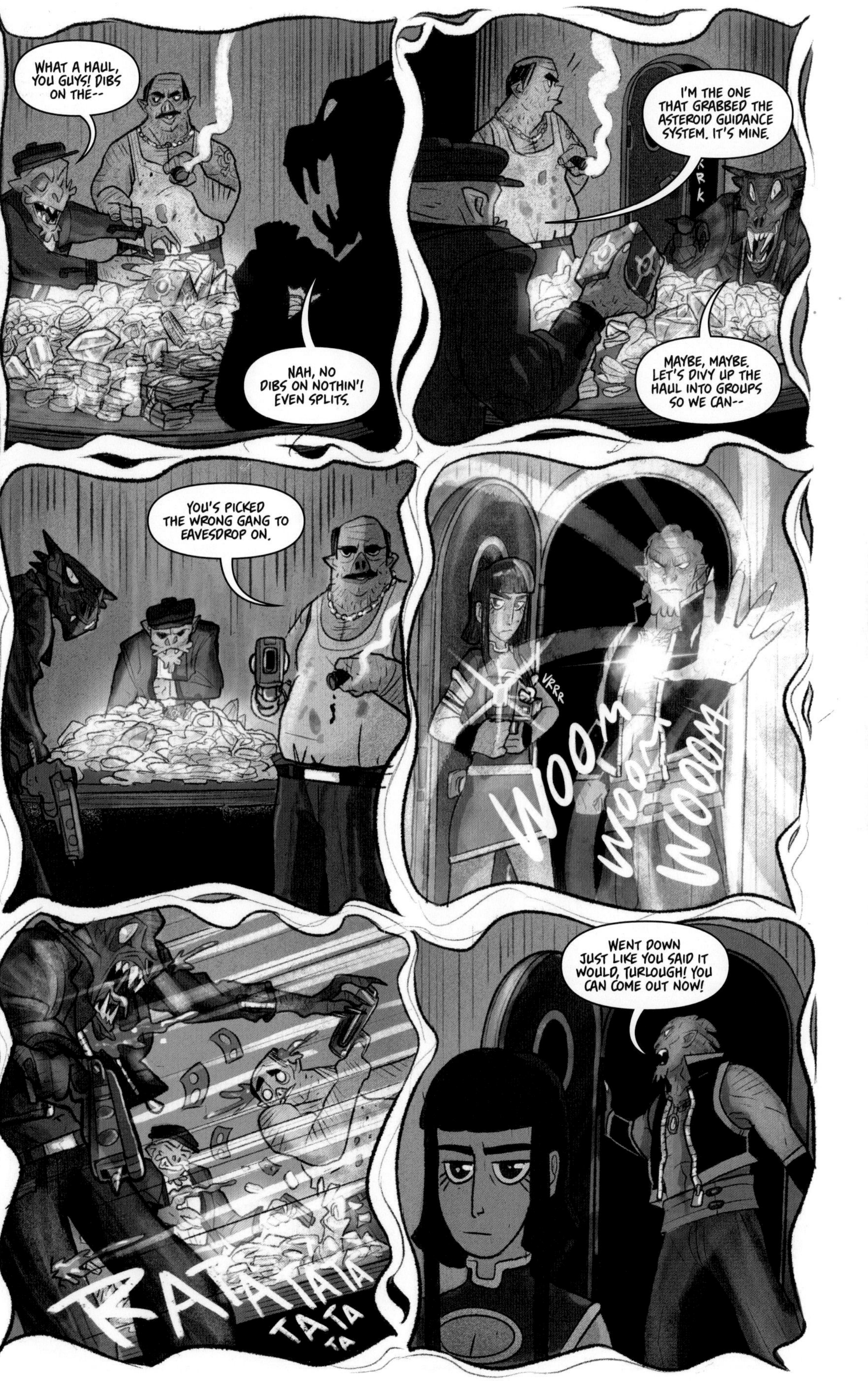
WHAT A HAUL, YOU GUYS! DIBS ON THE--
NAH, NO DIBS ON NOTHIN'! EVEN SPLITS.
I'M THE ONE THAT GRABBED THE ASTEROID GUIDANCE SYSTEM. IT'S MINE.
MAYBE, MAYBE. LET'S DIVY UP THE HAUL INTO GROUPS SO WE CAN--
YOU'S PICKED THE WRONG GANG TO EAVESDROP ON.
VRRR
WOOM WOOM WOOOM
RATATATA TATA TA
WENT DOWN JUST LIKE YOU SAID IT WOULD, TURLOUGH! YOU CAN COME OUT NOW!

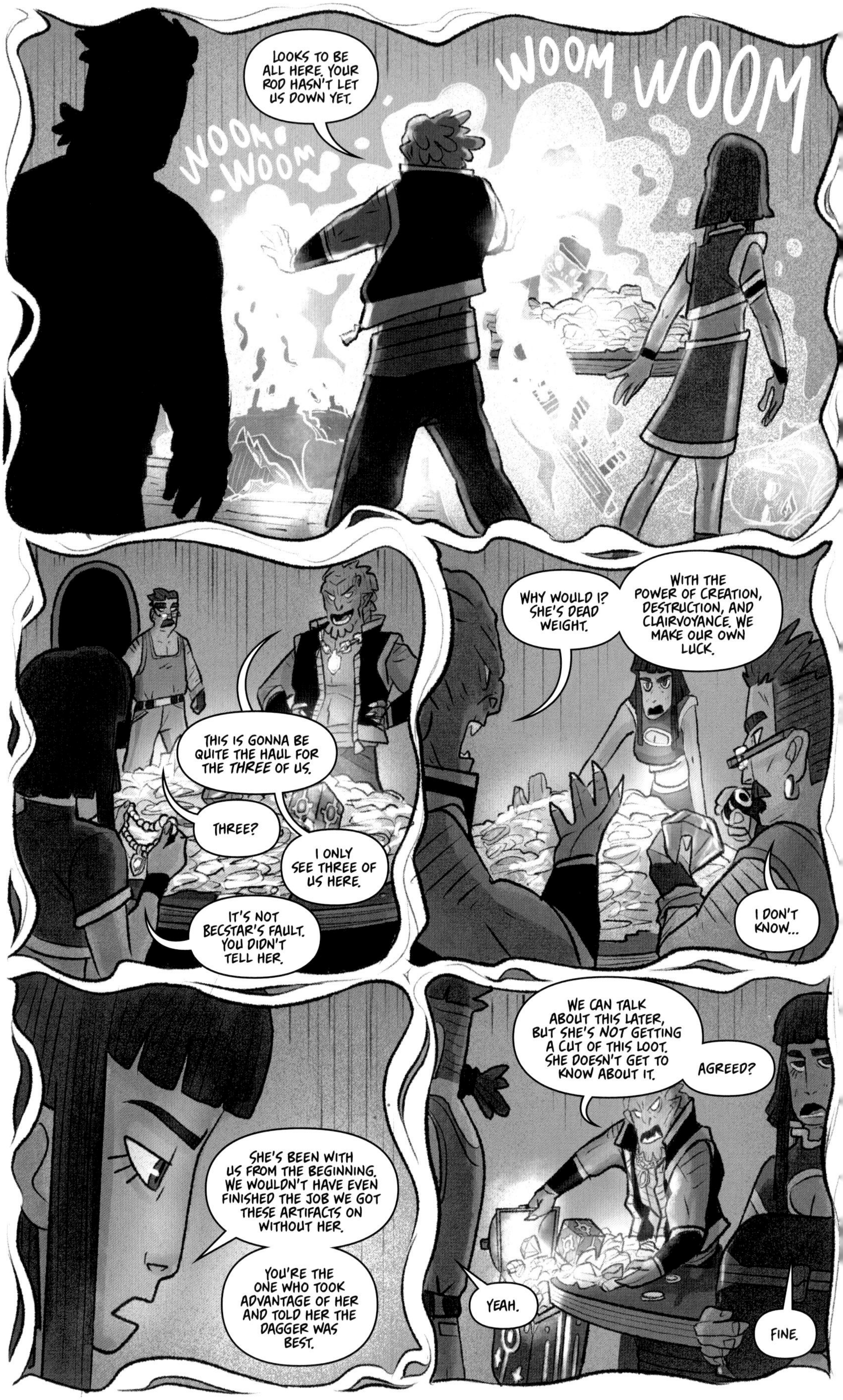
LOOKS TO BE ALL HERE. YOUR ROD HASN'T LET US DOWN YET.
WOOM WOOM
WOOM WOOM
THIS IS GONNA BE QUITE THE HAUL FOR THE THREE OF US.
THREE?
I ONLY SEE THREE OF US HERE.
IT'S NOT BECSTAR'S FAULT. YOU DIDN'T TELL HER.
WHY WOULD I? SHE'S DEAD WEIGHT.
WITH THE POWER OF CREATION, DESTRUCTION, AND CLAIRVOYANCE. WE MAKE OUR OWN LUCK.
I DON'T KNOW...
SHE'S BEEN WITH US FROM THE BEGINNING. WE WOULDN'T HAVE EVEN FINISHED THE JOB WE GOT THESE ARTIFACTS ON WITHOUT HER.
YOU'RE THE ONE WHO TOOK ADVANTAGE OF HER AND TOLD HER THE DAGGER WAS BEST.
WE CAN TALK ABOUT THIS LATER, BUT SHE'S NOT GETTING A CUT OF THIS LOOT. SHE DOESN'T GET TO KNOW ABOUT IT.
AGREED?
YEAH.
FINE.

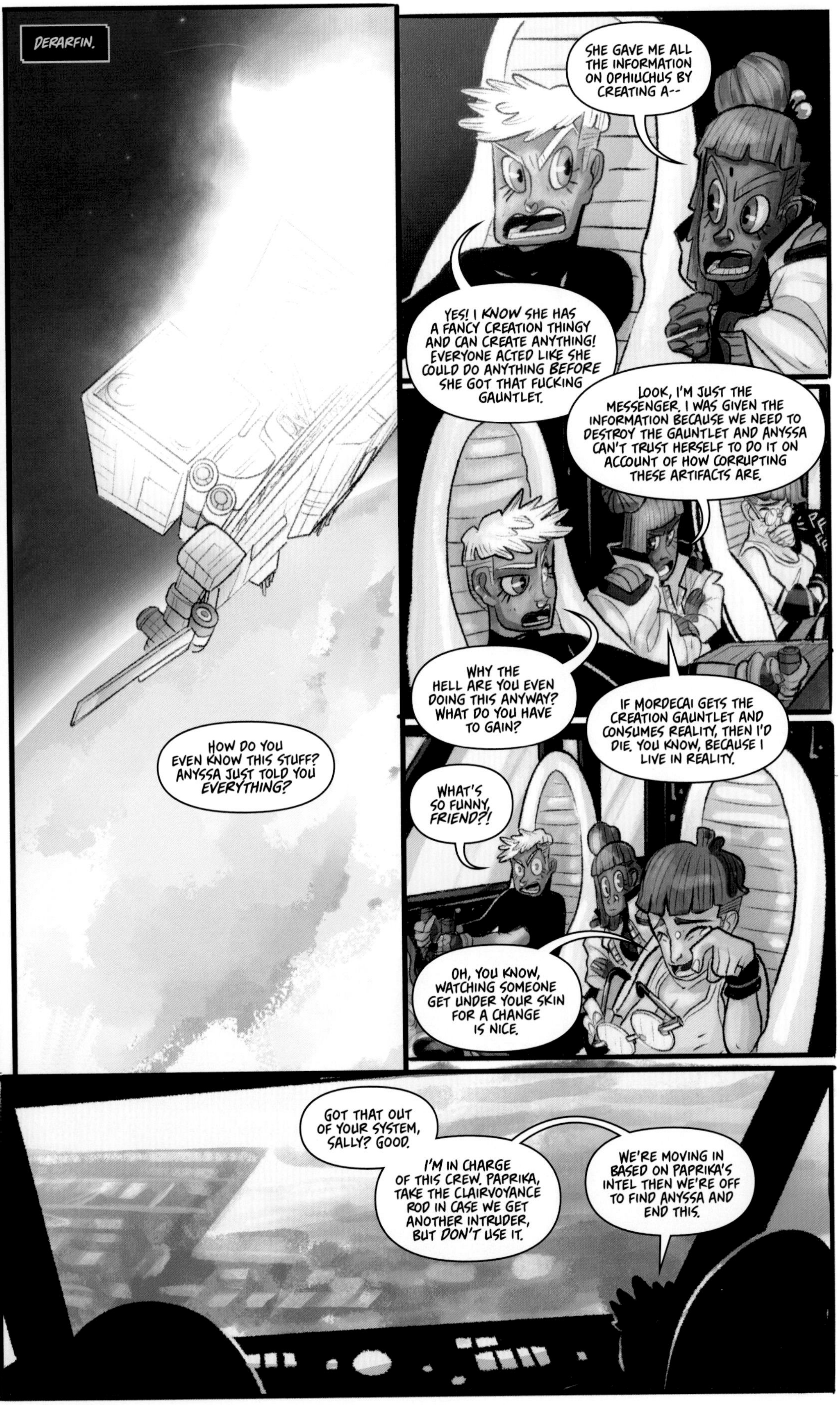
DERARFIN.
SHE GAVE ME ALL THE INFORMATION ON OPHIUCHUS BY CREATING A--
YES! I KNOW SHE HAS A FANCY CREATION THINGY AND CAN CREATE ANYTHING! EVERYONE ACTED LIKE SHE COULD DO ANYTHING *BEFORE* SHE GOT THAT FUCKING GAUNTLET.
LOOK, I'M JUST THE MESSENGER. I WAS GIVEN THE INFORMATION BECAUSE WE NEED TO DESTROY THE GAUNTLET AND ANYSSA CAN'T TRUST HERSELF TO DO IT ON ACCOUNT OF HOW CORRUPTING THESE ARTIFACTS ARE.
PFFF
WHY THE HELL ARE YOU EVEN DOING THIS ANYWAY? WHAT DO YOU HAVE TO GAIN?
IF MORDECAI GETS THE CREATION GAUNTLET AND CONSUMES REALITY, THEN I'D DIE. YOU KNOW, BECAUSE I LIVE IN REALITY.
HOW DO YOU EVEN KNOW THIS STUFF? ANYSSA JUST TOLD YOU *EVERYTHING?*
WHAT'S SO FUNNY, *FRIEND?!*
OH, YOU KNOW, WATCHING SOMEONE GET UNDER YOUR SKIN FOR A CHANGE IS NICE.
GOT THAT OUT OF YOUR SYSTEM, SALLY? GOOD.
I'M IN CHARGE OF THIS CREW. PAPRIKA, TAKE THE CLAIRVOYANCE ROD IN CASE WE GET ANOTHER INTRUDER, BUT *DON'T* USE IT.
WE'RE MOVING IN BASED ON PAPRIKA'S INTEL THEN WE'RE OFF TO FIND ANYSSA AND END THIS.

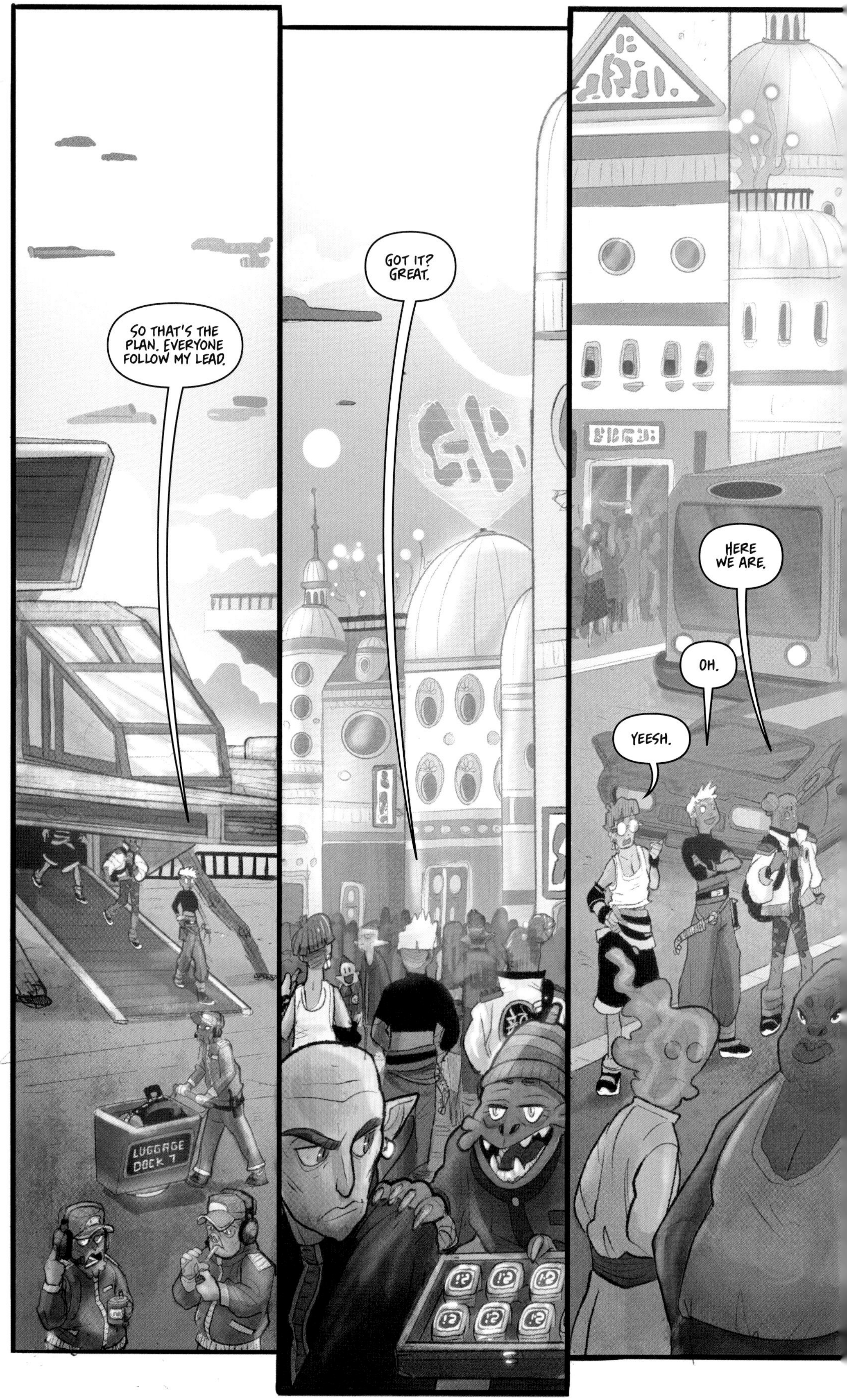
SO THAT'S THE PLAN. EVERYONE FOLLOW MY LEAD.
LUGGAGE DOCK 7
GOT IT? GREAT.
HERE WE ARE.
OH.
YEESH.

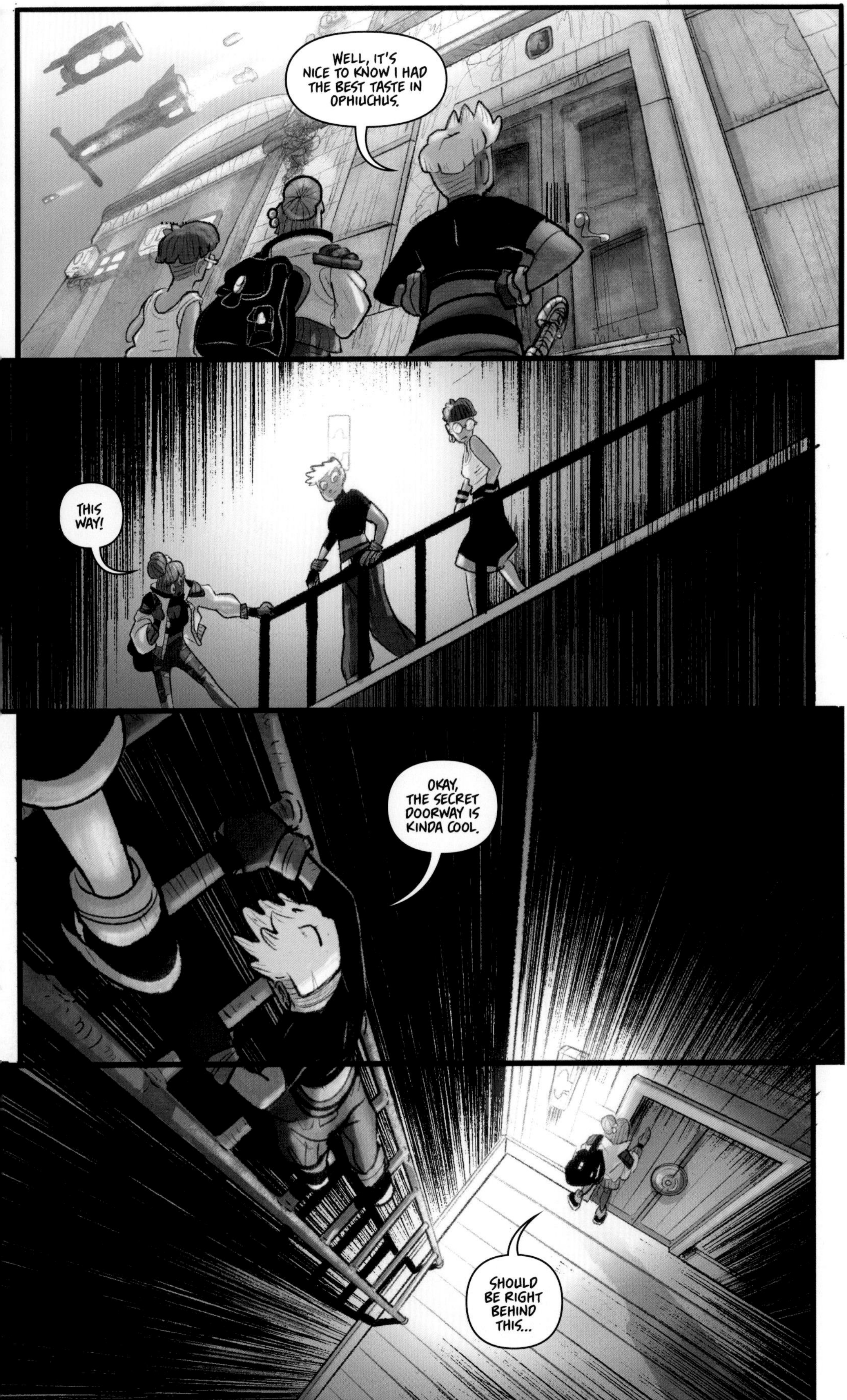
WELL, IT'S NICE TO KNOW I HAD THE BEST TASTE IN OPHIUCHUS.
THIS WAY!
OKAY, THE SECRET DOORWAY IS KINDA COOL.
SHOULD BE RIGHT BEHIND THIS...

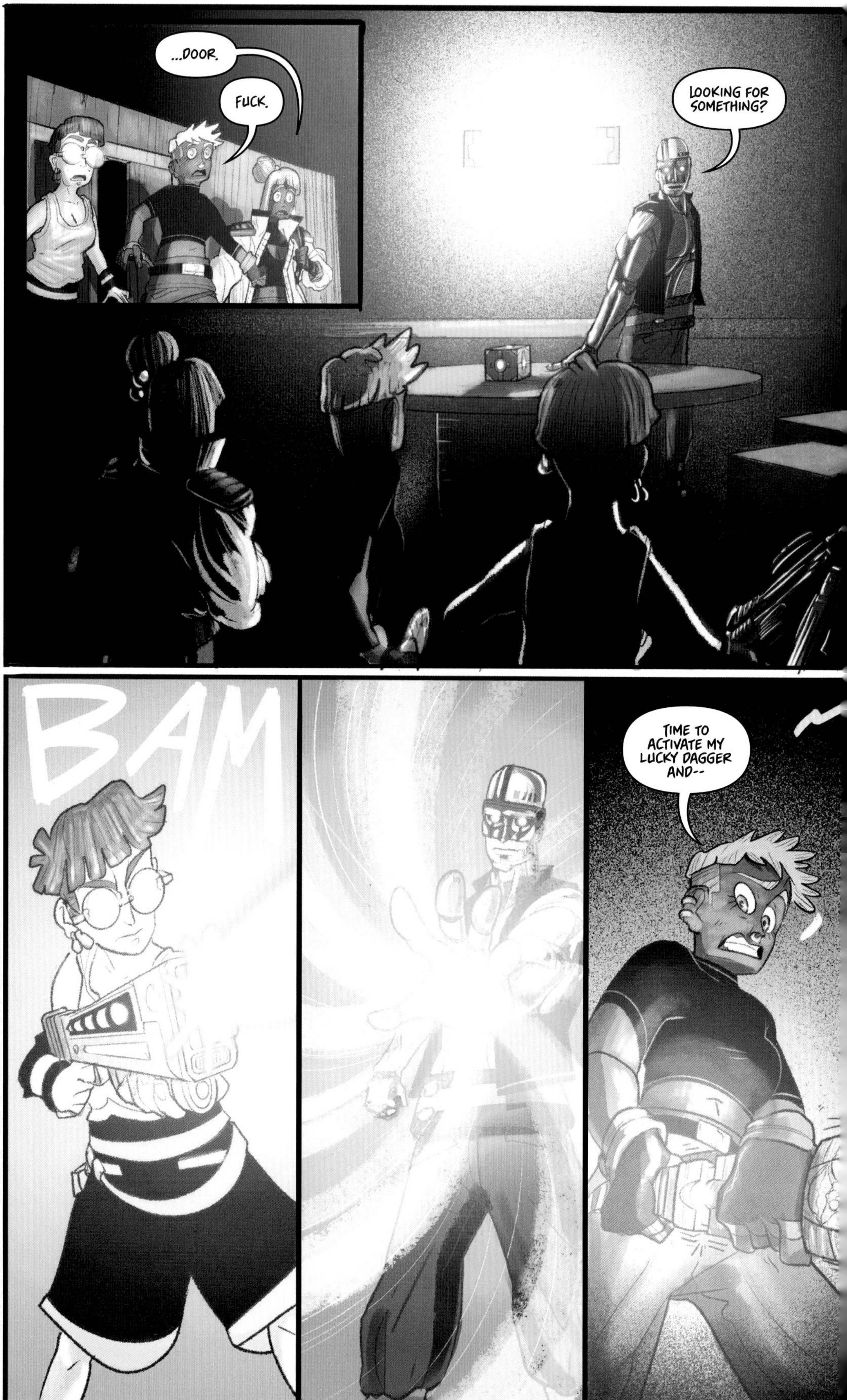
...DOOR.
FUCK.
LOOKING FOR SOMETHING?
BAM
TIME TO ACTIVATE MY LUCKY DAGGER AND--

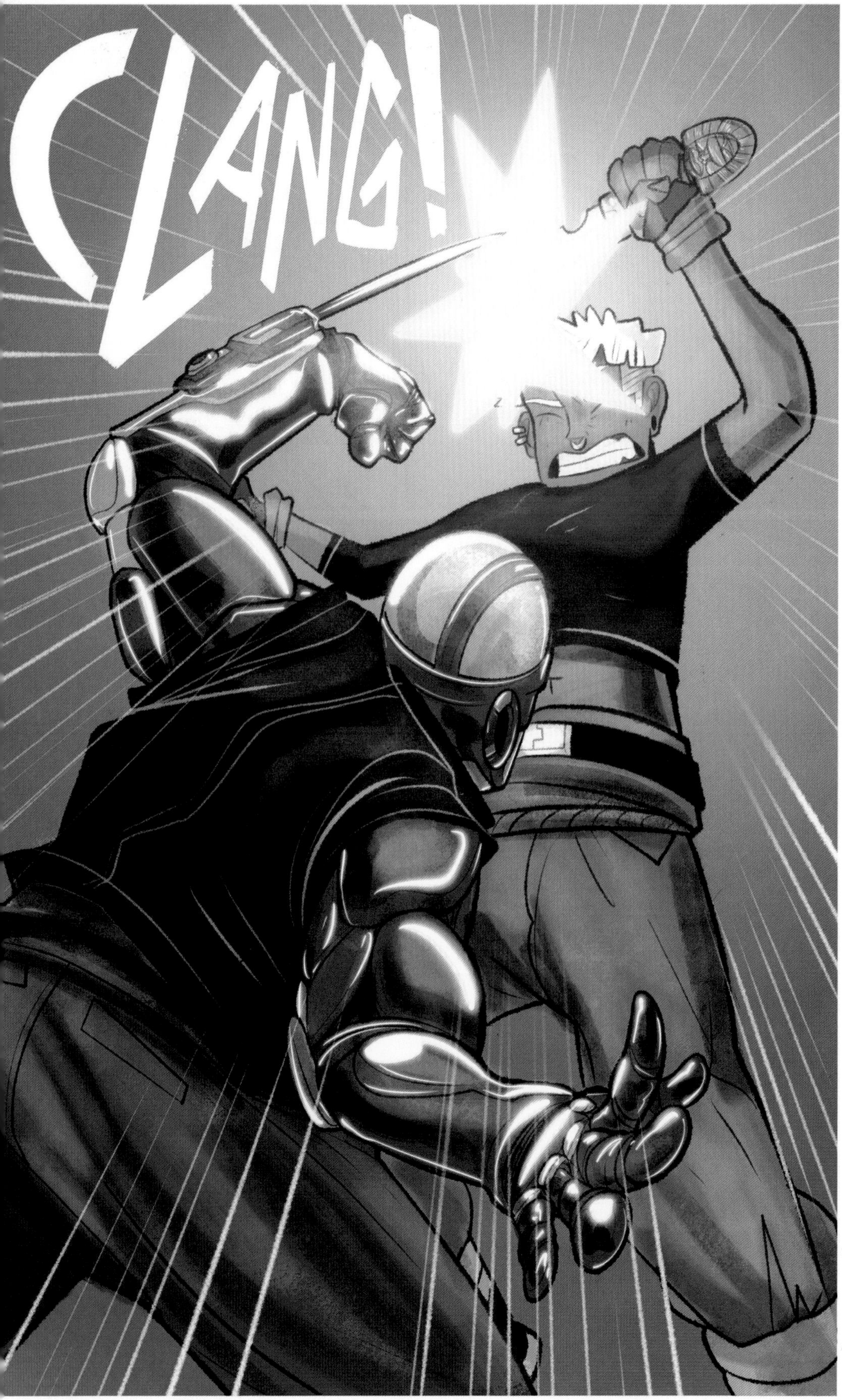
CLANG!

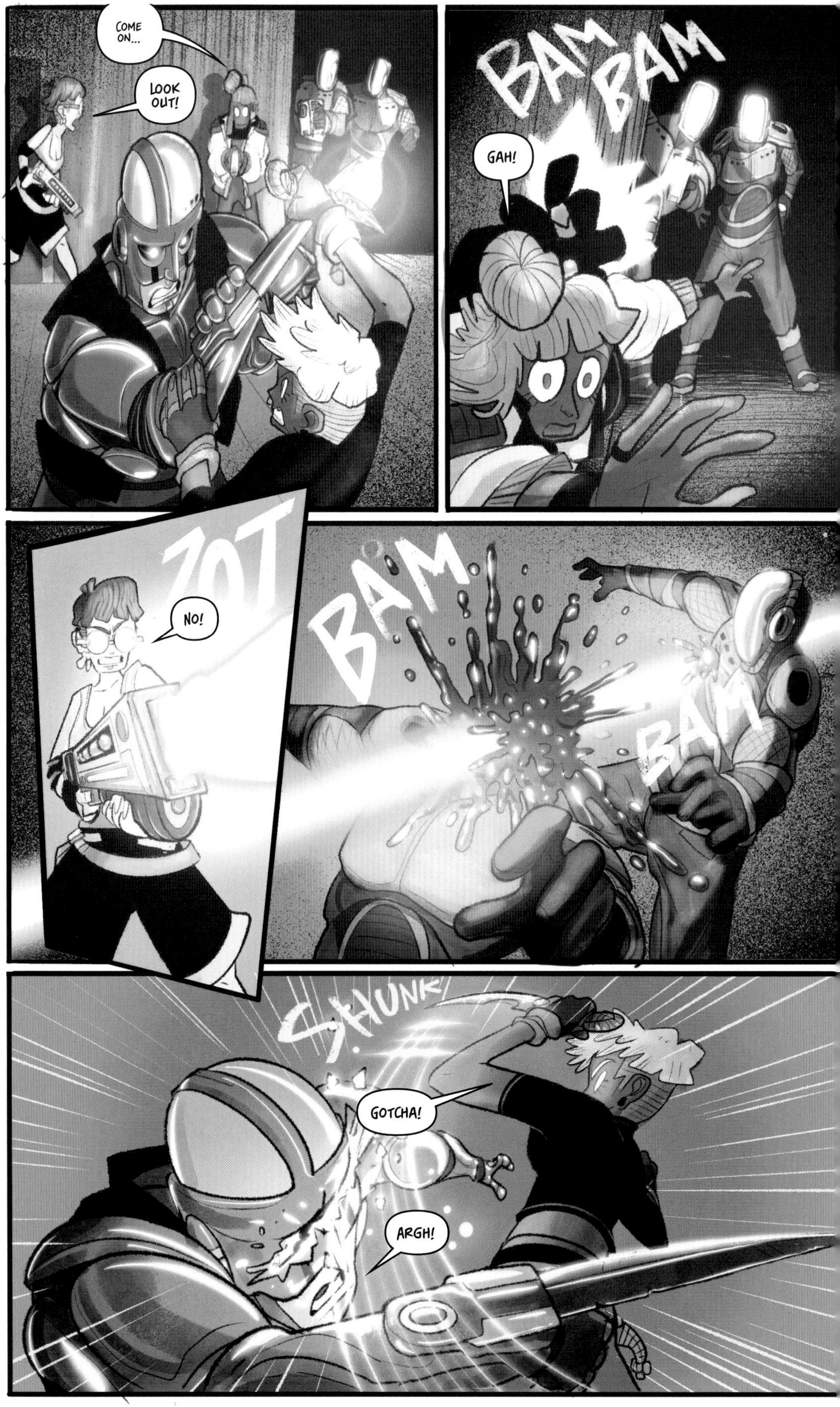
COME ON...
LOOK OUT!
BAM BAM
GAH!
ZOT
NO!
BAM
BAM
SHUNK
GOTCHA!
ARGH!

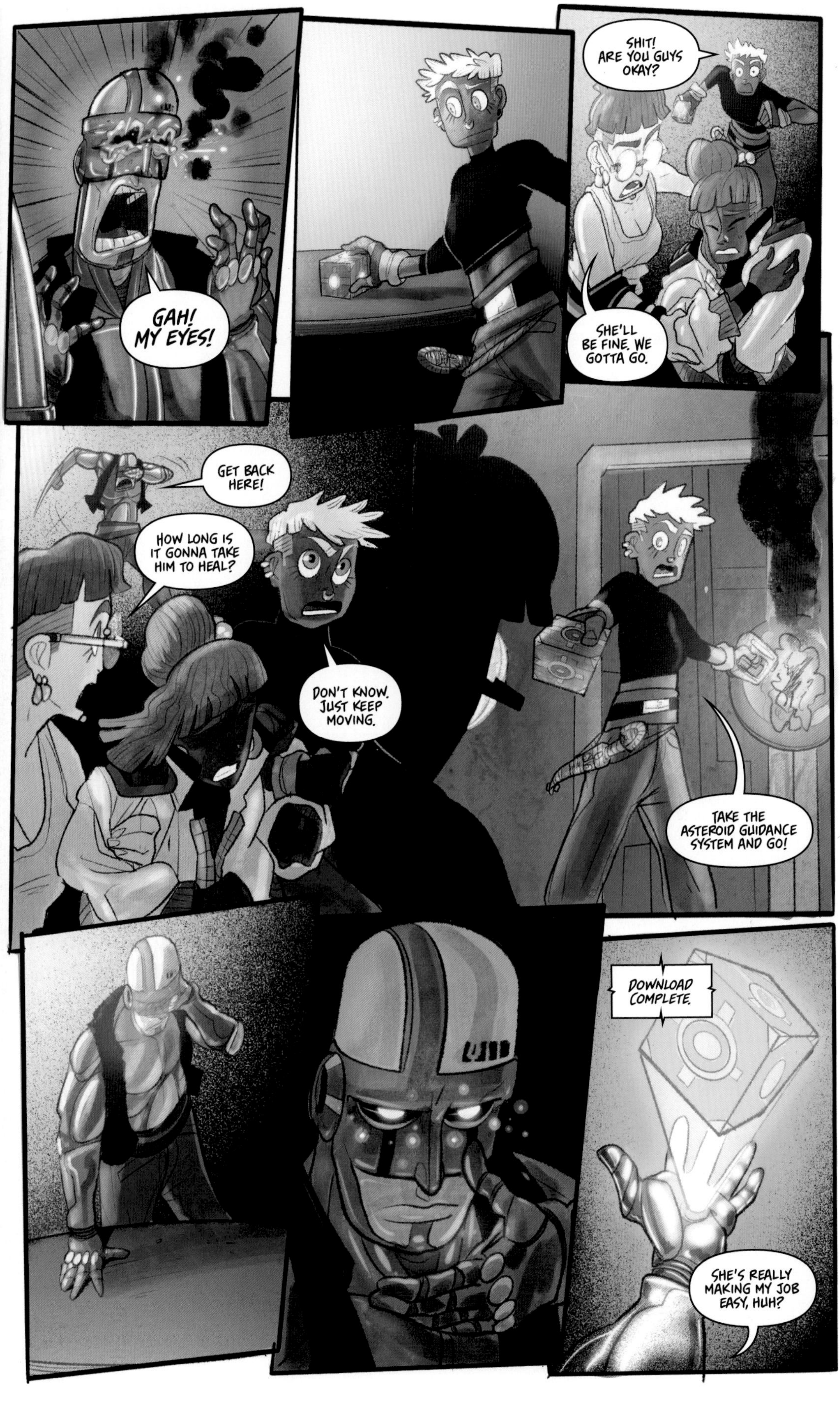

GAH! MY EYES!
SHIT! ARE YOU GUYS OKAY?
SHE'LL BE FINE. WE GOTTA GO.
GET BACK HERE!
HOW LONG IS IT GONNA TAKE HIM TO HEAL?
DON'T KNOW. JUST KEEP MOVING.
TAKE THE ASTEROID GUIDANCE SYSTEM AND GO!
DOWNLOAD COMPLETE.
SHE'S REALLY MAKING MY JOB EASY, HUH?

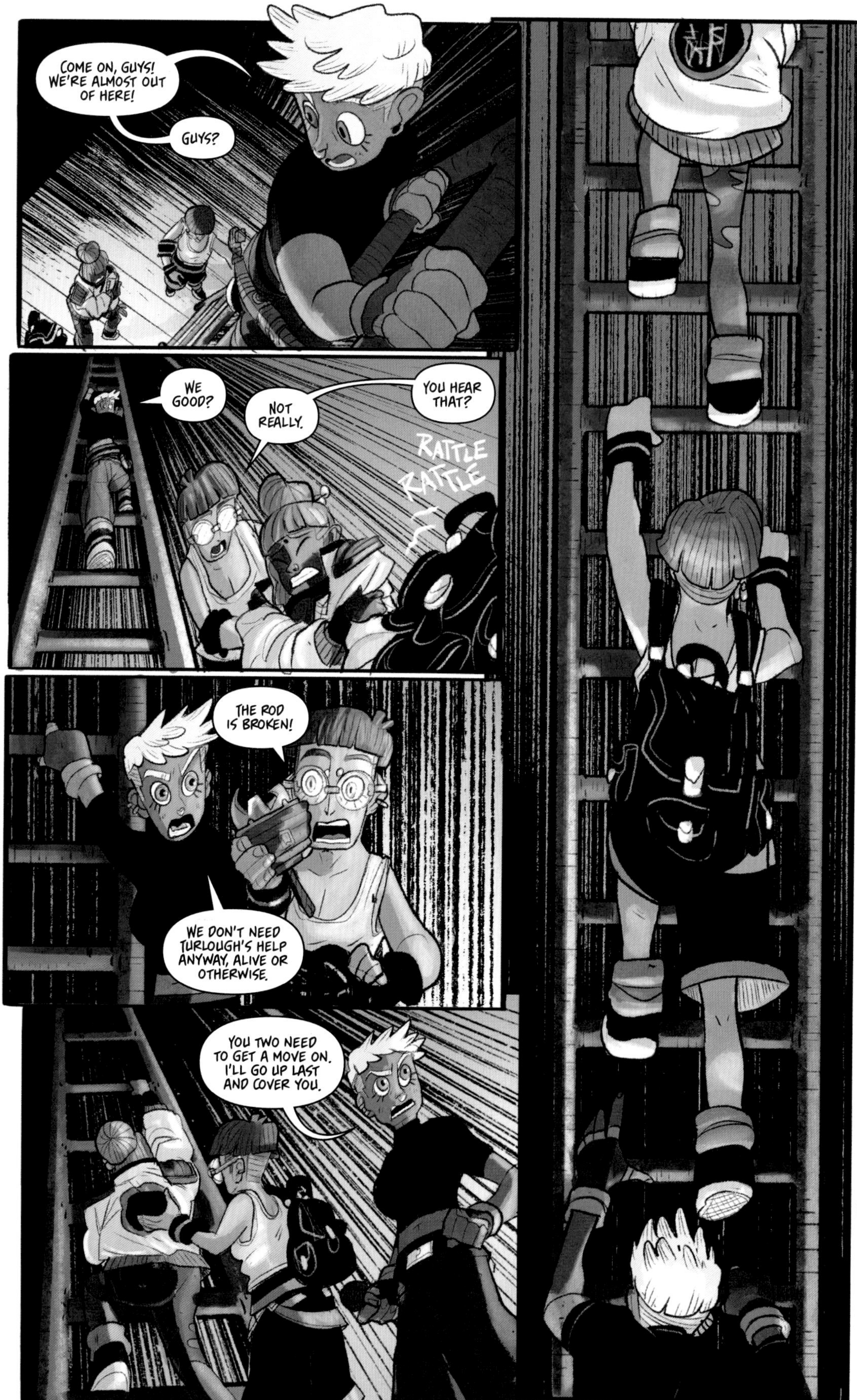
COME ON, GUYS! WE'RE ALMOST OUT OF HERE!
GUYS?
WE GOOD?
NOT REALLY.
YOU HEAR THAT?
RATTLE RATTLE
THE ROD IS BROKEN!
WE DON'T NEED TURLOUGH'S HELP ANYWAY, ALIVE OR OTHERWISE.
YOU TWO NEED TO GET A MOVE ON. I'LL GO UP LAST AND COVER YOU.

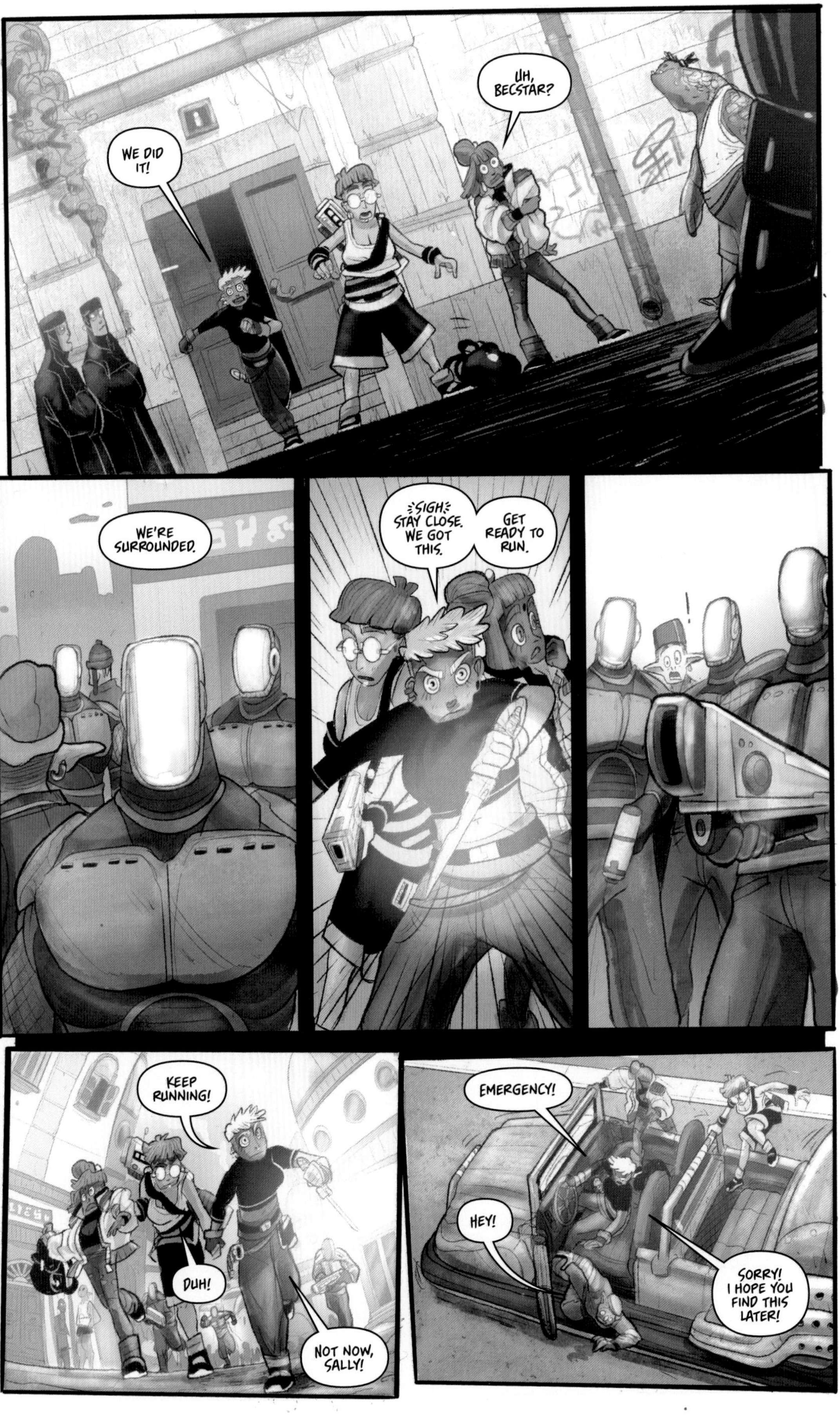
WE DID IT!
UH, BECSTAR?
WE'RE SURROUNDED.
SIGH STAY CLOSE. WE GOT THIS.
GET READY TO RUN.
!
KEEP RUNNING!
DUH!
NOT NOW, SALLY!
EMERGENCY!
HEY!
SORRY! I HOPE YOU FIND THIS LATER!

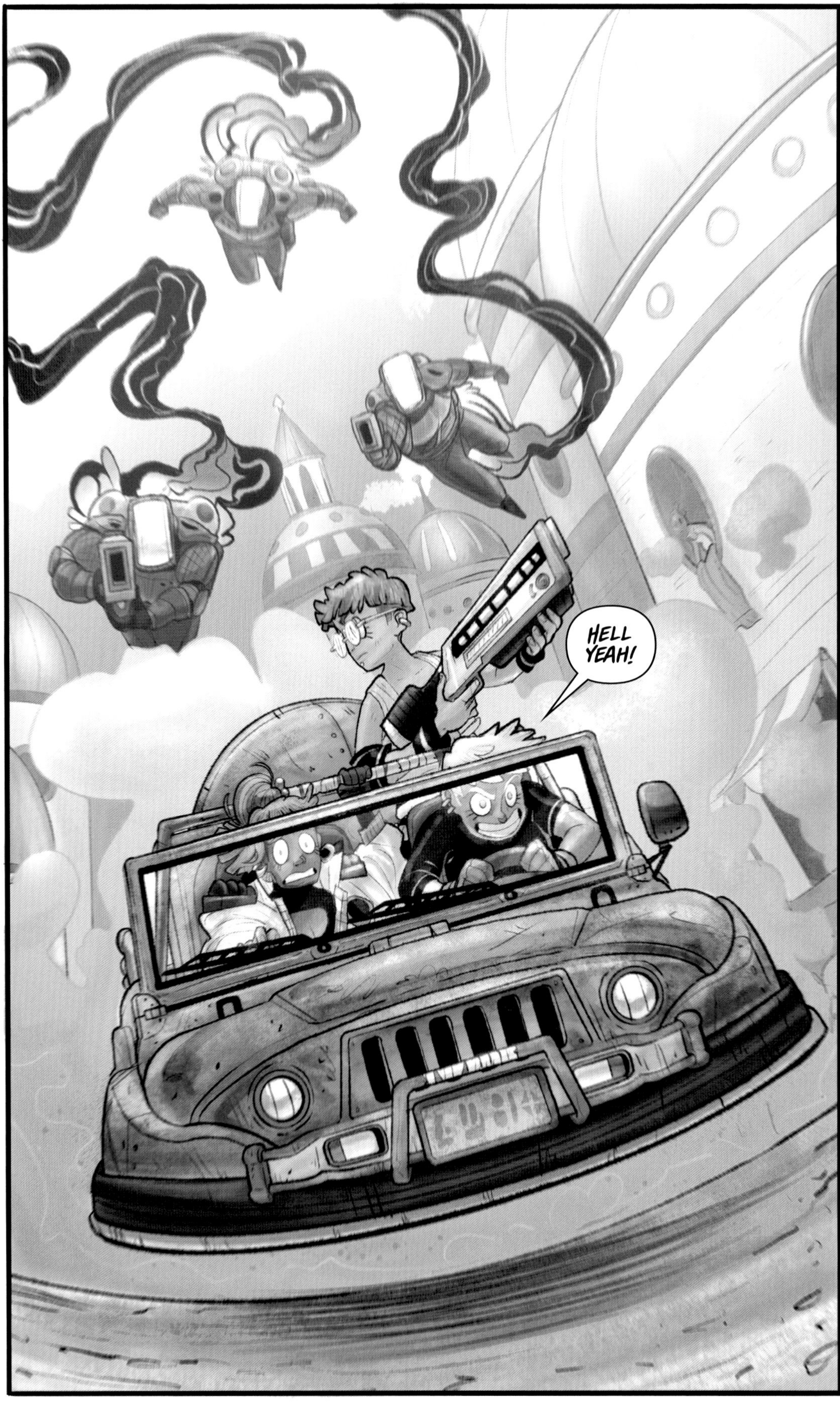
HELL YEAH!

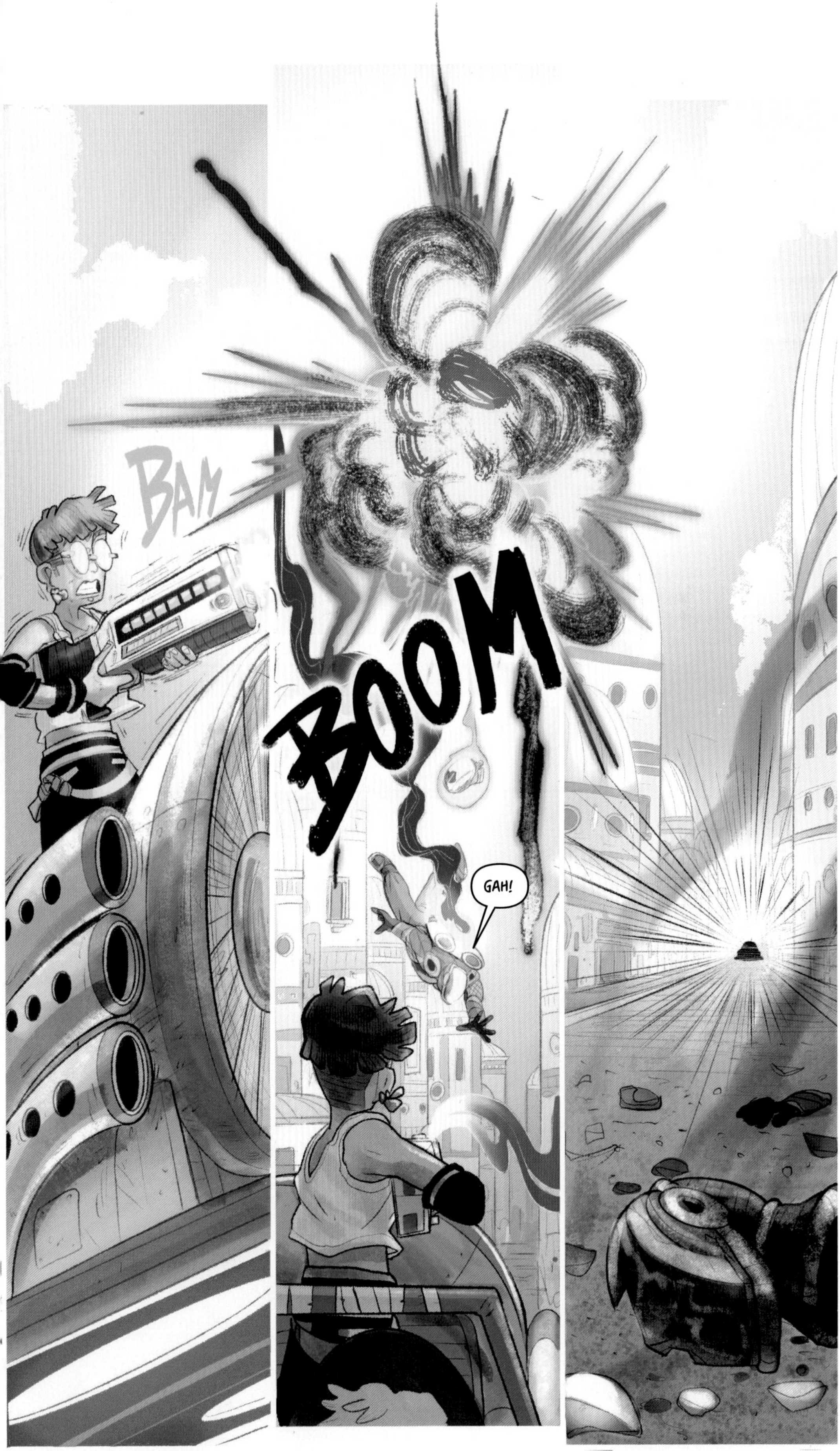
BAM
BOOM
GAH!

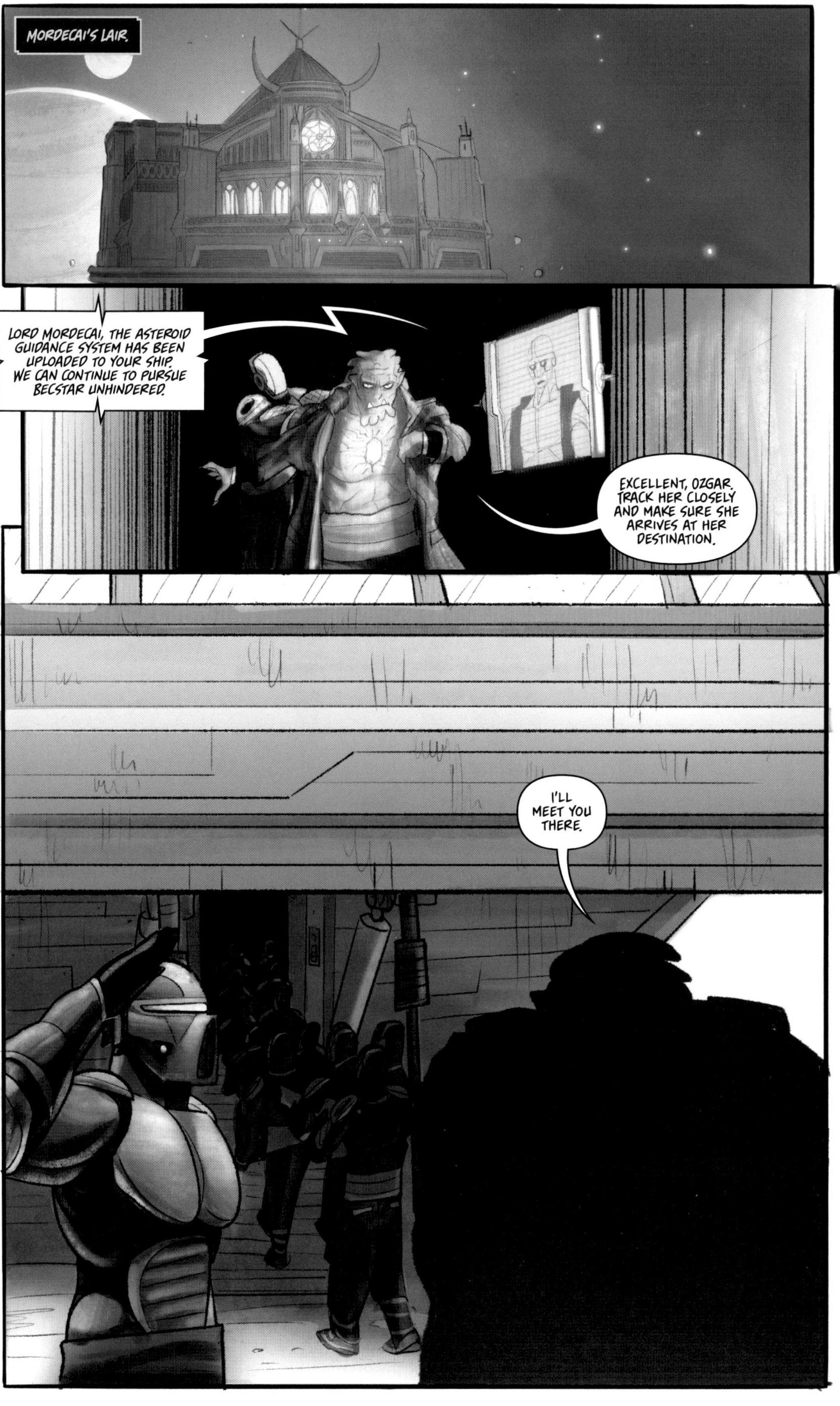
MORDECAI'S LAIR.
LORD MORDECAI, THE ASTEROID GUIDANCE SYSTEM HAS BEEN UPLOADED TO YOUR SHIP. WE CAN CONTINUE TO PURSUE BECSTAR UNHINDERED.
EXCELLENT, OZGAR. TRACK HER CLOSELY AND MAKE SURE SHE ARRIVES AT HER DESTINATION.
I'LL MEET YOU THERE.

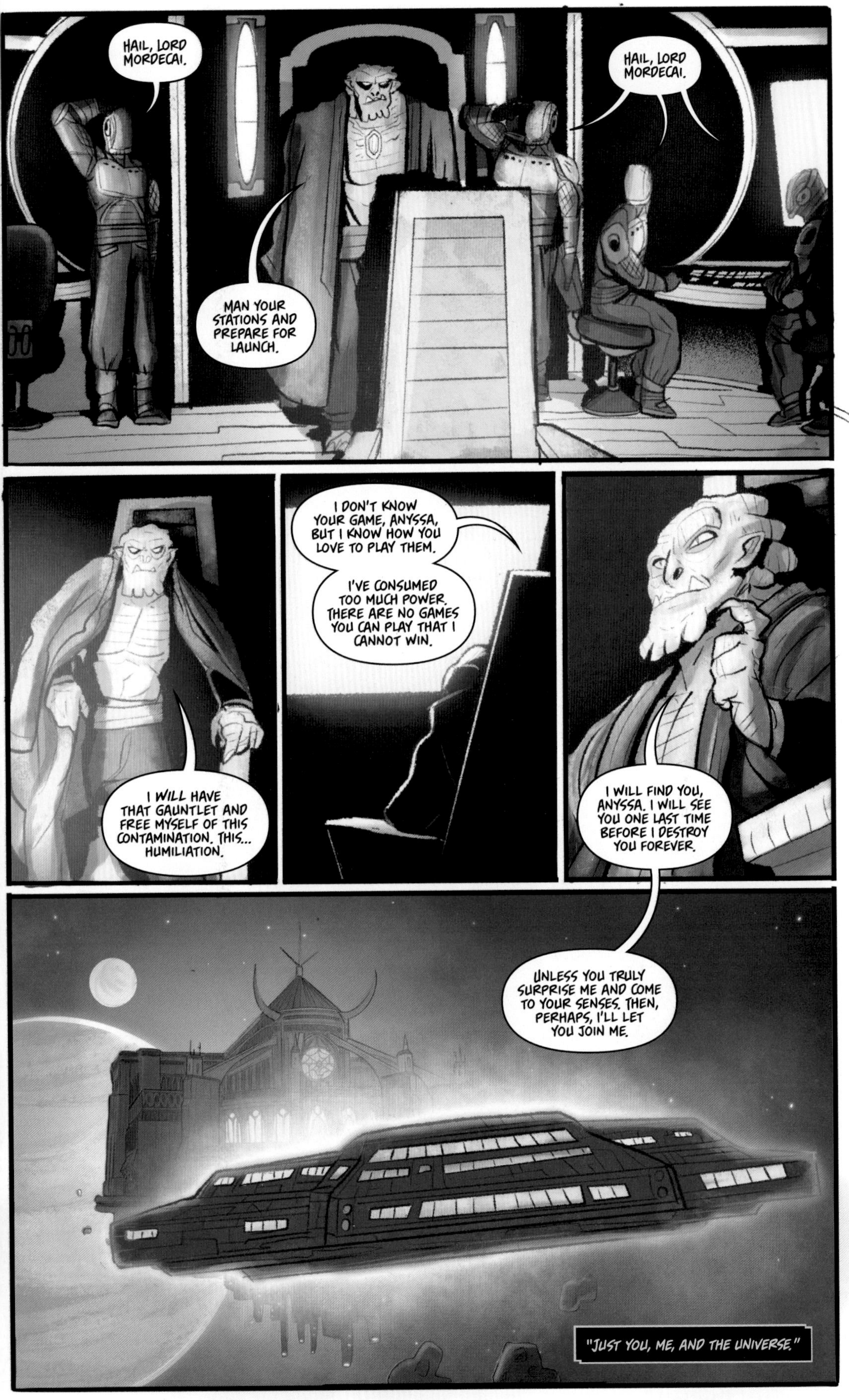
HAIL, LORD MORDECAI.
HAIL, LORD MORDECAI.
MAN YOUR STATIONS AND PREPARE FOR LAUNCH.
I WILL HAVE THAT GAUNTLET AND FREE MYSELF OF THIS CONTAMINATION. THIS... HUMILIATION.
I DON'T KNOW YOUR GAME, ANYSSA, BUT I KNOW HOW YOU LOVE TO PLAY THEM.
I'VE CONSUMED TOO MUCH POWER. THERE ARE NO GAMES YOU CAN PLAY THAT I CANNOT WIN.
I WILL FIND YOU, ANYSSA. I WILL SEE YOU ONE LAST TIME BEFORE I DESTROY YOU FOREVER.
UNLESS YOU TRULY SURPRISE ME AND COME TO YOUR SENSES. THEN, PERHAPS, I'LL LET YOU JOIN ME.
"JUST YOU, ME, AND THE UNIVERSE."

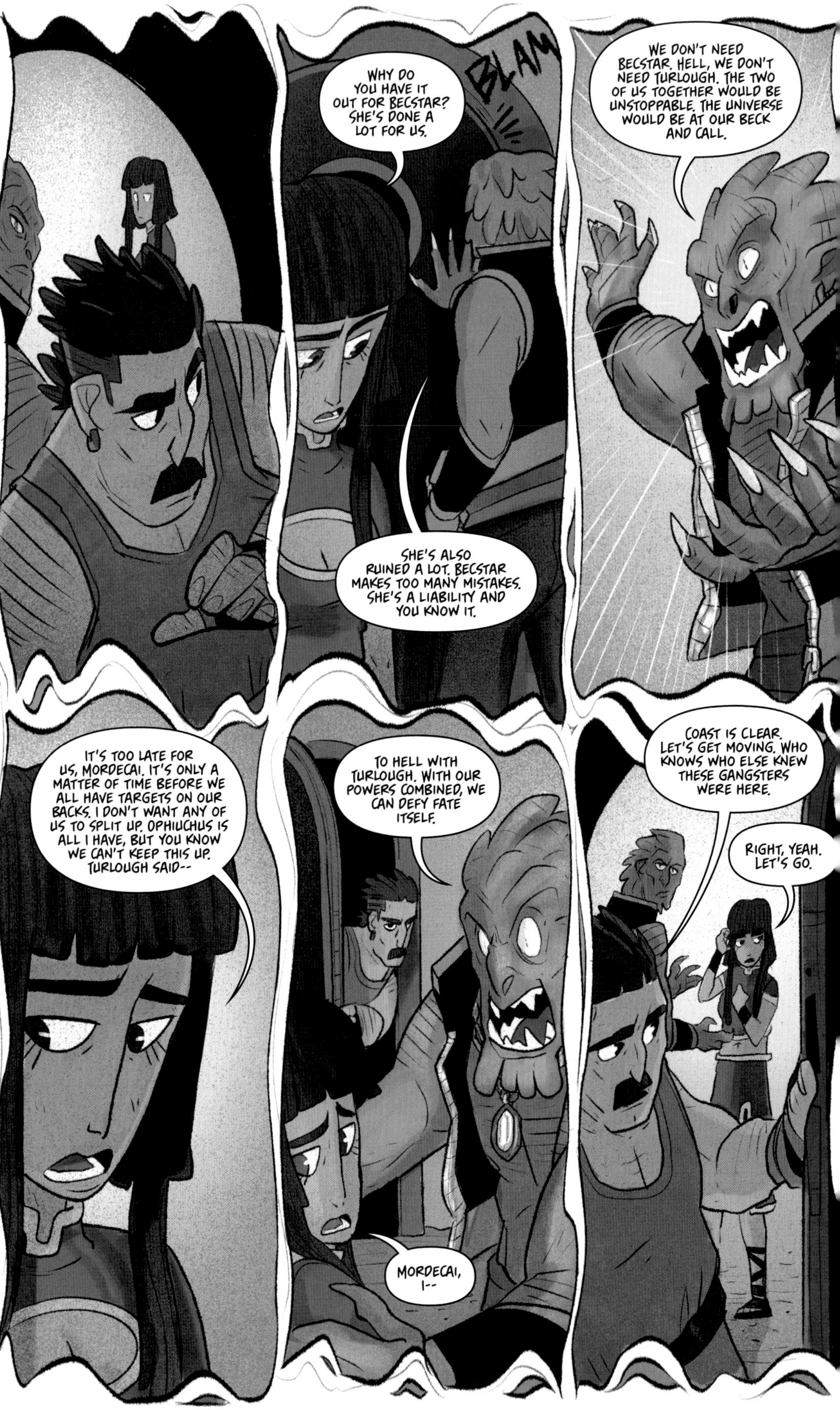
WHY DO YOU HAVE IT OUT FOR BECSTAR? SHE'S DONE A LOT FOR US.
BLAM
SHE'S ALSO RUINED A LOT. BECSTAR MAKES TOO MANY MISTAKES. SHE'S A LIABILITY AND YOU KNOW IT.
WE DON'T NEED BECSTAR. HELL, WE DON'T NEED TURLOUGH. THE TWO OF US TOGETHER WOULD BE UNSTOPPABLE. THE UNIVERSE WOULD BE AT OUR BECK AND CALL.
IT'S TOO LATE FOR US, MORDECAI. IT'S ONLY A MATTER OF TIME BEFORE WE ALL HAVE TARGETS ON OUR BACKS. I DON'T WANT ANY OF US TO SPLIT UP. OPHIUCHUS IS ALL I HAVE, BUT YOU KNOW WE CAN'T KEEP THIS UP. TURLOUGH SAID--
TO HELL WITH TURLOUGH. WITH OUR POWERS COMBINED, WE CAN DEFY FATE ITSELF.
MORDECAI, I--
COAST IS CLEAR. LET'S GET MOVING. WHO KNOWS WHO ELSE KNEW THESE GANGSTERS WERE HERE.
RIGHT, YEAH. LET'S GO.

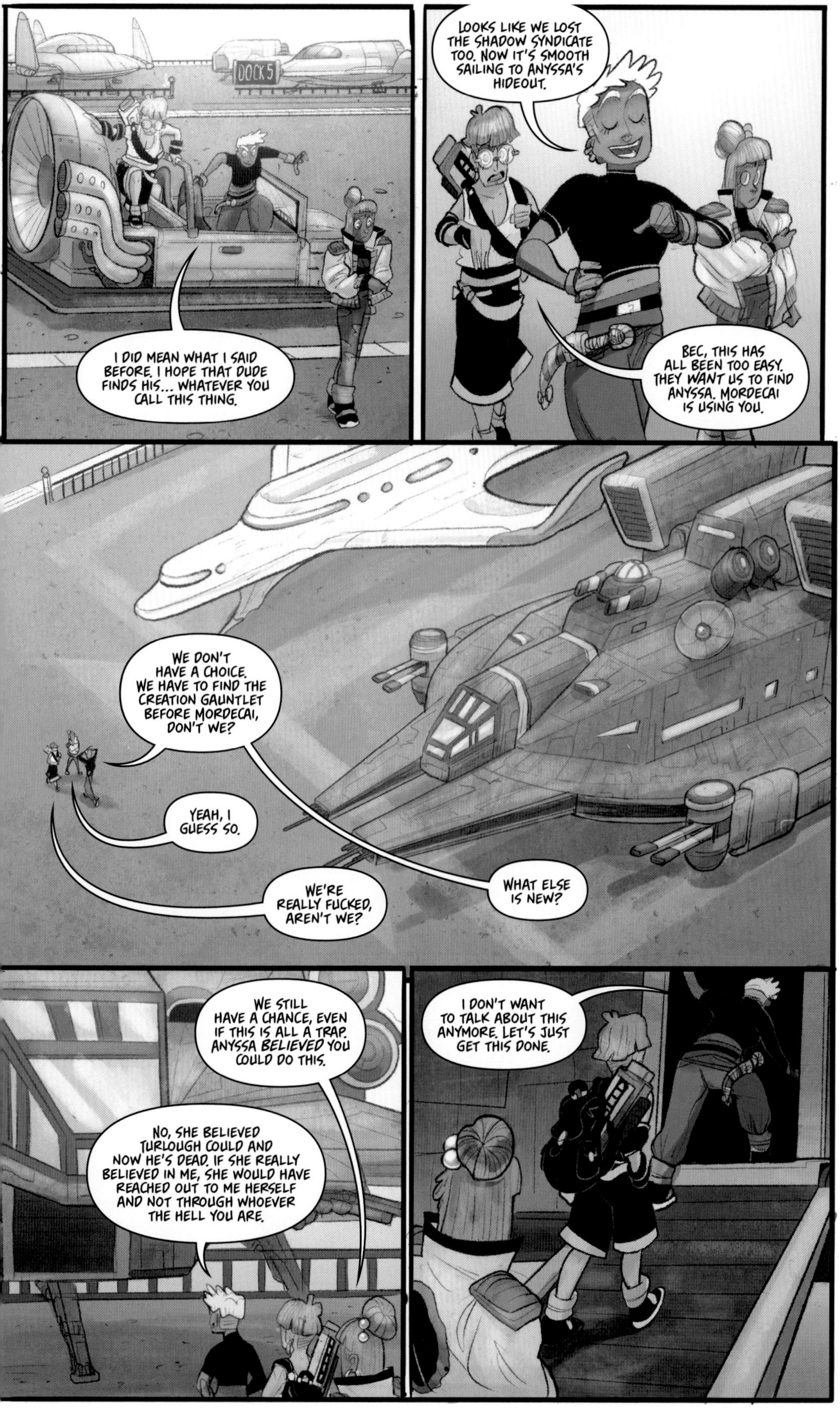
DOCK 5
I DID MEAN WHAT I SAID BEFORE. I HOPE THAT DUDE FINDS HIS... WHATEVER YOU CALL THIS THING.
LOOKS LIKE WE LOST THE SHADOW SYNDICATE TOO. NOW IT'S SMOOTH SAILING TO ANYSSA'S HIDEOUT.
BEC, THIS HAS ALL BEEN TOO EASY. THEY WANT US TO FIND ANYSSA. MORDECAI IS USING YOU.
WE DON'T HAVE A CHOICE. WE HAVE TO FIND THE CREATION GAUNTLET BEFORE MORDECAI, DON'T WE?
YEAH, I GUESS SO.
WE'RE REALLY FUCKED, AREN'T WE?
WHAT ELSE IS NEW?
WE STILL HAVE A CHANCE, EVEN IF THIS IS ALL A TRAP. ANYSSA BELIEVED YOU COULD DO THIS.
NO, SHE BELIEVED TURLOUGH COULD AND NOW HE'S DEAD. IF SHE REALLY BELIEVED IN ME, SHE WOULD HAVE REACHED OUT TO ME HERSELF AND NOT THROUGH WHOEVER THE HELL YOU ARE.
I DON'T WANT TO TALK ABOUT THIS ANYMORE. LET'S JUST GET THIS DONE.

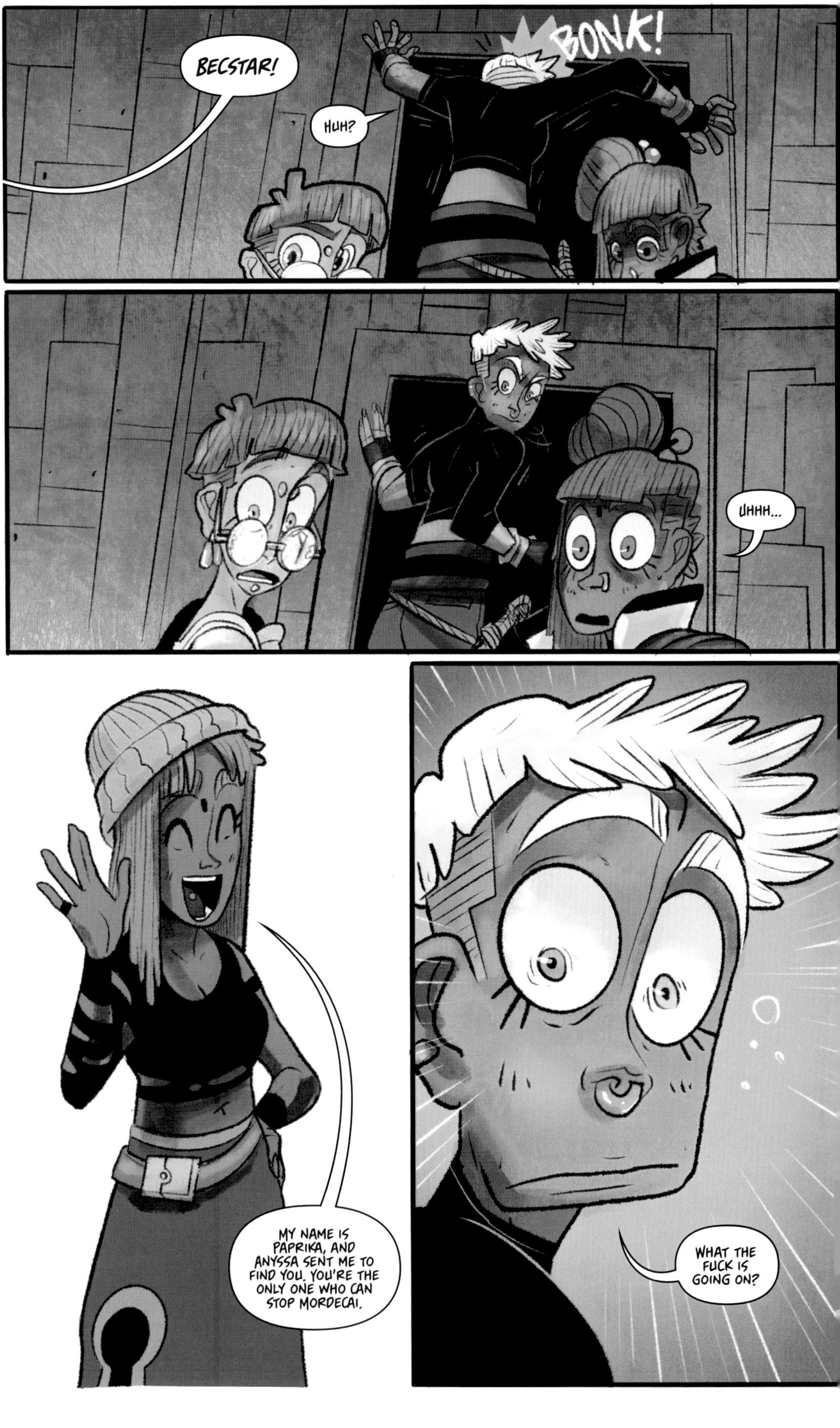
BONK!
BECSTAR!
HUH?
UHHH...
MY NAME IS PAPRIKA, AND ANYSSA SENT ME TO FIND YOU. YOU'RE THE ONLY ONE WHO CAN STOP MORDECAI.
WHAT THE FUCK IS GOING ON?

PART 04

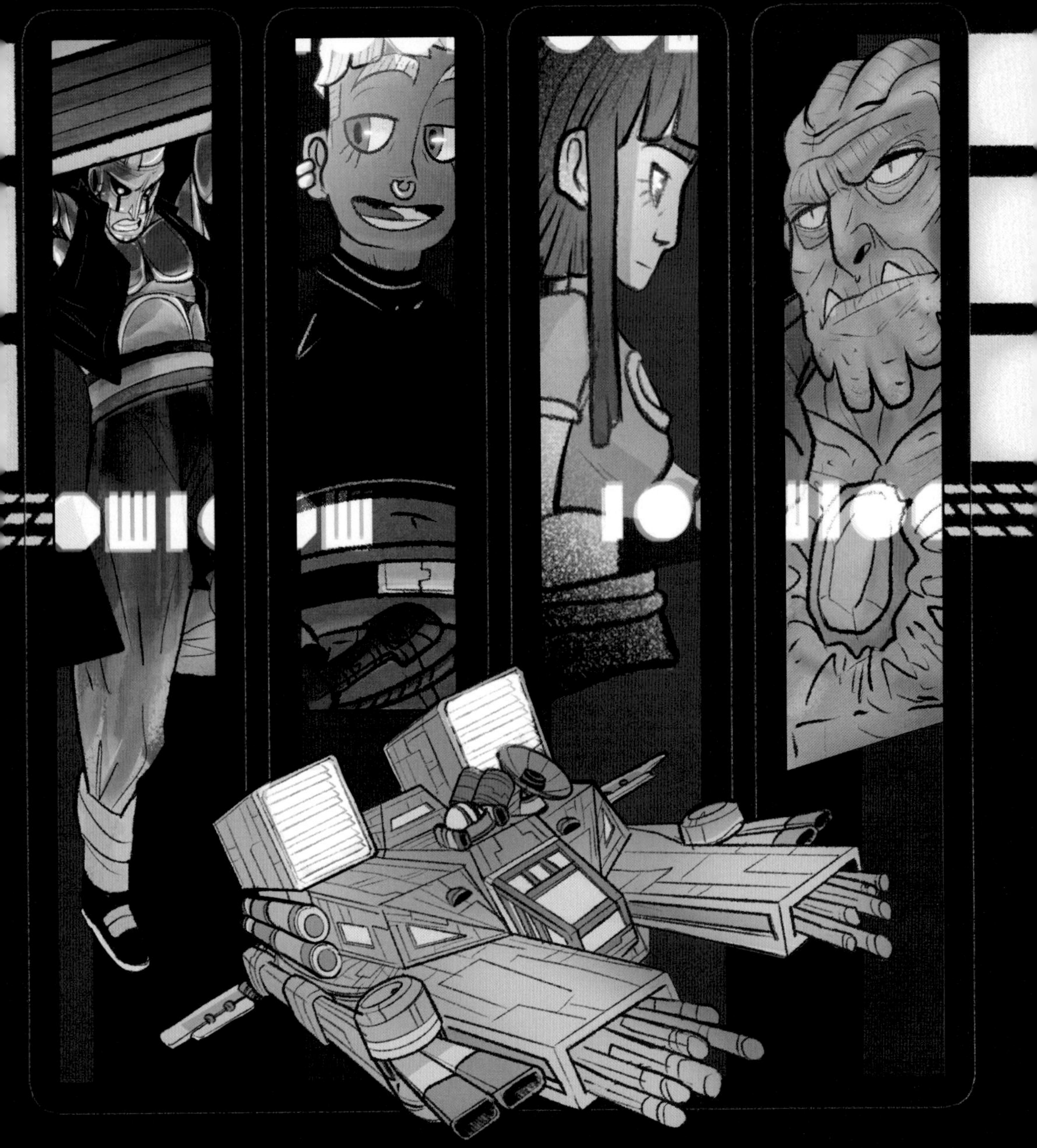

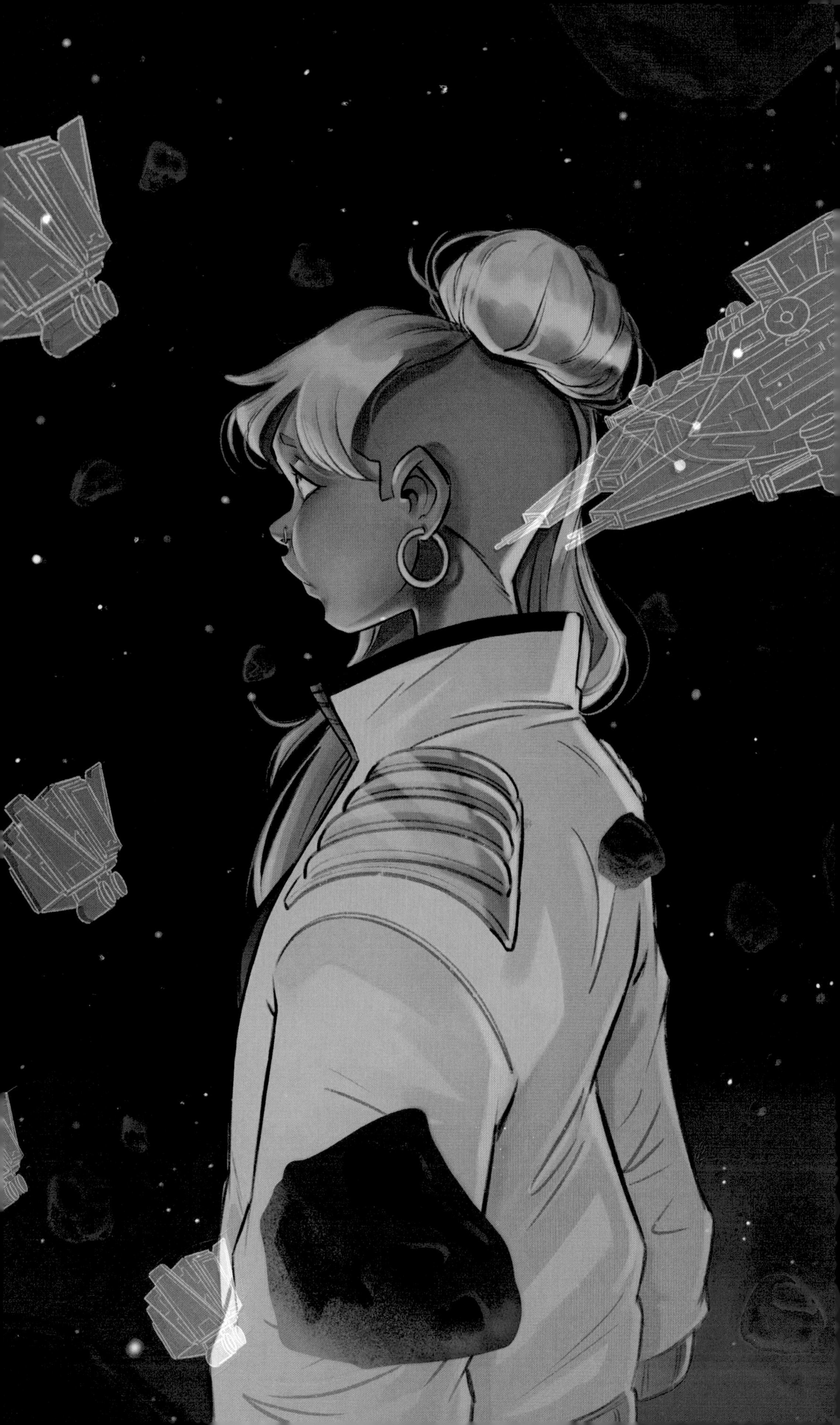

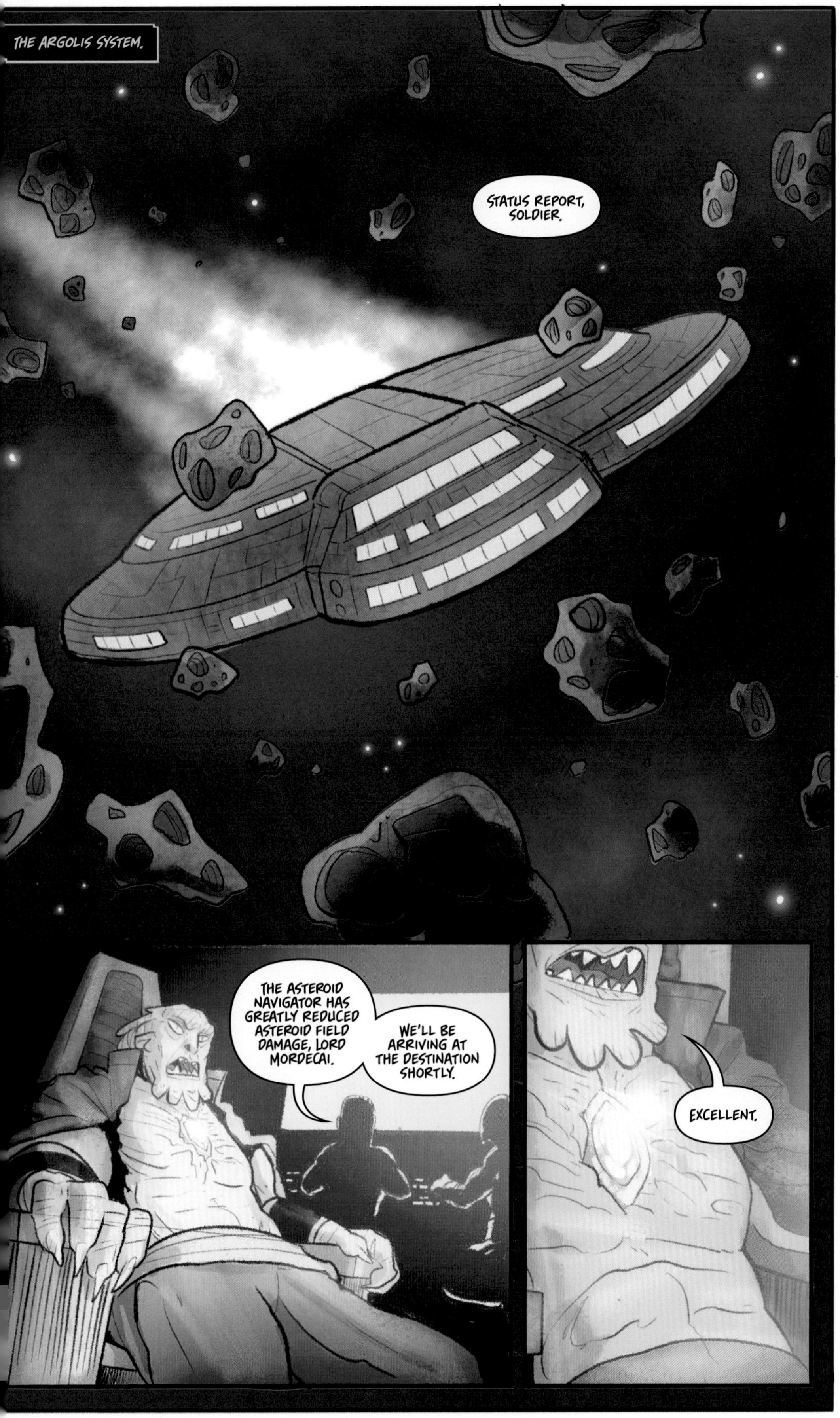
THE ARGOLIS SYSTEM.
STATUS REPORT, SOLDIER.
THE ASTEROID NAVIGATOR HAS GREATLY REDUCED ASTEROID FIELD DAMAGE, LORD MORDECAI.
WE'LL BE ARRIVING AT THE DESTINATION SHORTLY.
EXCELLENT.

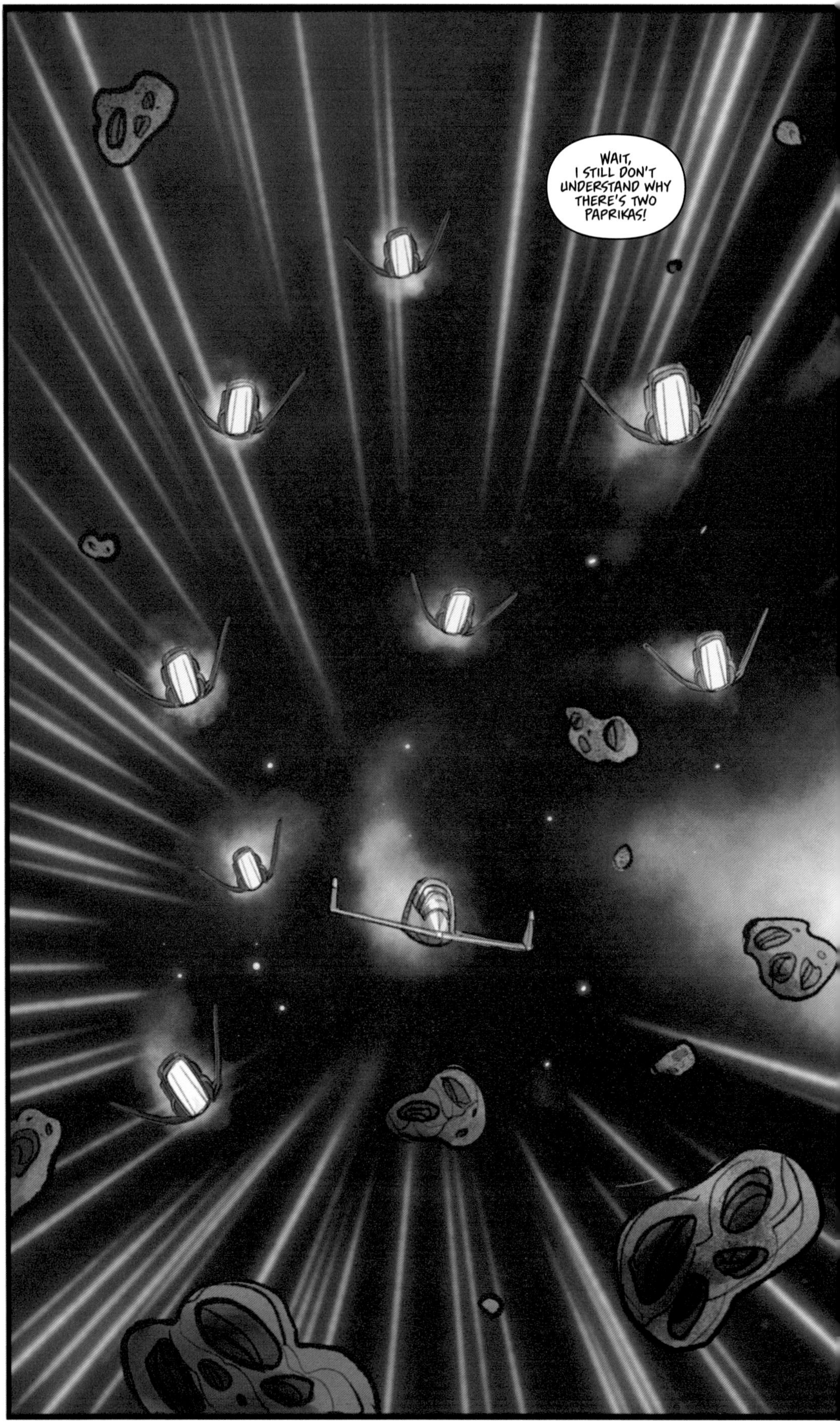
WAIT, I STILL DON'T UNDERSTAND WHY THERE'S TWO PAPRIKAS!

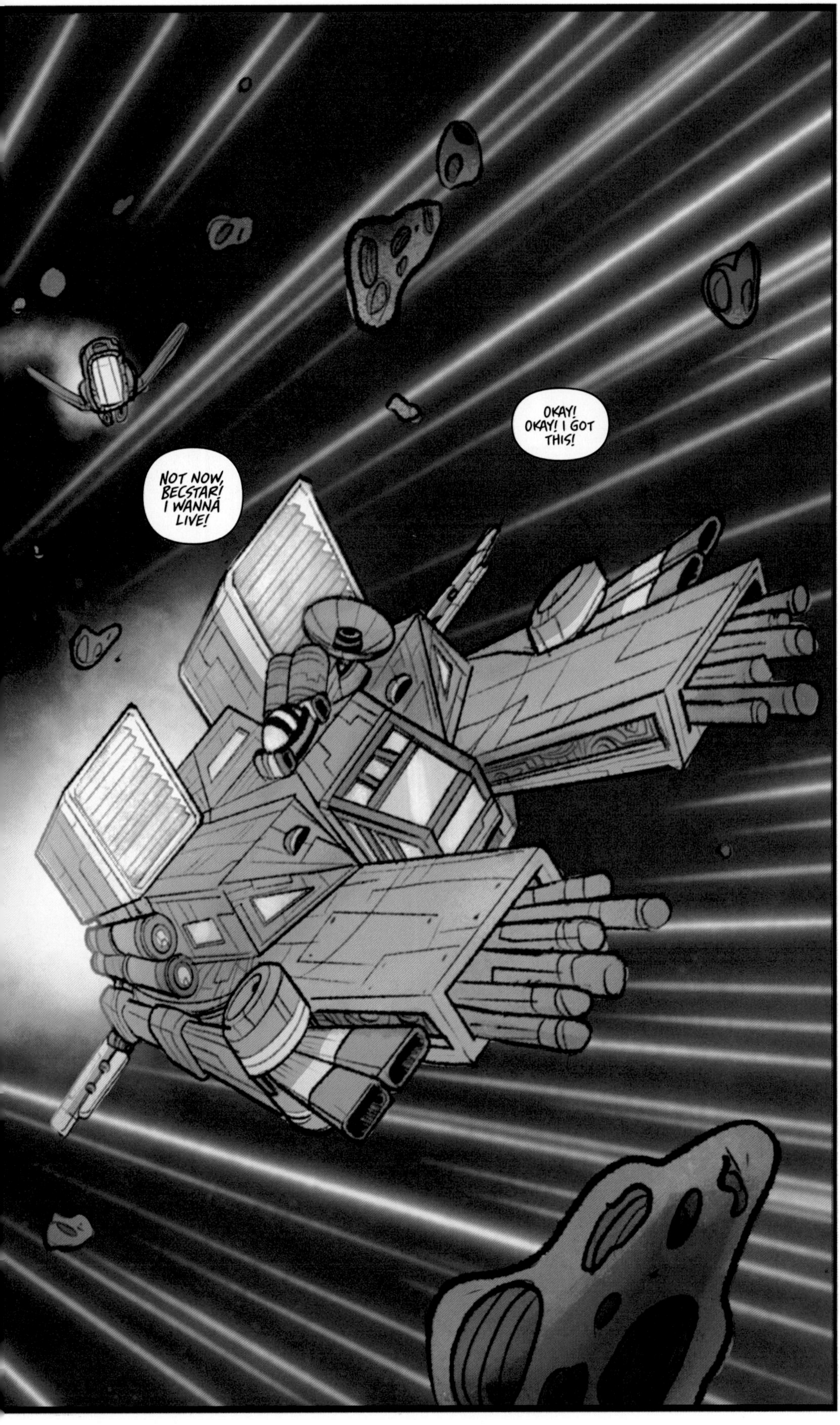
OKAY! OKAY! I GOT THIS!
NOT NOW, BECSTAR! I WANNA LIVE!

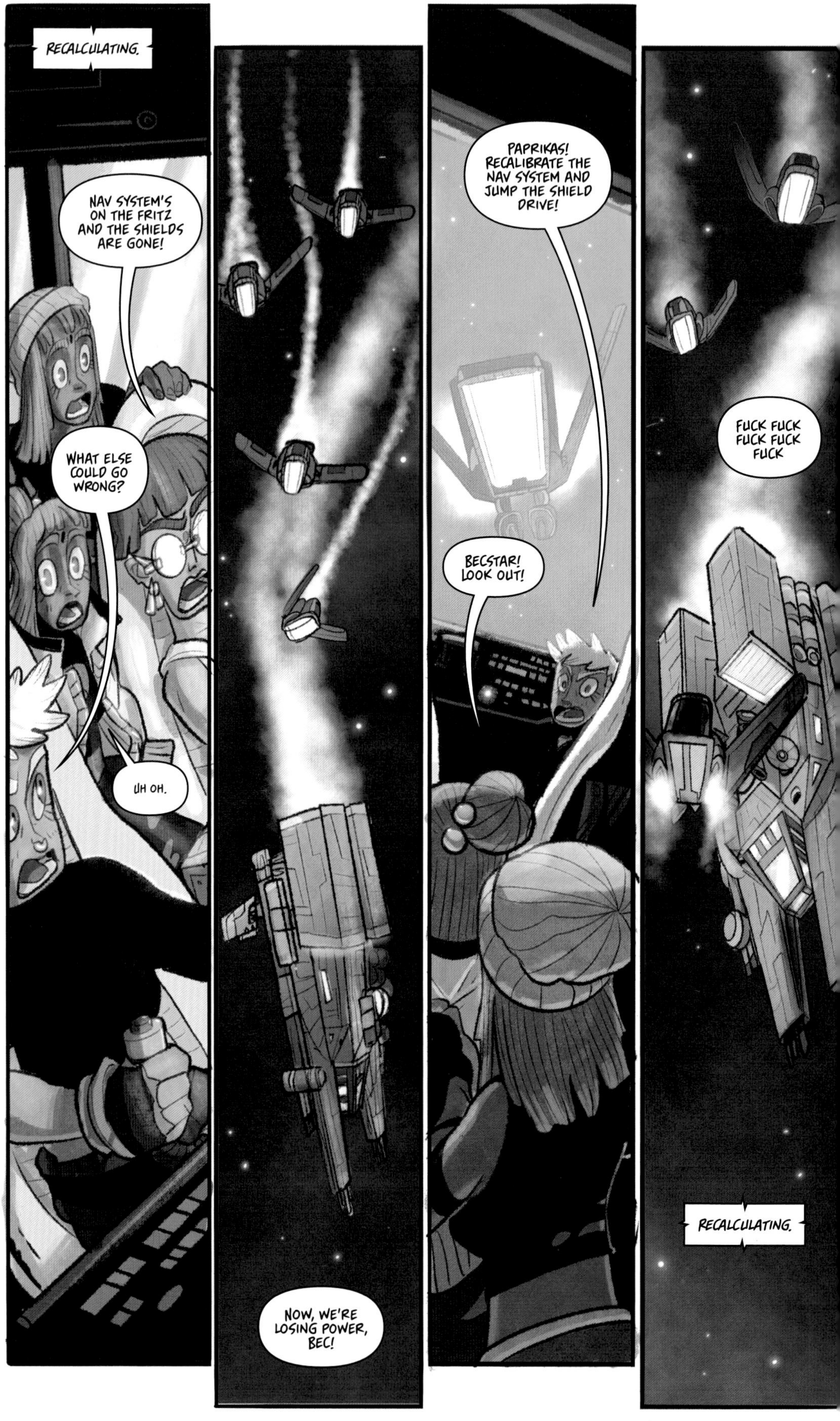
RECALCULATING.
NAV SYSTEM'S ON THE FRITZ AND THE SHIELDS ARE GONE!
WHAT ELSE COULD GO WRONG?
UH OH.
NOW, WE'RE LOSING POWER, BEC!
PAPRIKAS! RECALIBRATE THE NAV SYSTEM AND JUMP THE SHIELD DRIVE!
BECSTAR! LOOK OUT!
FUCK FUCK FUCK FUCK FUCK
RECALCULATING.

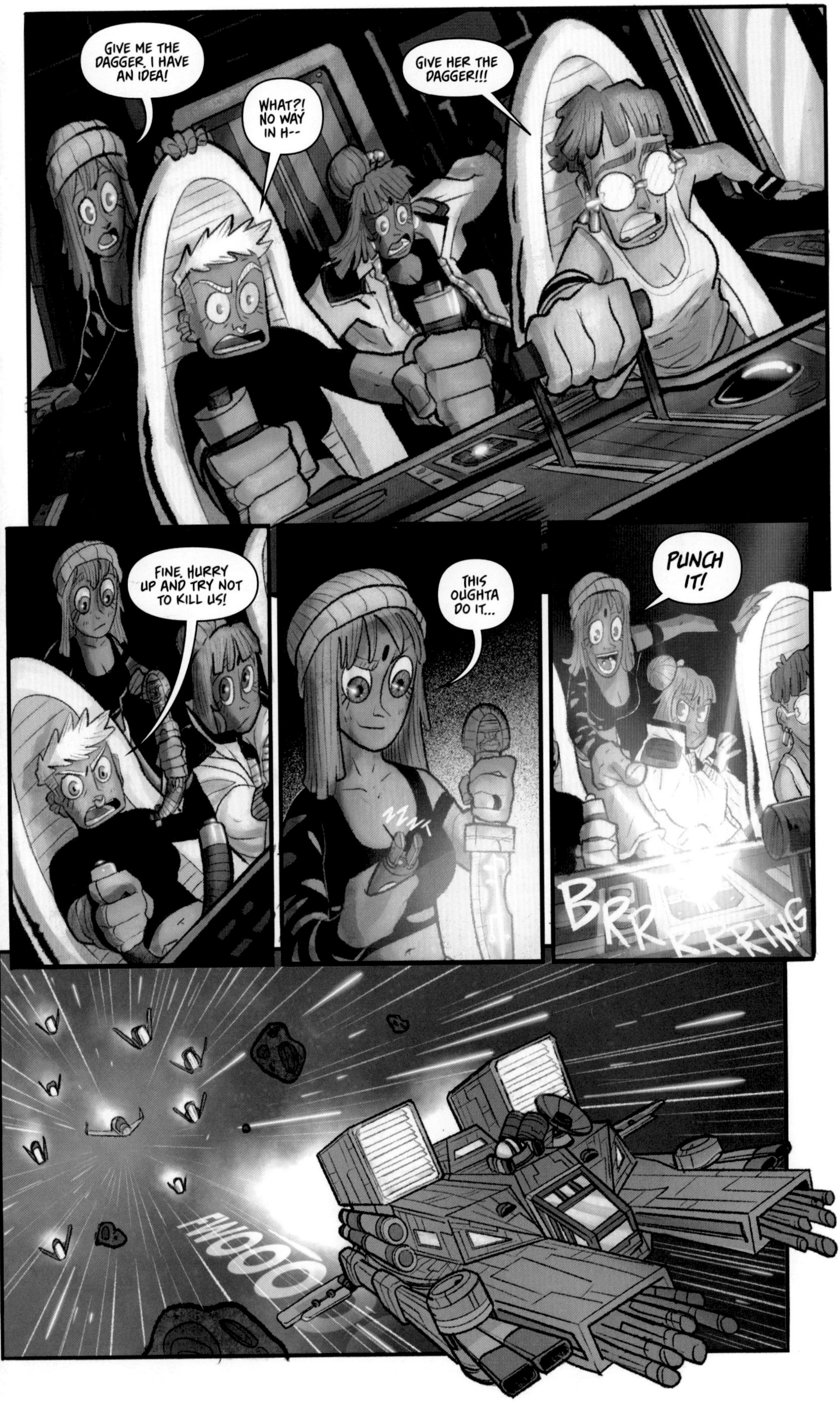
GIVE ME THE DAGGER. I HAVE AN IDEA!
WHAT?! NO WAY IN H--
GIVE HER THE DAGGER!!!
FINE. HURRY UP AND TRY NOT TO KILL US!
THIS OUGHTA DO IT...
ZZZNT
PUNCH IT!
BRRRRRRING
FWOOO

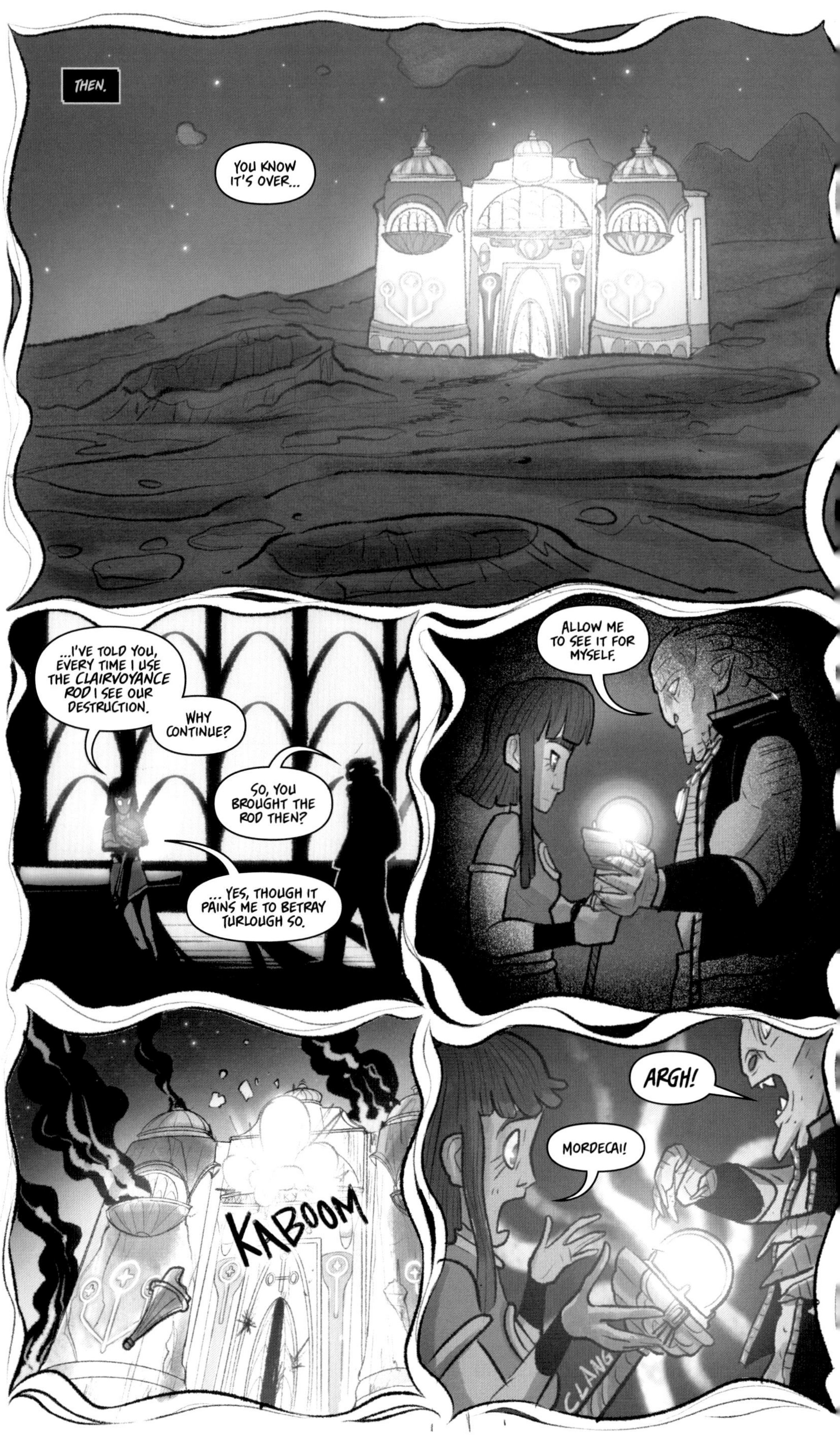
THEN.
YOU KNOW IT'S OVER...
...I'VE TOLD YOU, EVERY TIME I USE THE CLAIRVOYANCE ROD I SEE OUR DESTRUCTION.
WHY CONTINUE?
SO, YOU BROUGHT THE ROD THEN?
... YES, THOUGH IT PAINS ME TO BETRAY TURLOUGH SO.
ALLOW ME TO SEE IT FOR MYSELF.
KABOOM
ARGH!
MORDECAI!
CLANG

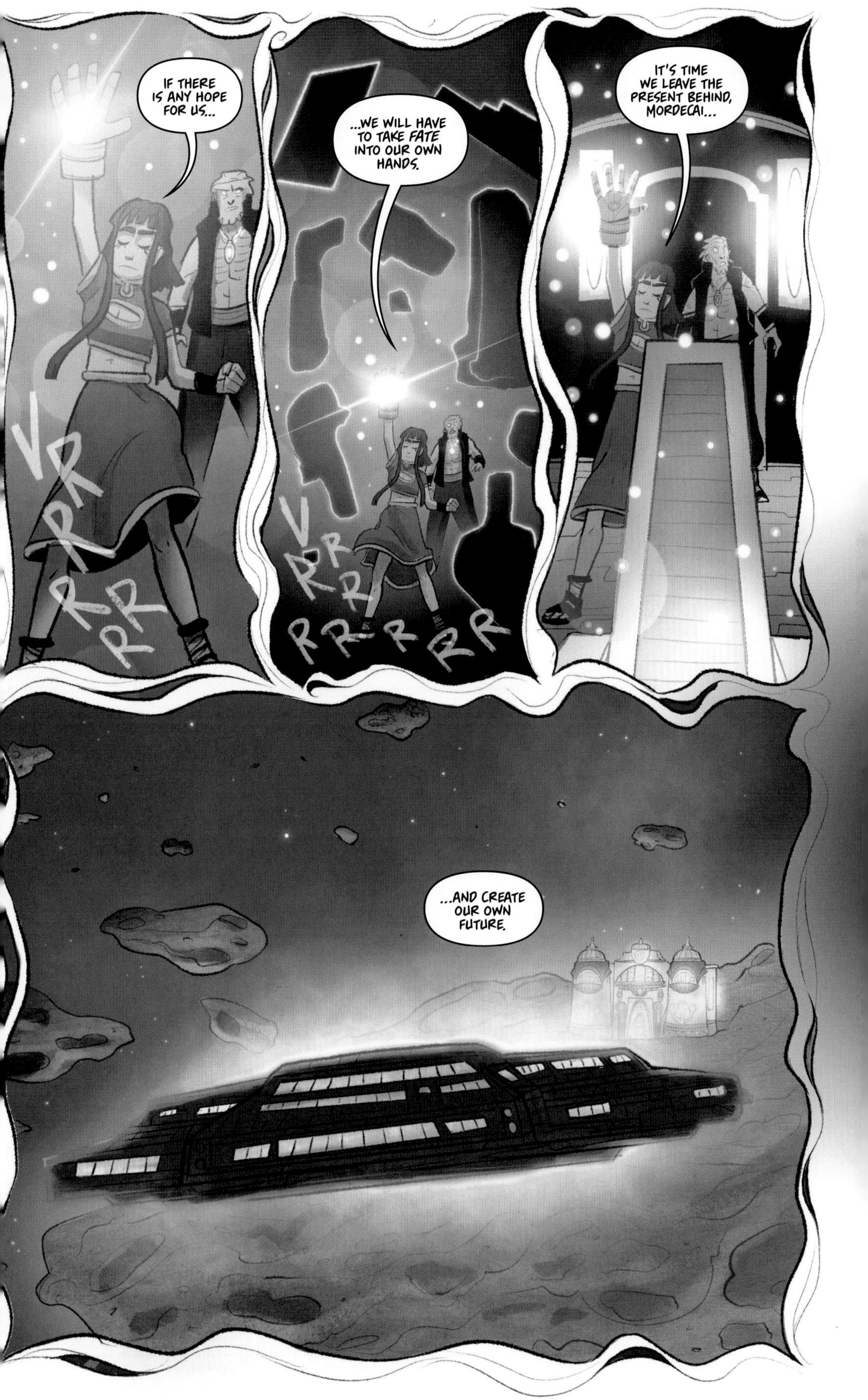
IF THERE IS ANY HOPE FOR US...
VRRRRR
...WE WILL HAVE TO TAKE FATE INTO OUR OWN HANDS.
VRRRRRRRRR
IT'S TIME WE LEAVE THE PRESENT BEHIND, MORDECAI...
...AND CREATE OUR OWN FUTURE.

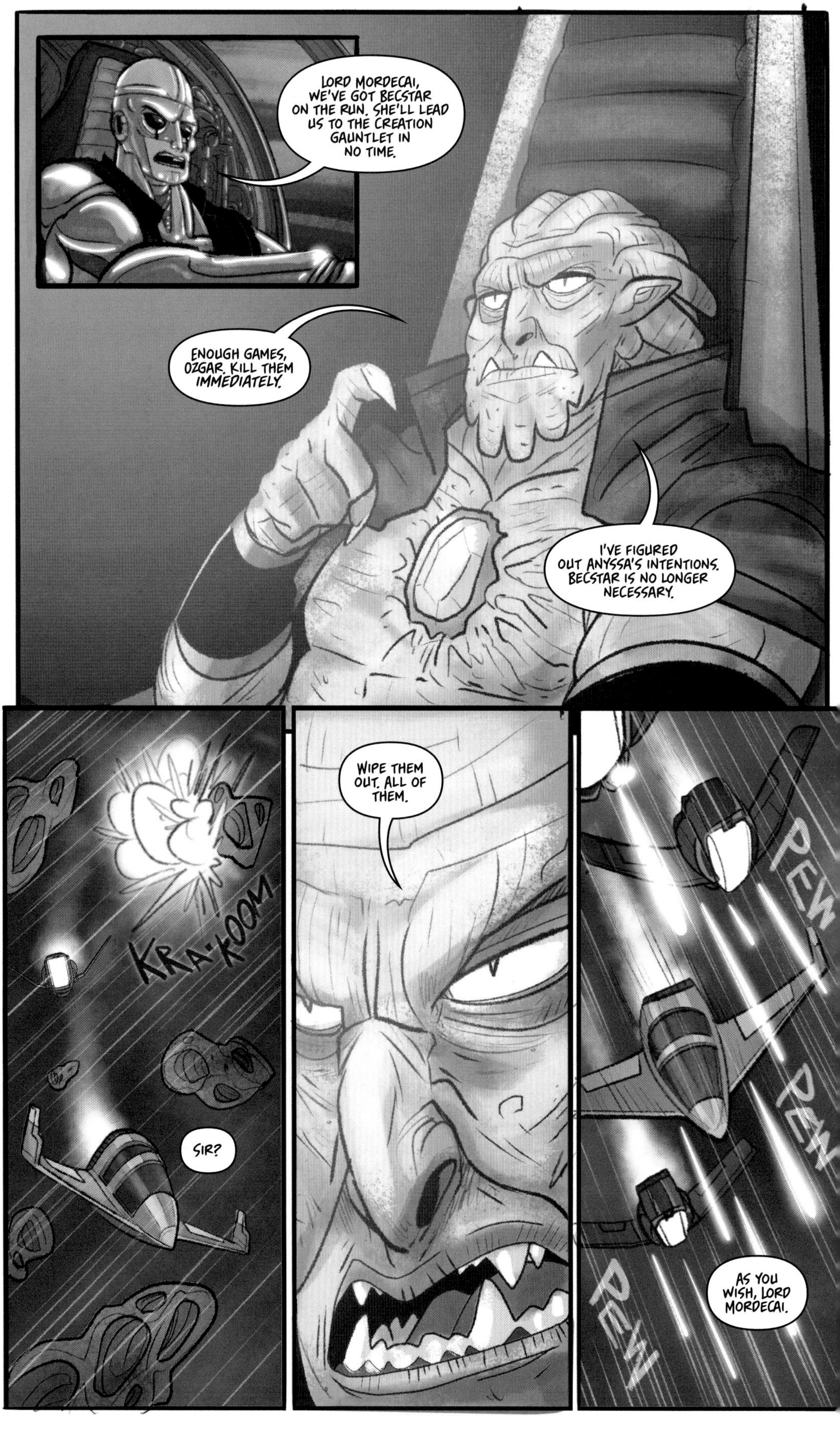
LORD MORDECAI, WE'VE GOT BECSTAR ON THE RUN. SHE'LL LEAD US TO THE CREATION GAUNTLET IN NO TIME.
ENOUGH GAMES, OZGAR. KILL THEM IMMEDIATELY.
I'VE FIGURED OUT ANYSSA'S INTENTIONS. BECSTAR IS NO LONGER NECESSARY.
KRA-KOOM
SIR?
WIPE THEM OUT. ALL OF THEM.
PEW
PEW
PEW
AS YOU WISH, LORD MORDECAI.

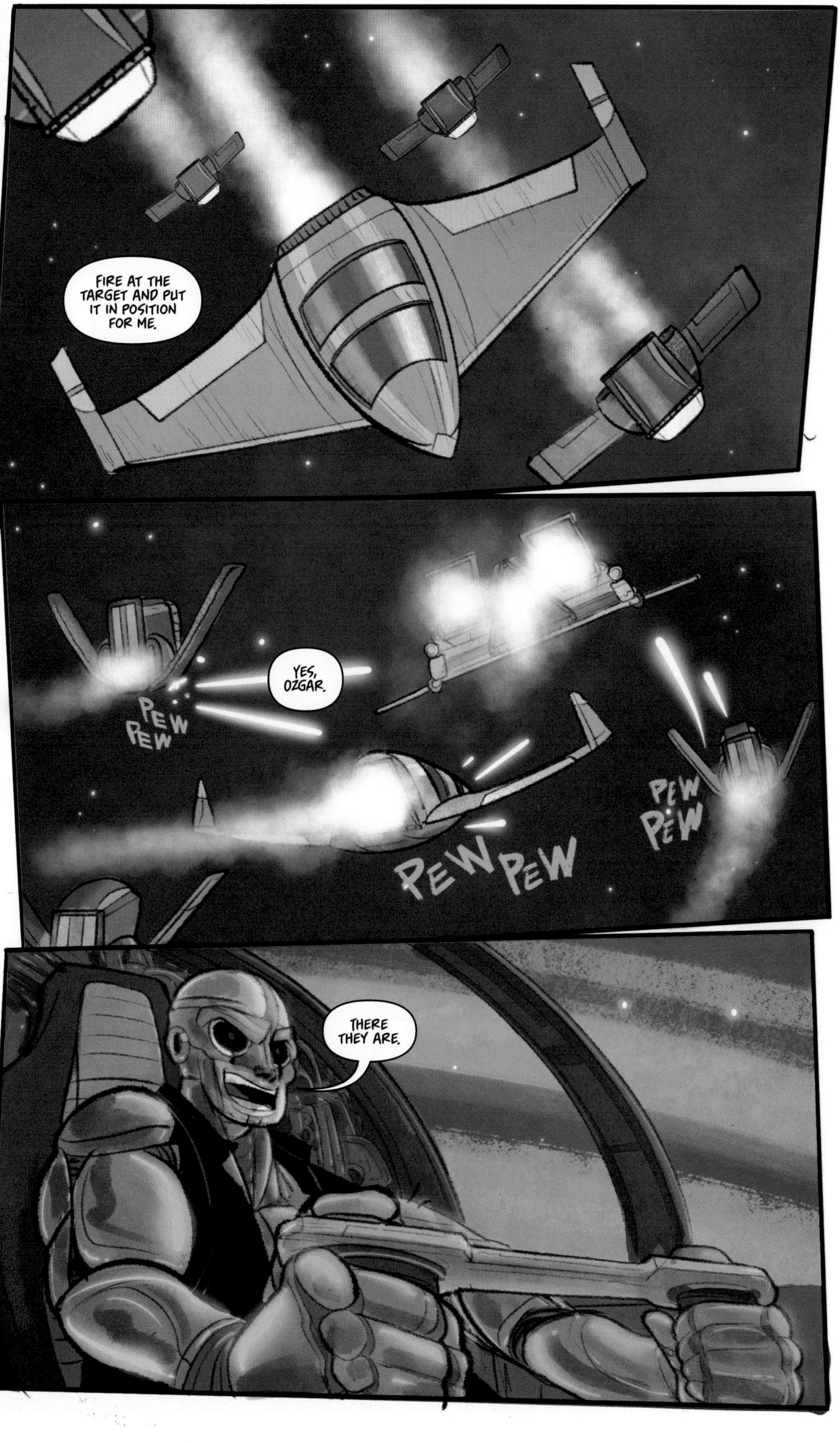
FIRE AT THE TARGET AND PUT IT IN POSITION FOR ME.
YES, OZGAR.
PEW PEW
PEW PEW
PEW PEW
THERE THEY ARE.

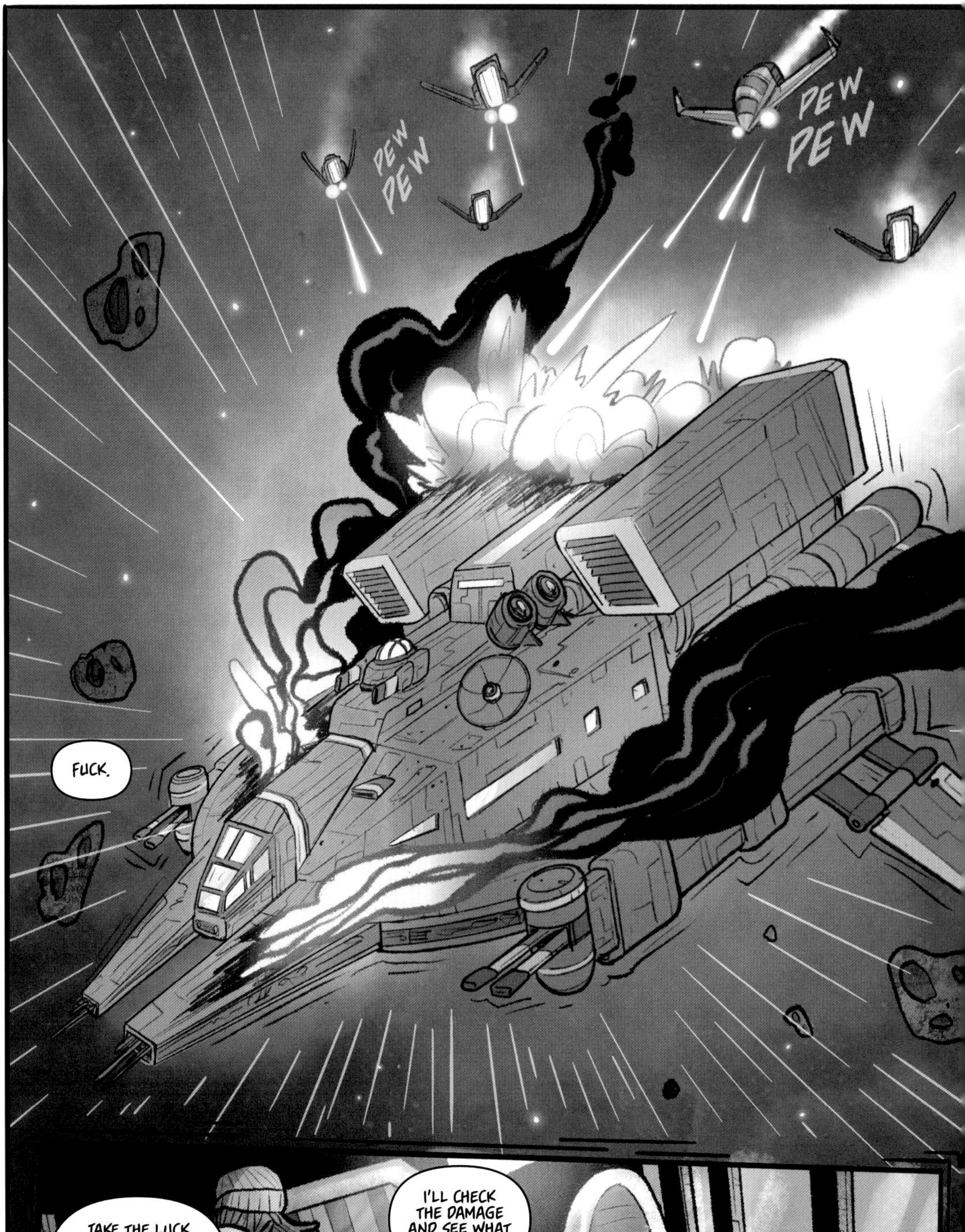
PEW
PEW
PEW
PEW
FUCK.

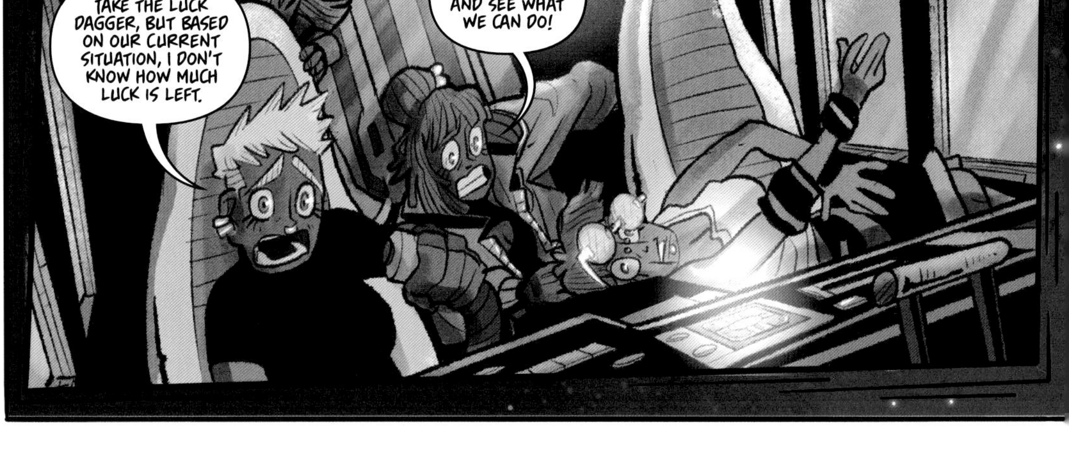
TAKE THE LUCK DAGGER, BUT BASED ON OUR CURRENT SITUATION, I DON'T KNOW HOW MUCH LUCK IS LEFT.
I'LL CHECK THE DAMAGE AND SEE WHAT WE CAN DO!

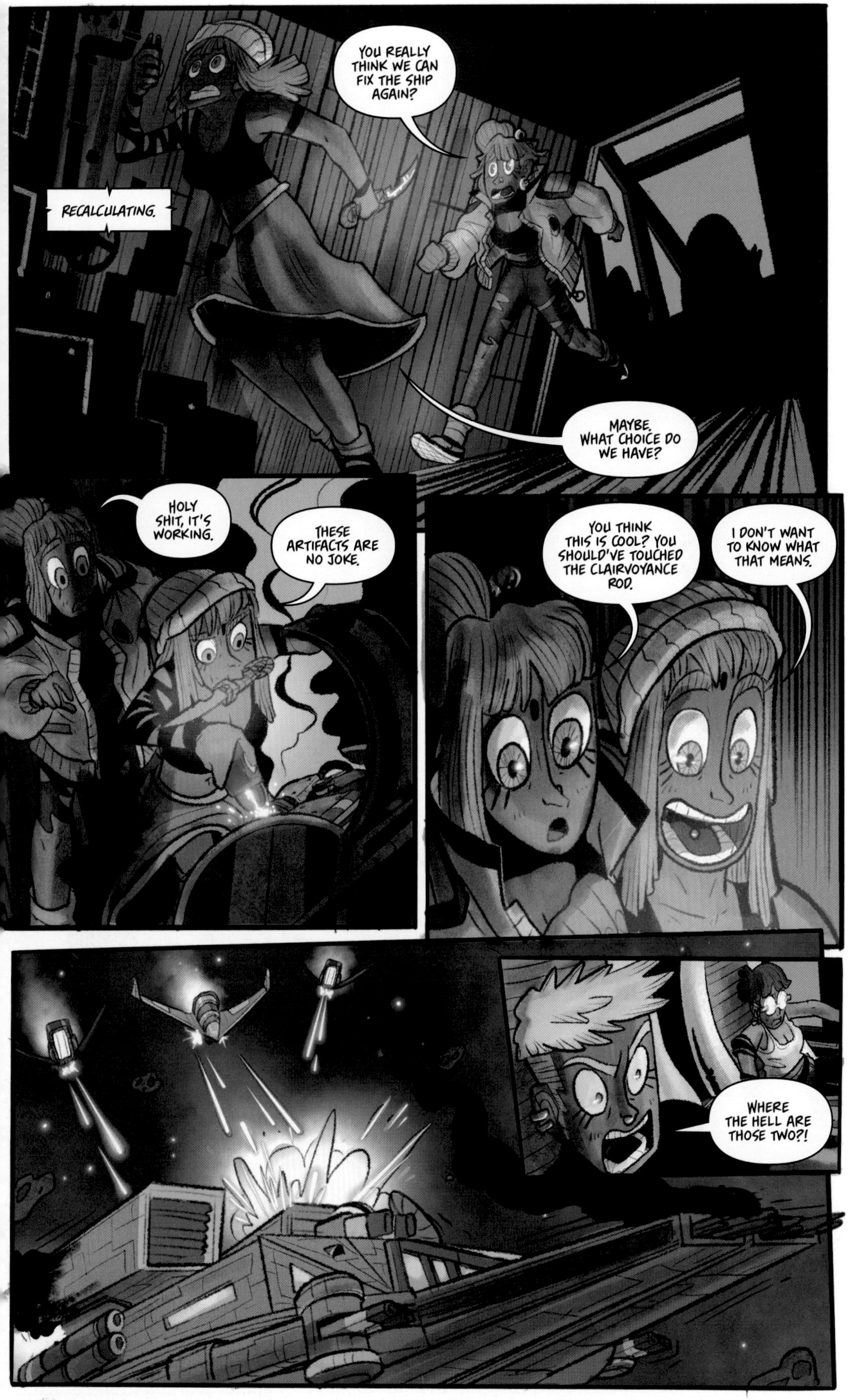
RECALCULATING.
YOU REALLY THINK WE CAN FIX THE SHIP AGAIN?
MAYBE. WHAT CHOICE DO WE HAVE?
HOLY SHIT, IT'S WORKING.
THESE ARTIFACTS ARE NO JOKE.
YOU THINK THIS IS COOL? YOU SHOULD'VE TOUCHED THE CLAIRVOYANCE ROD.
I DON'T WANT TO KNOW WHAT THAT MEANS.
WHERE THE HELL ARE THOSE TWO?!

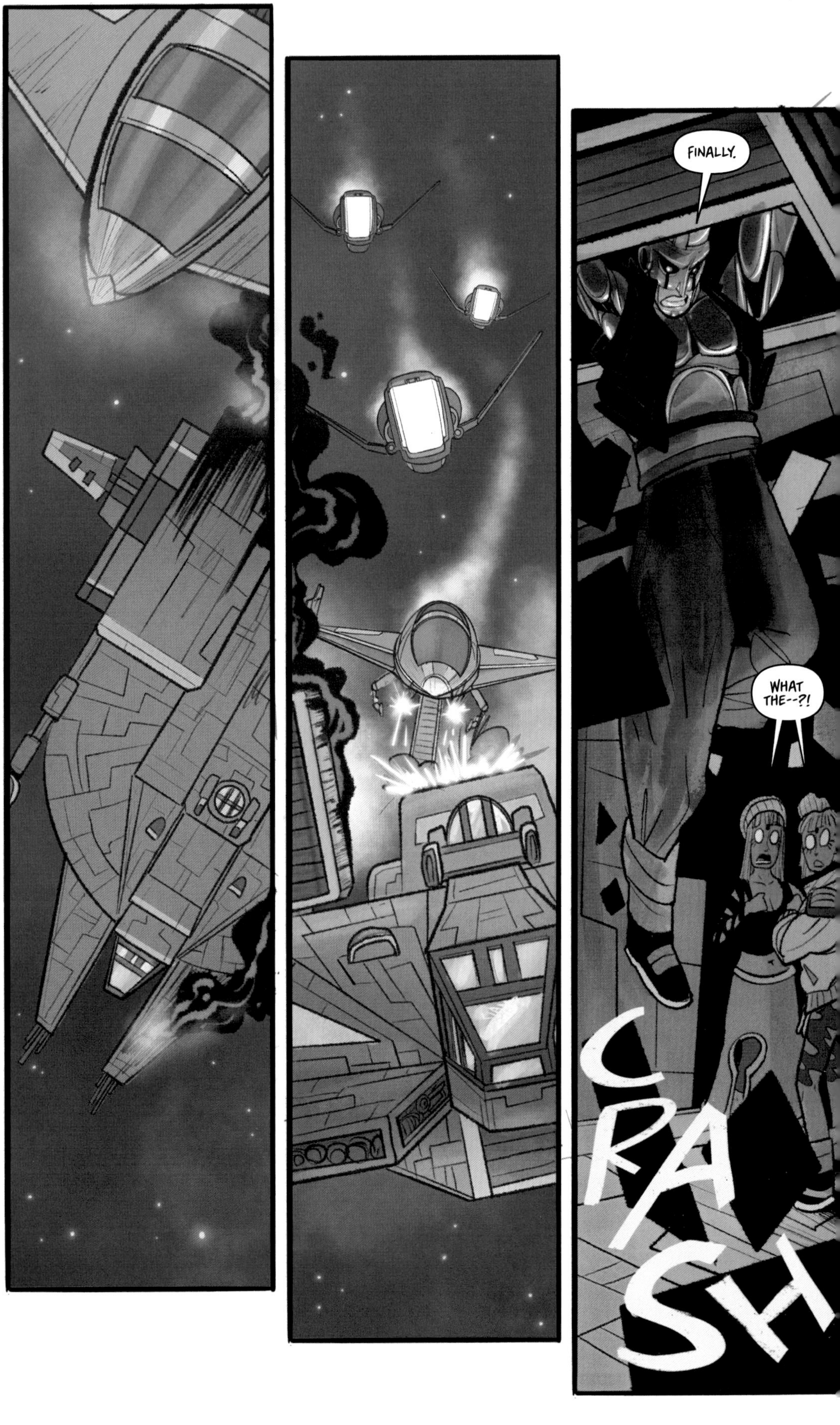
FINALLY.
WHAT THE--?!
CRASH

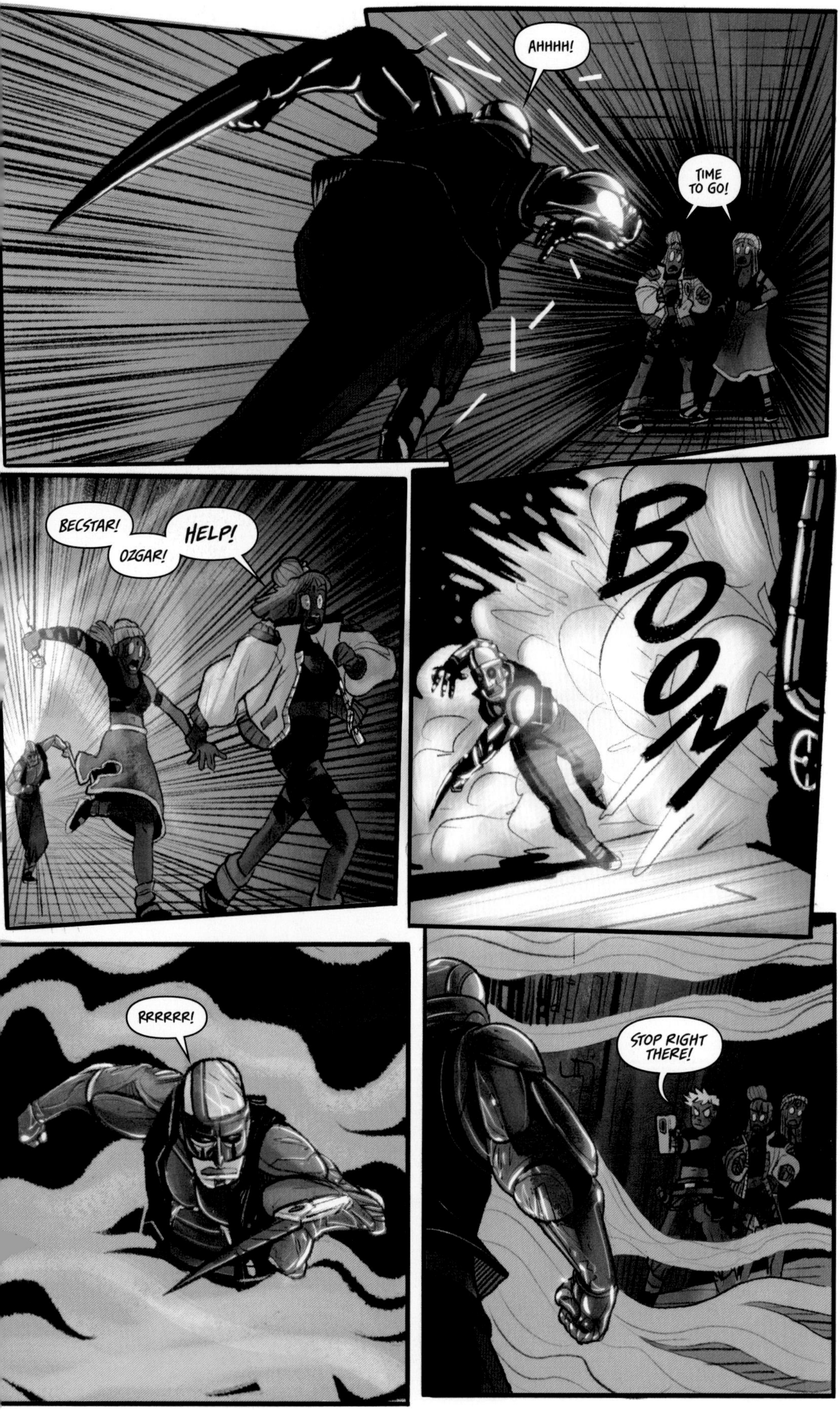
AHHHH!
TIME TO GO!
BECSTAR!
OZGAR!
HELP!
BOOM
RRRRRR!
STOP RIGHT THERE!

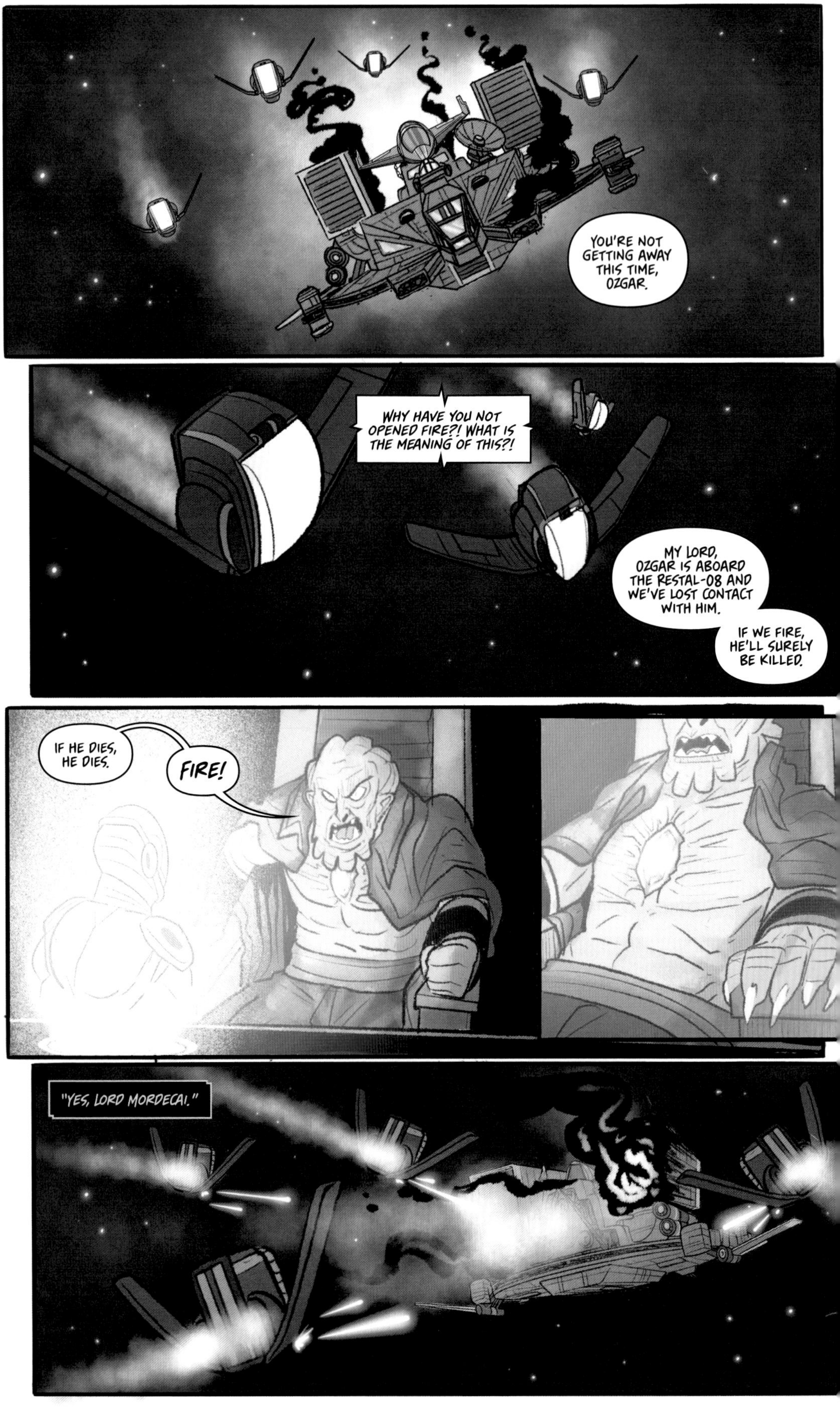
YOU'RE NOT GETTING AWAY THIS TIME, OZGAR.
WHY HAVE YOU NOT OPENED FIRE?! WHAT IS THE MEANING OF THIS?!
MY LORD, OZGAR IS ABOARD THE RESTAL-08 AND WE'VE LOST CONTACT WITH HIM.
IF WE FIRE, HE'LL SURELY BE KILLED.
IF HE DIES, HE DIES.
FIRE!
"YES, LORD MORDECAI."

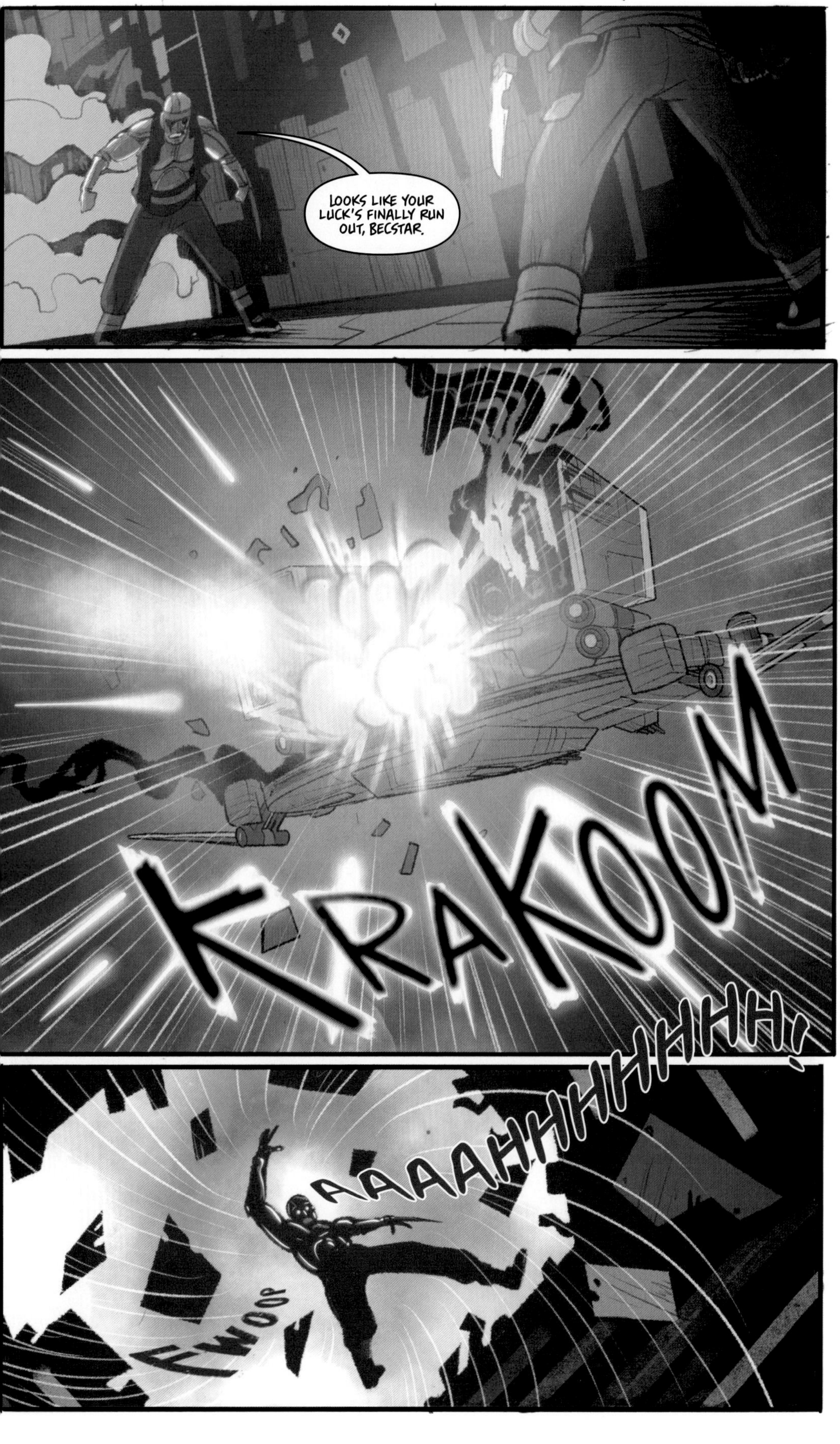
LOOKS LIKE YOUR LUCK'S FINALLY RUN OUT, BECSTAR.
KRAKOOM
AAAAHHHHHHHHH!
FWOOP

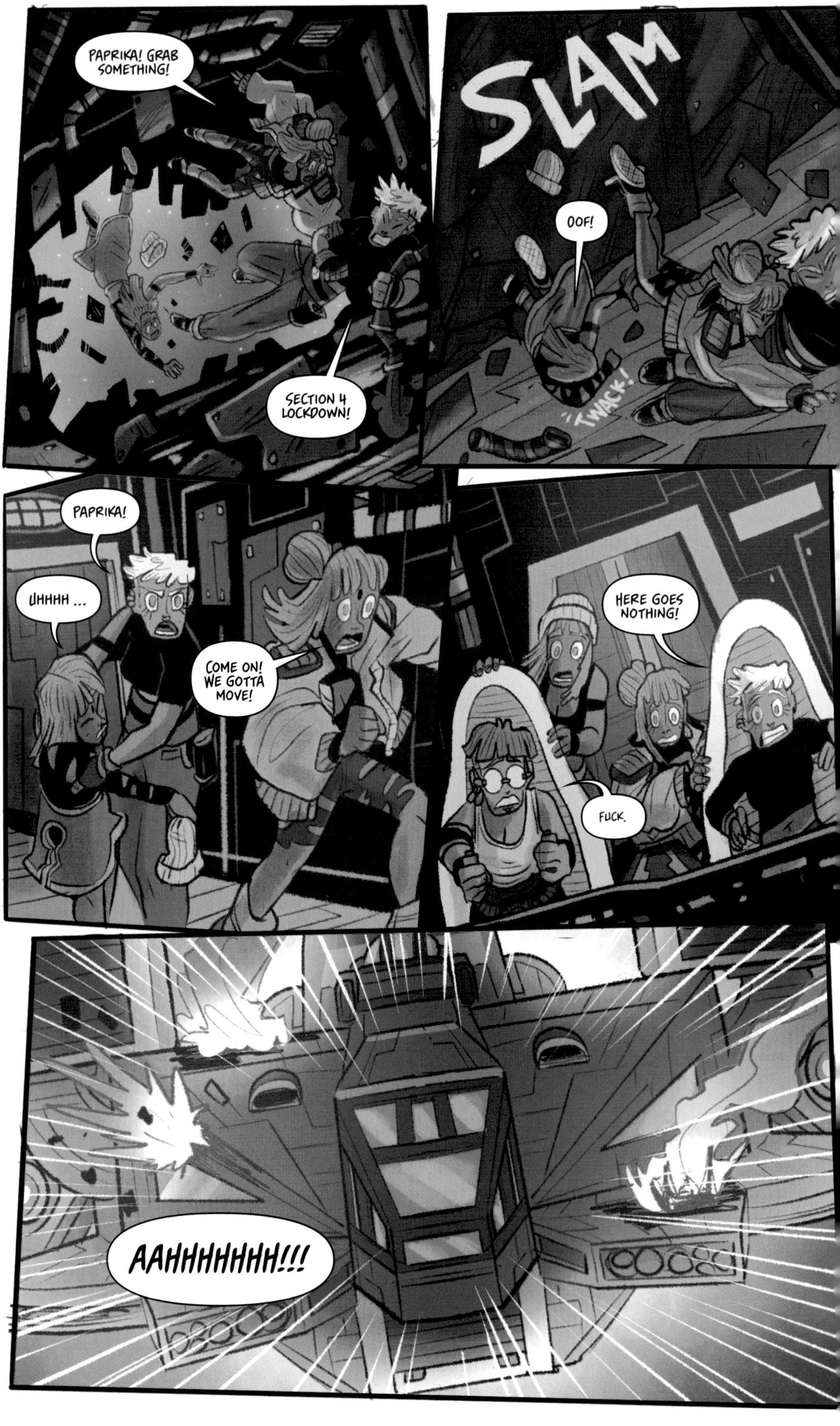
PAPRIKA! GRAB SOMETHING!
SECTION 4 LOCKDOWN!
SLAM
OOF!
TWACK!
PAPRIKA!
UHHHH ...
COME ON! WE GOTTA MOVE!
HERE GOES NOTHING!
FUCK.
AAHHHHHHH!!!

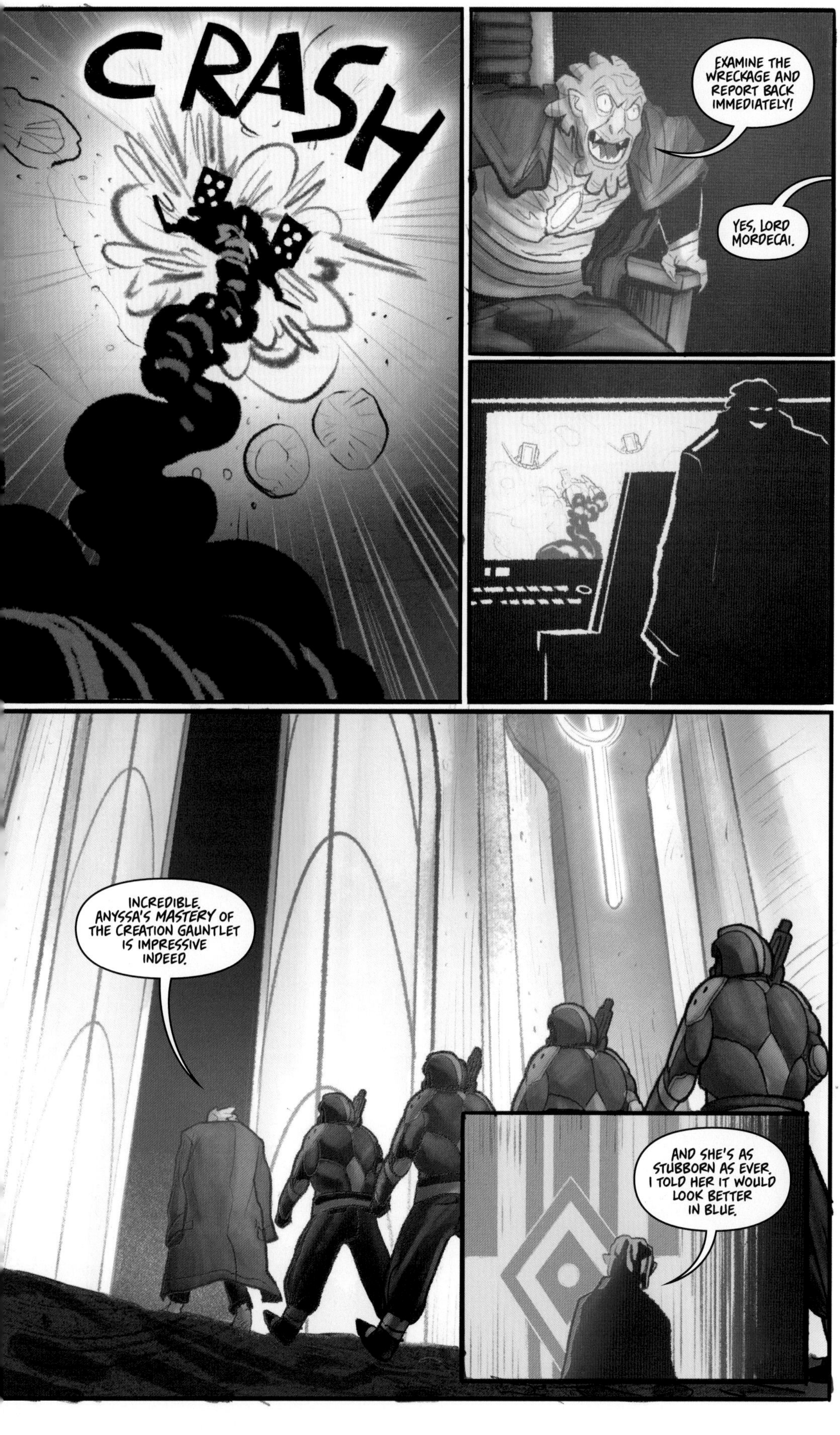
CRASH
EXAMINE THE WRECKAGE AND REPORT BACK IMMEDIATELY!
YES, LORD MORDECAI.
INCREDIBLE. ANYSSA'S MASTERY OF THE CREATION GAUNTLET IS IMPRESSIVE INDEED.
AND SHE'S AS STUBBORN AS EVER. I TOLD HER IT WOULD LOOK BETTER IN BLUE.

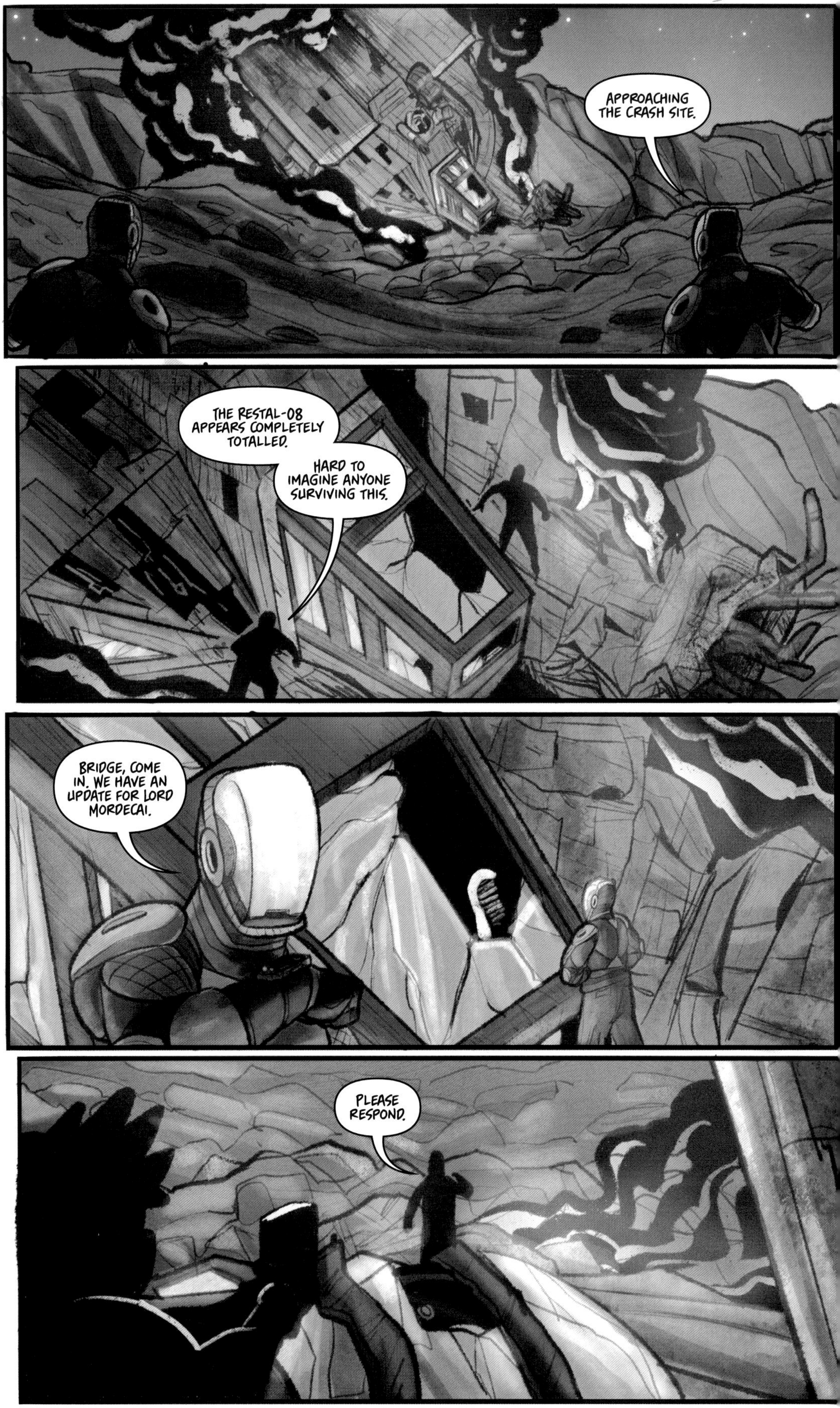
APPROACHING THE CRASH SITE.
THE RESTAL-08 APPEARS COMPLETELY TOTALLED.
HARD TO IMAGINE ANYONE SURVIVING THIS.
BRIDGE, COME IN. WE HAVE AN UPDATE FOR LORD MORDECAI.
PLEASE RESPOND.

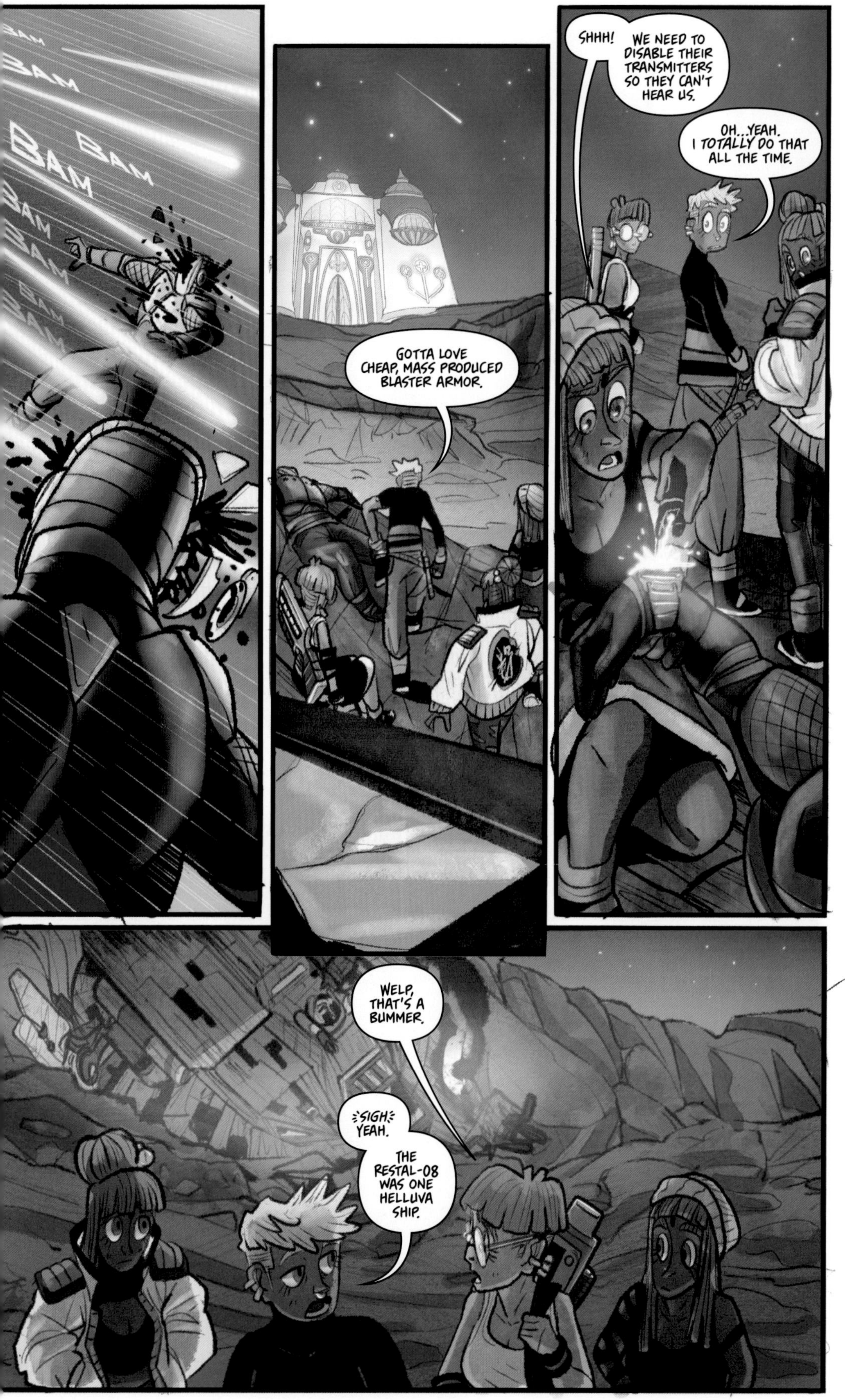
BAM
BAM
BAM
BAM
BAM
BAM
BAM
BAM
BAM
GOTTA LOVE CHEAP, MASS PRODUCED BLASTER ARMOR.
SHHH!
WE NEED TO DISABLE THEIR TRANSMITTERS SO THEY CAN'T HEAR US.
OH...YEAH. I TOTALLY DO THAT ALL THE TIME.
WELP, THAT'S A BUMMER.
SIGH YEAH.
THE RESTAL-08 WAS ONE HELLUVA SHIP.

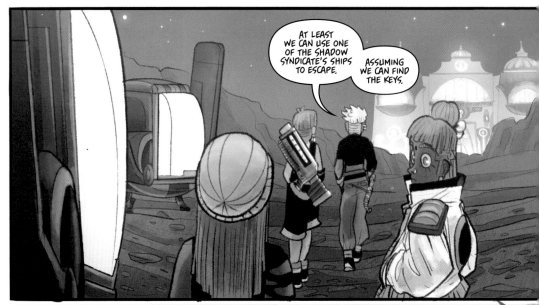

AT LEAST WE CAN USE ONE OF THE SHADOW SYNDICATE'S SHIPS TO ESCAPE.

ASSUMING WE CAN FIND THE KEYS.

ALREADY SNAGGED THEM.

YOU'RE MY FAVORITE PAPRIKA.

FEH.

THERE! THAT'S THE ASTEROID BASE!

HEY, YOU'RE A GREAT PAPRIKA, TOO. SORRY FOR JUMPING THE GUN BACK THERE...

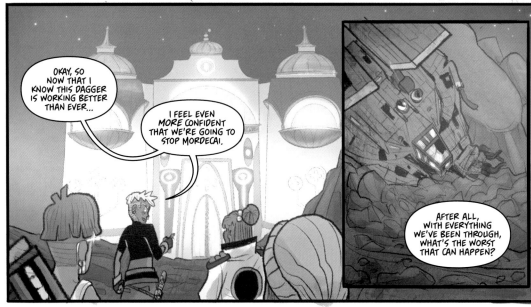

OKAY, SO NOW THAT I KNOW THIS DAGGER IS WORKING BETTER THAN EVER...

I FEEL EVEN MORE CONFIDENT THAT WE'RE GOING TO STOP MORDECAI.

AFTER ALL, WITH EVERYTHING WE'VE BEEN THROUGH, WHAT'S THE WORST THAT CAN HAPPEN?

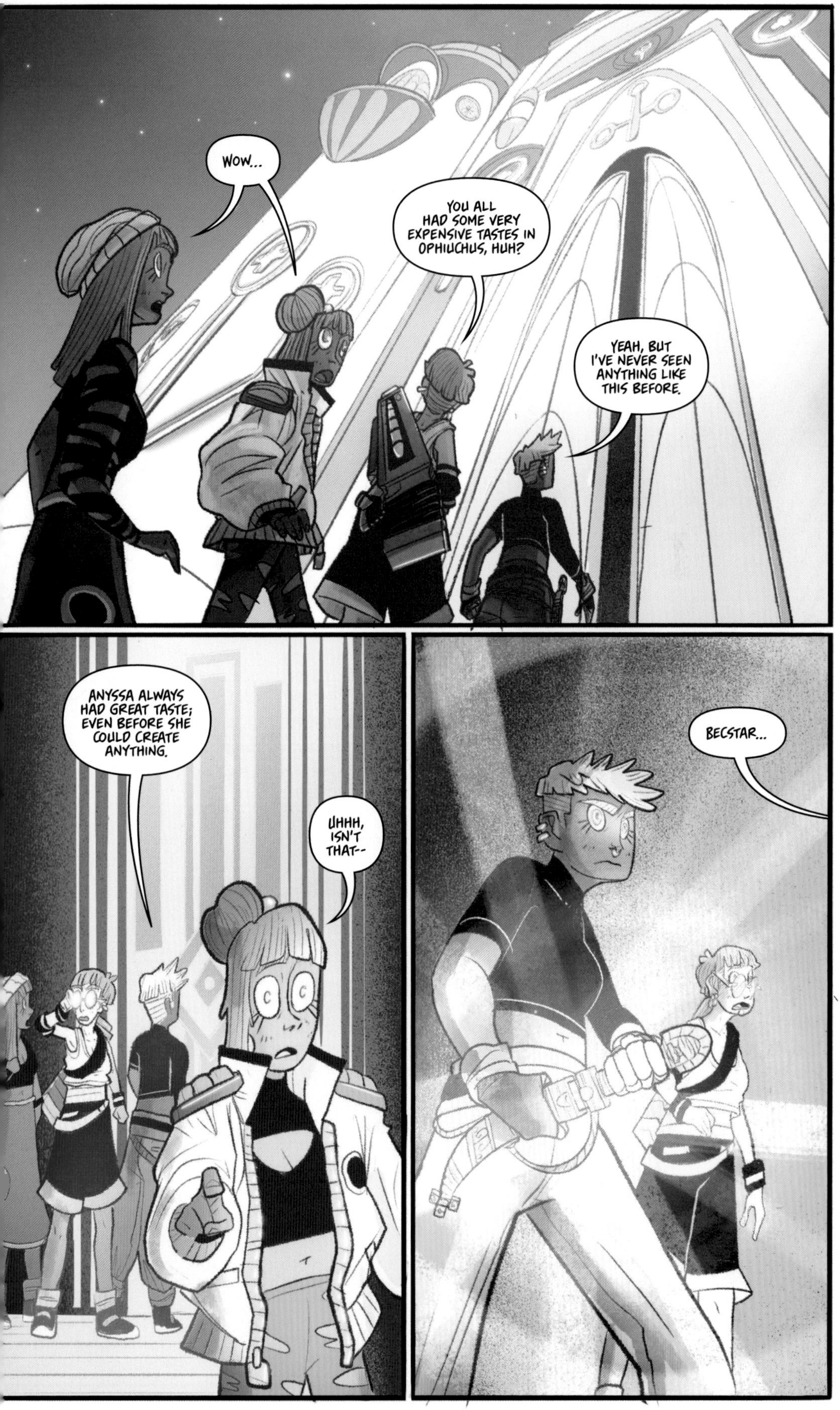
WOW...
YOU ALL HAD SOME VERY EXPENSIVE TASTES IN OPHIUCHUS, HUH?
YEAH, BUT I'VE NEVER SEEN ANYTHING LIKE THIS BEFORE.
ANYSSA ALWAYS HAD GREAT TASTE; EVEN BEFORE SHE COULD CREATE ANYTHING.
UHHH, ISN'T THAT--
BECSTAR...

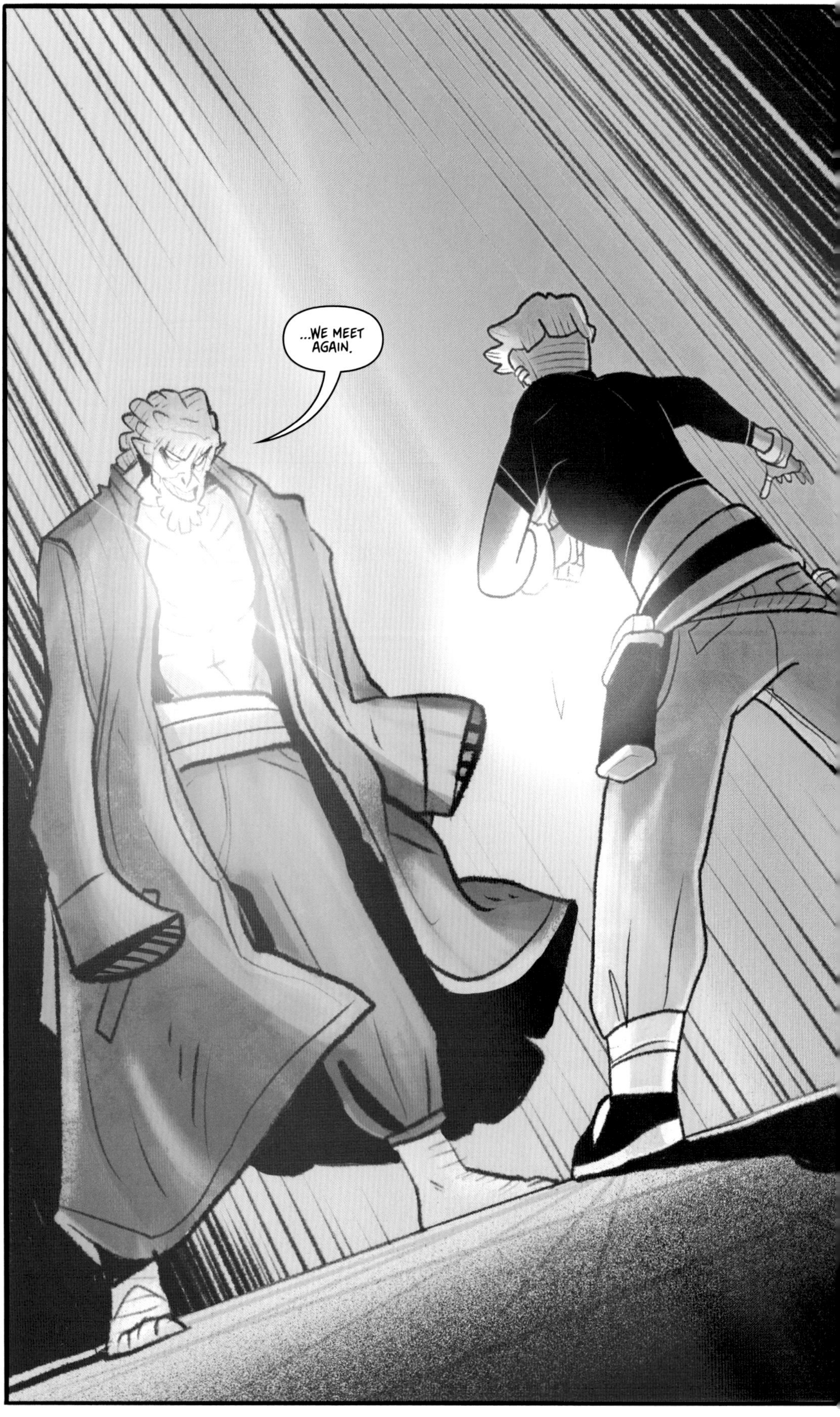
...WE MEET AGAIN.

PART 05

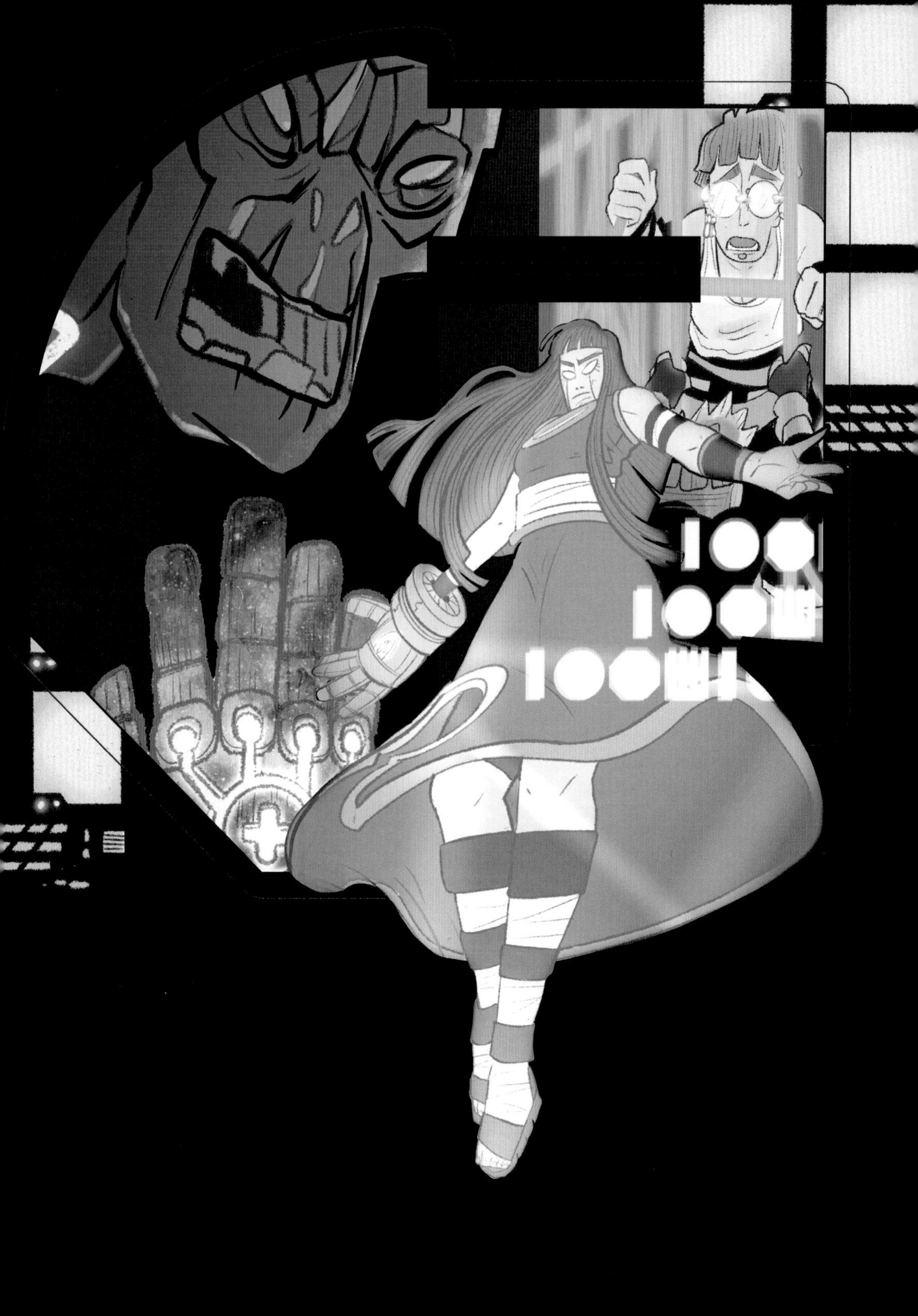

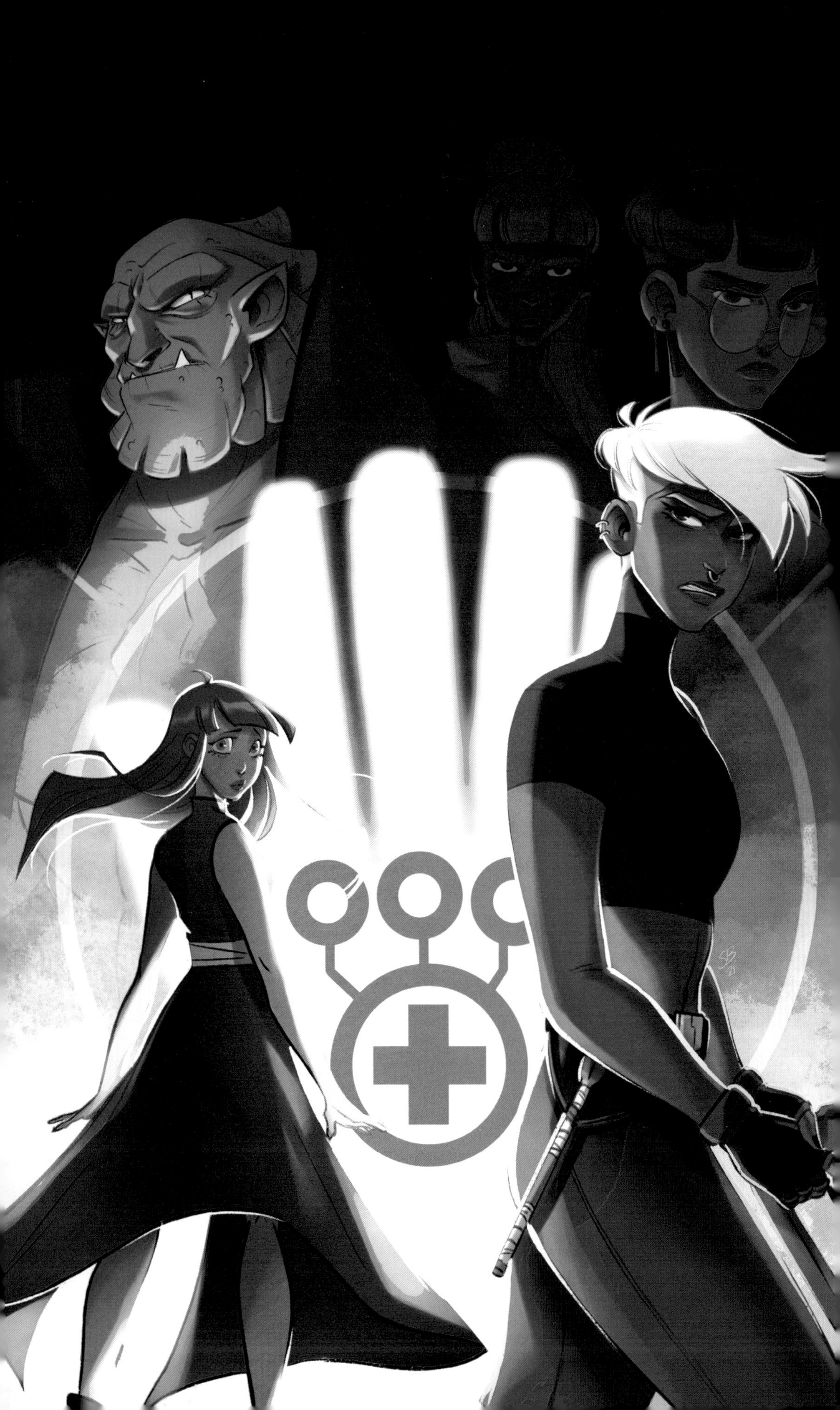

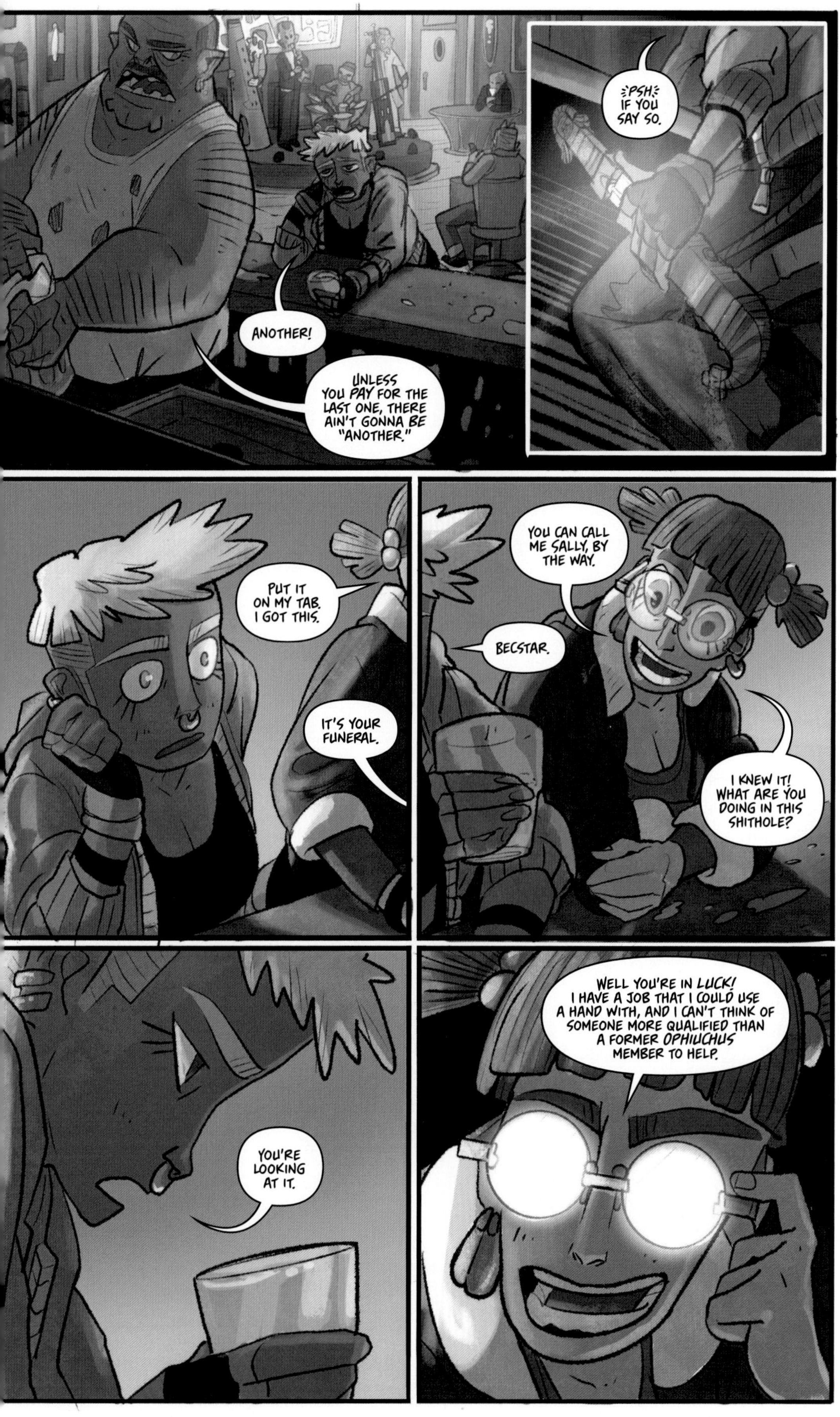
ANOTHER!
UNLESS YOU PAY FOR THE LAST ONE, THERE AIN'T GONNA BE "ANOTHER."
PSH IF YOU SAY SO.
PUT IT ON MY TAB. I GOT THIS.
IT'S YOUR FUNERAL.
YOU CAN CALL ME SALLY, BY THE WAY.
BECSTAR.
I KNEW IT! WHAT ARE YOU DOING IN THIS SHITHOLE?
YOU'RE LOOKING AT IT.
WELL YOU'RE IN LUCK! I HAVE A JOB THAT I COULD USE A HAND WITH, AND I CAN'T THINK OF SOMEONE MORE QUALIFIED THAN A FORMER OPHIUCHUS MEMBER TO HELP.

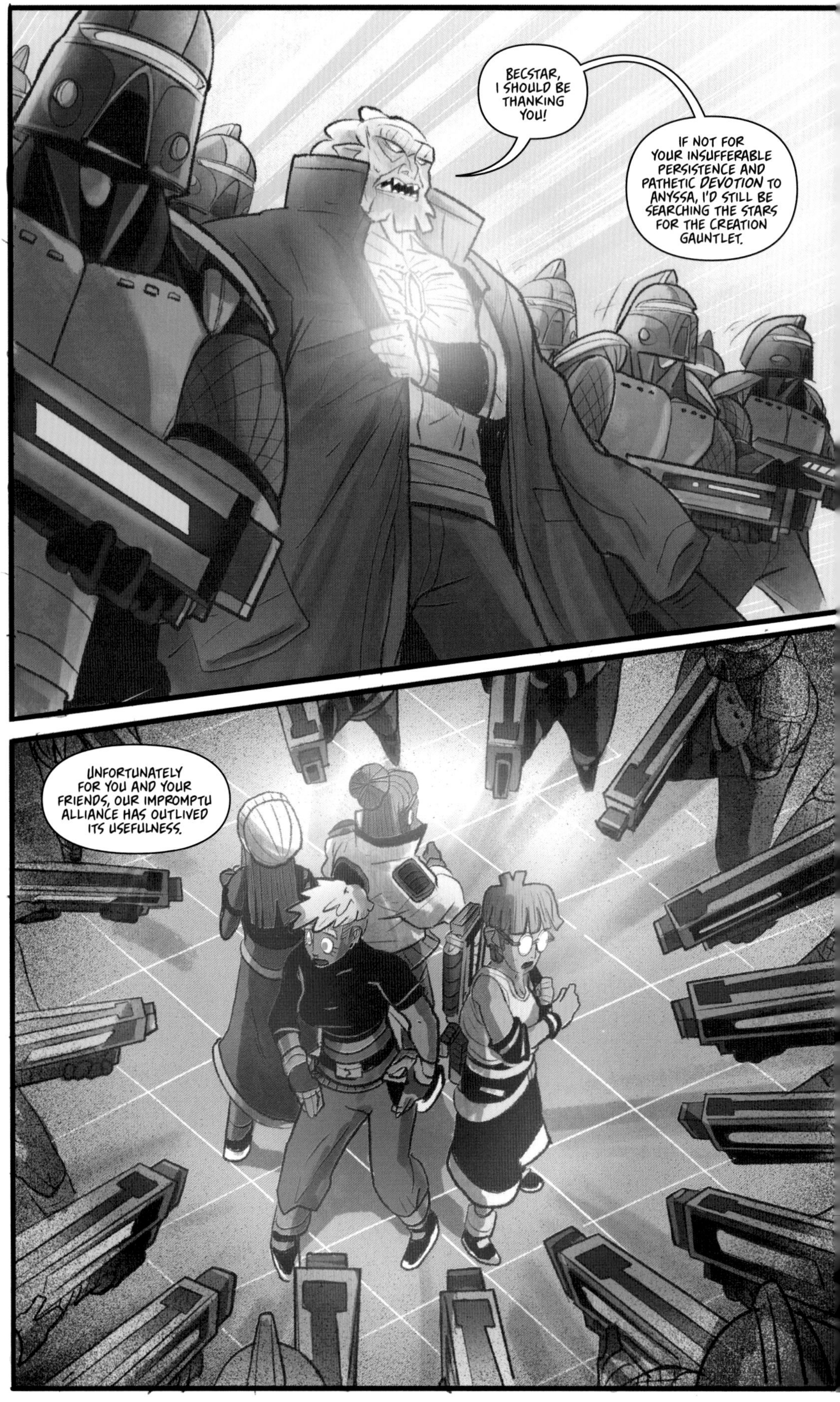
BECSTAR, I SHOULD BE THANKING YOU!
IF NOT FOR YOUR INSUFFERABLE PERSISTENCE AND PATHETIC *DEVOTION* TO ANYSSA, I'D STILL BE SEARCHING THE STARS FOR THE CREATION GAUNTLET.
UNFORTUNATELY FOR YOU AND YOUR FRIENDS, OUR IMPROMPTU ALLIANCE HAS OUTLIVED ITS USEFULNESS.

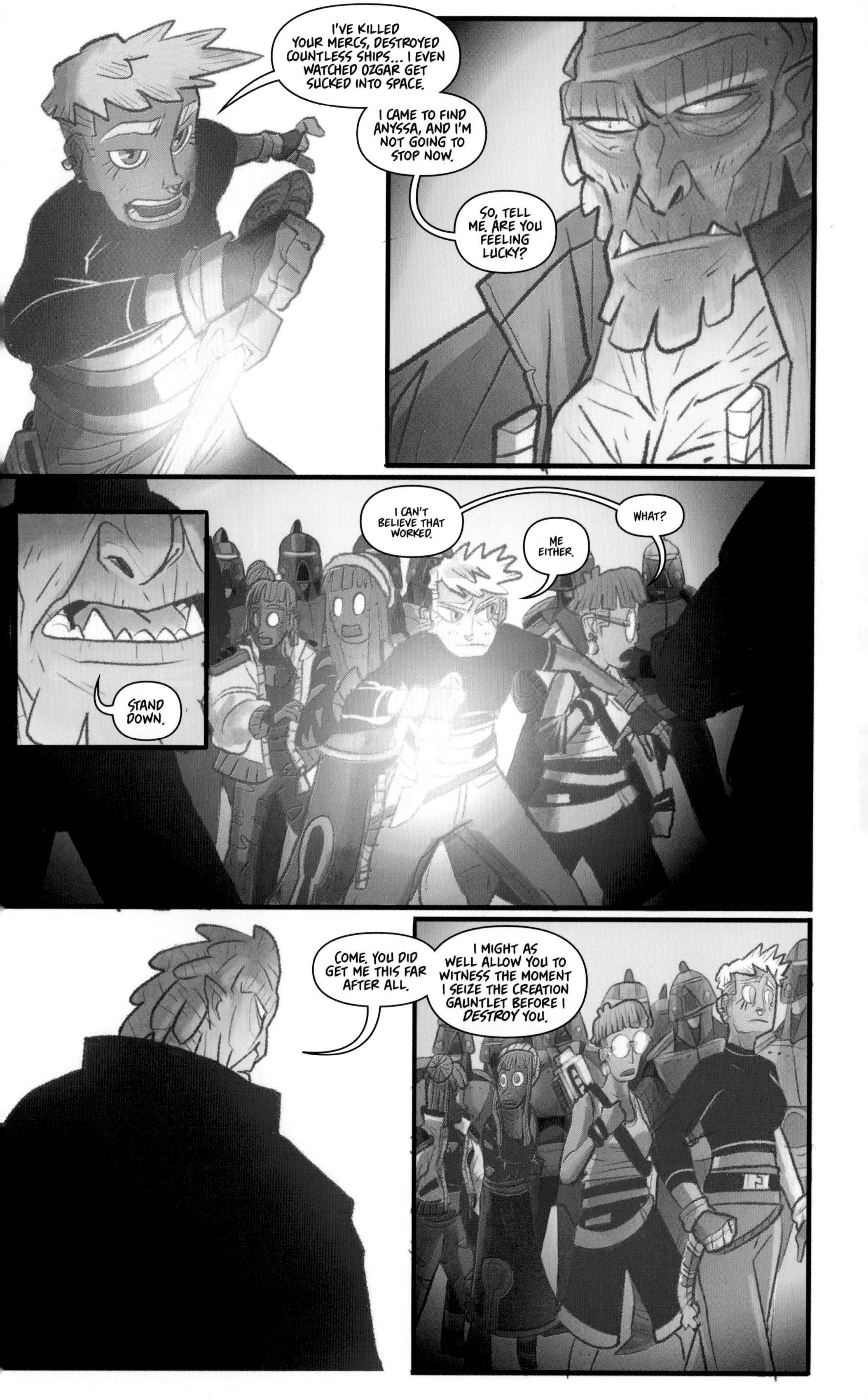
I'VE KILLED YOUR MERCS, DESTROYED COUNTLESS SHIPS... I EVEN WATCHED OZGAR GET SUCKED INTO SPACE.
I CAME TO FIND ANYSSA, AND I'M NOT GOING TO STOP NOW.
SO, TELL ME. ARE YOU FEELING LUCKY?
STAND DOWN.
I CAN'T BELIEVE THAT WORKED.
WHAT?
ME EITHER.
COME. YOU DID GET ME THIS FAR AFTER ALL.
I MIGHT AS WELL ALLOW YOU TO WITNESS THE MOMENT I SEIZE THE CREATION GAUNTLET BEFORE I DESTROY YOU.

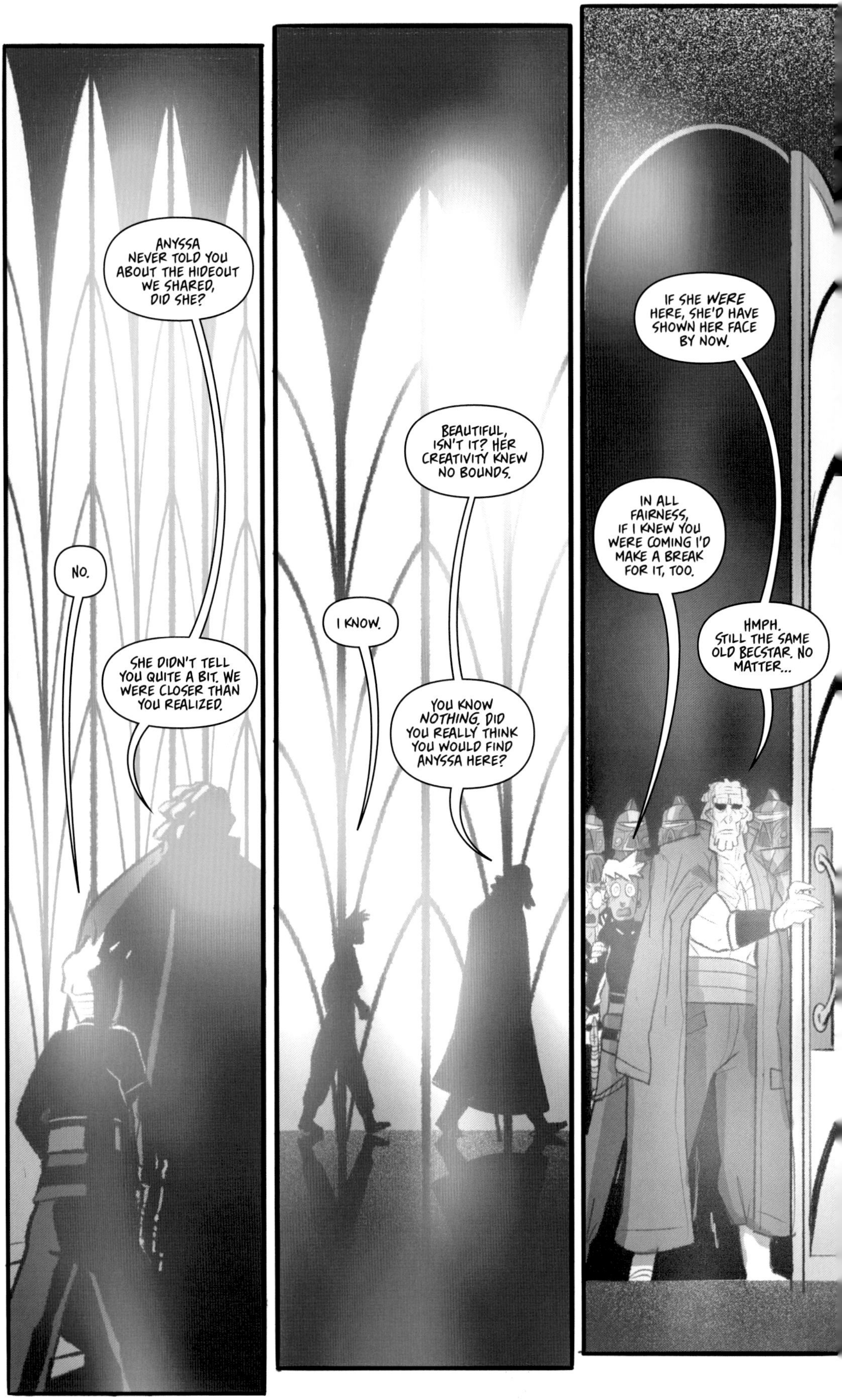
ANYSSA NEVER TOLD YOU ABOUT THE HIDEOUT WE SHARED, DID SHE?
NO.
SHE DIDN'T TELL YOU QUITE A BIT. WE WERE CLOSER THAN YOU REALIZED.
BEAUTIFUL, ISN'T IT? HER CREATIVITY KNEW NO BOUNDS.
I KNOW.
YOU KNOW NOTHING. DID YOU REALLY THINK YOU WOULD FIND ANYSSA HERE?
IF SHE WERE HERE, SHE'D HAVE SHOWN HER FACE BY NOW.
IN ALL FAIRNESS, IF I KNEW YOU WERE COMING I'D MAKE A BREAK FOR IT, TOO.
HMPH. STILL THE SAME OLD BECSTAR. NO MATTER...

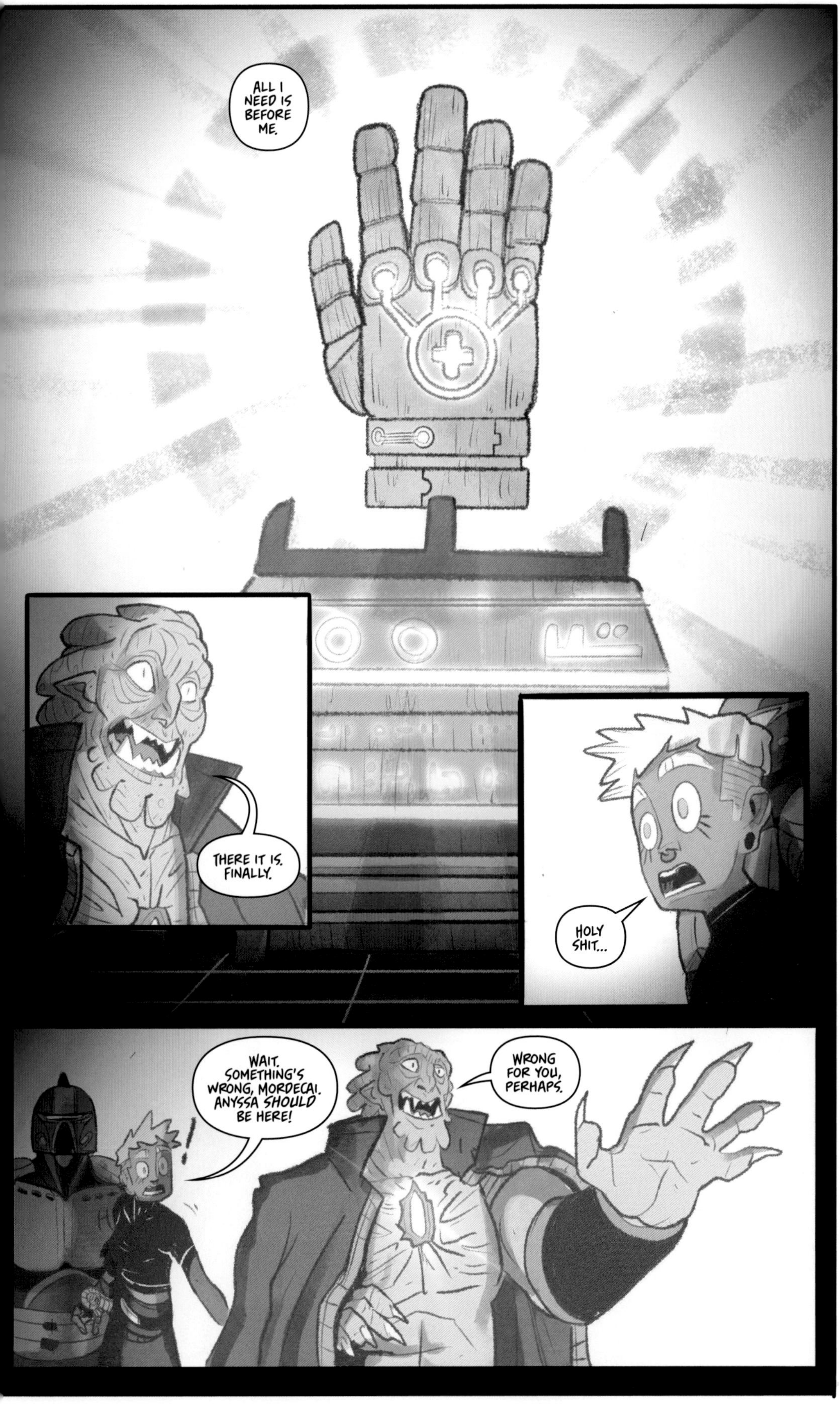
ALL I NEED IS BEFORE ME.
THERE IT IS. FINALLY.
HOLY SHIT...
WAIT. SOMETHING'S WRONG, MORDECAI. ANYSSA SHOULD BE HERE!
!
WRONG FOR YOU, PERHAPS.

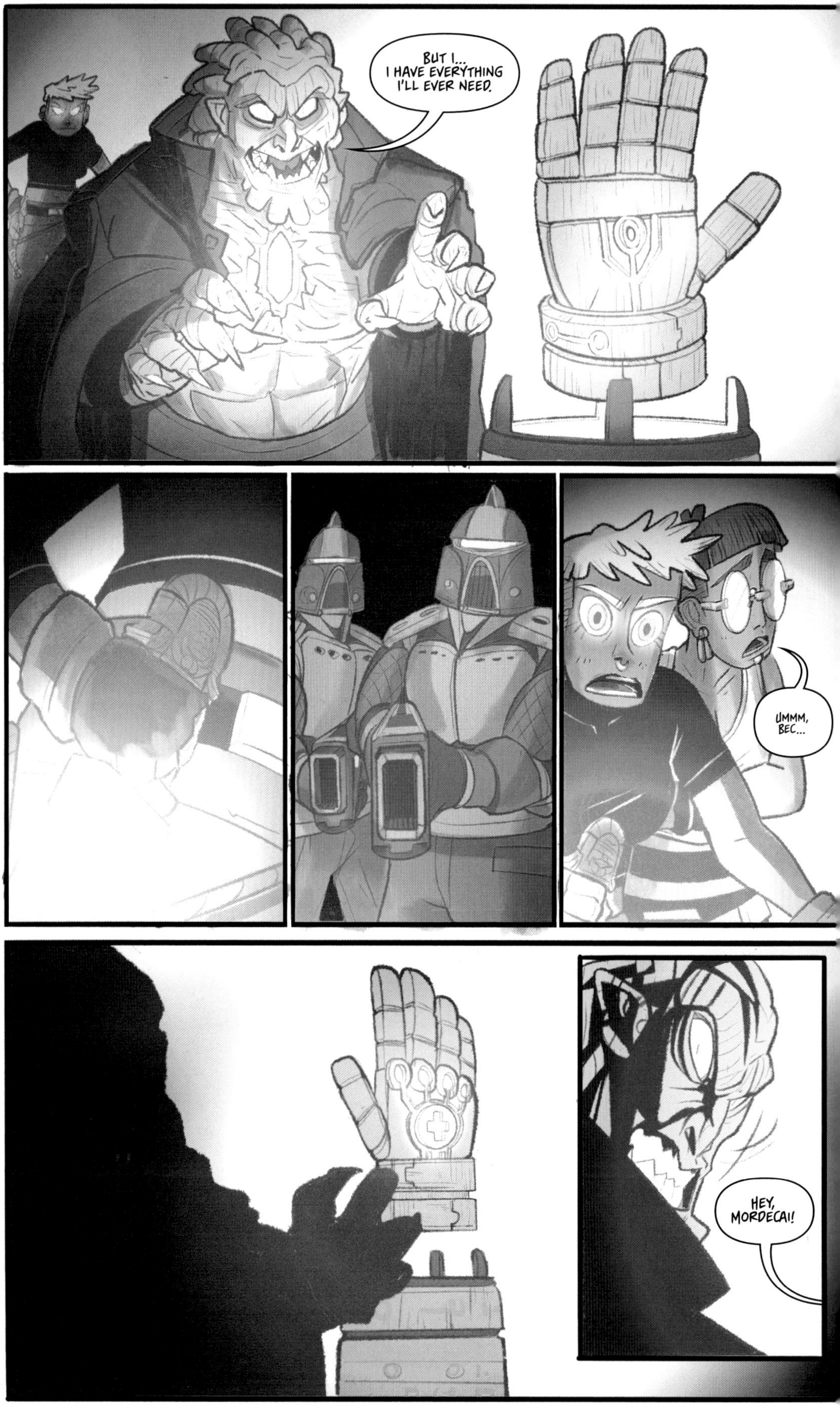
BUT I...
I HAVE EVERYTHING
I'LL EVER NEED.
UMMM,
BEC...
HEY,
MORDECAI!

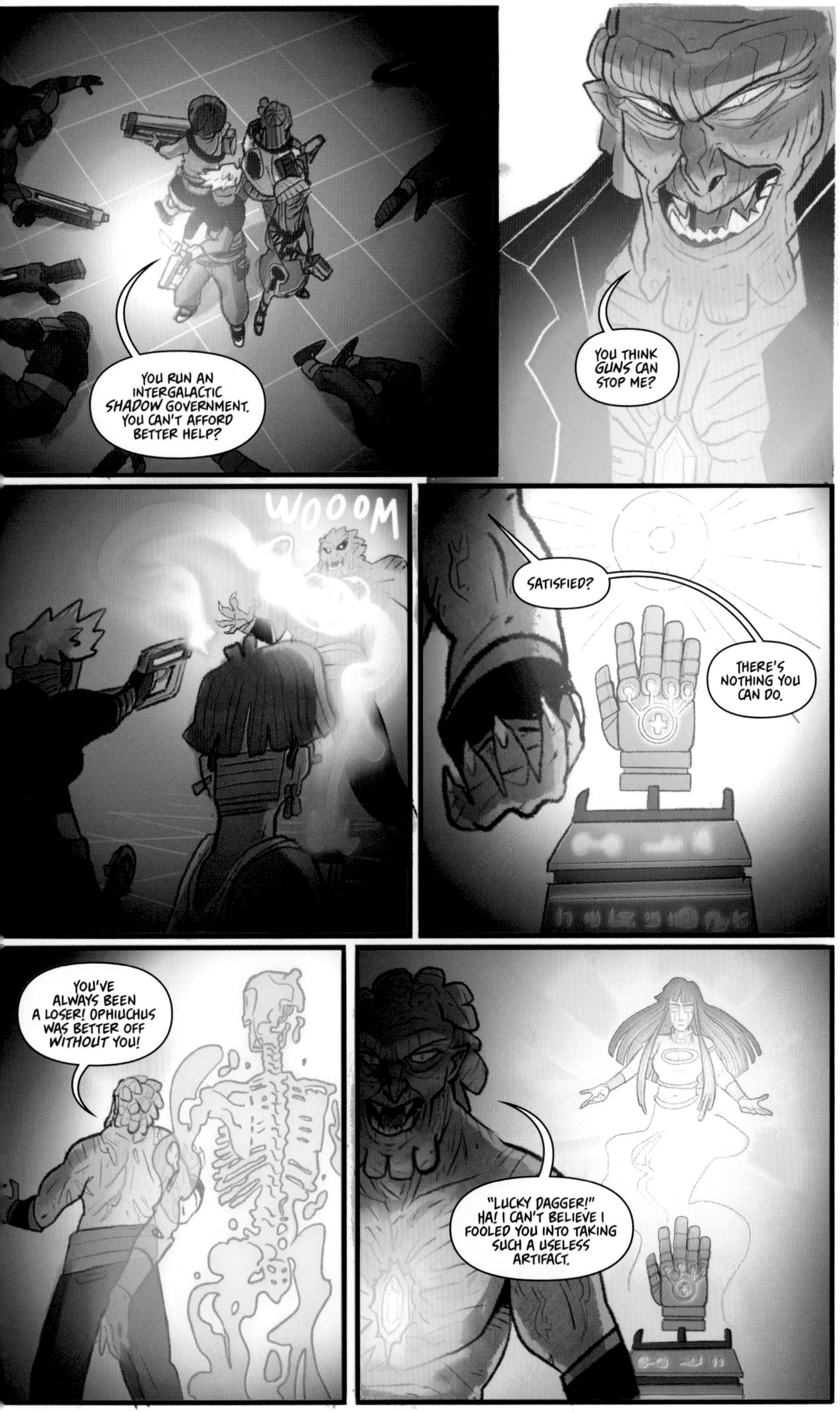
YOU RUN AN INTERGALACTIC SHADOW GOVERNMENT. YOU CAN'T AFFORD BETTER HELP?
YOU THINK GUNS CAN STOP ME?
WOOOM
SATISFIED?
THERE'S NOTHING YOU CAN DO.
YOU'VE ALWAYS BEEN A LOSER! OPHIUCHUS WAS BETTER OFF WITHOUT YOU!
"LUCKY DAGGER!" HA! I CAN'T BELIEVE I FOOLED YOU INTO TAKING SUCH A USELESS ARTIFACT.

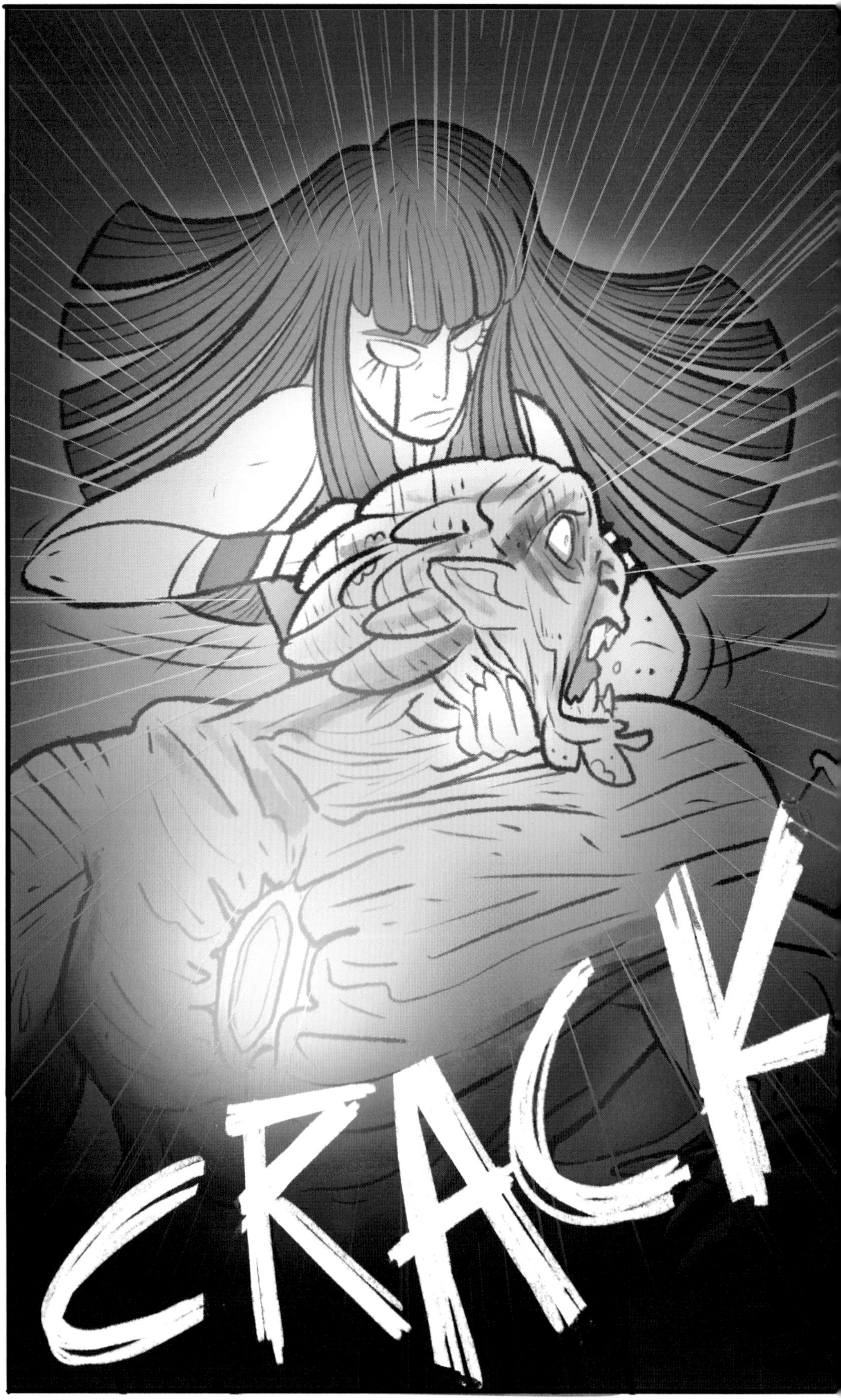
CRACK

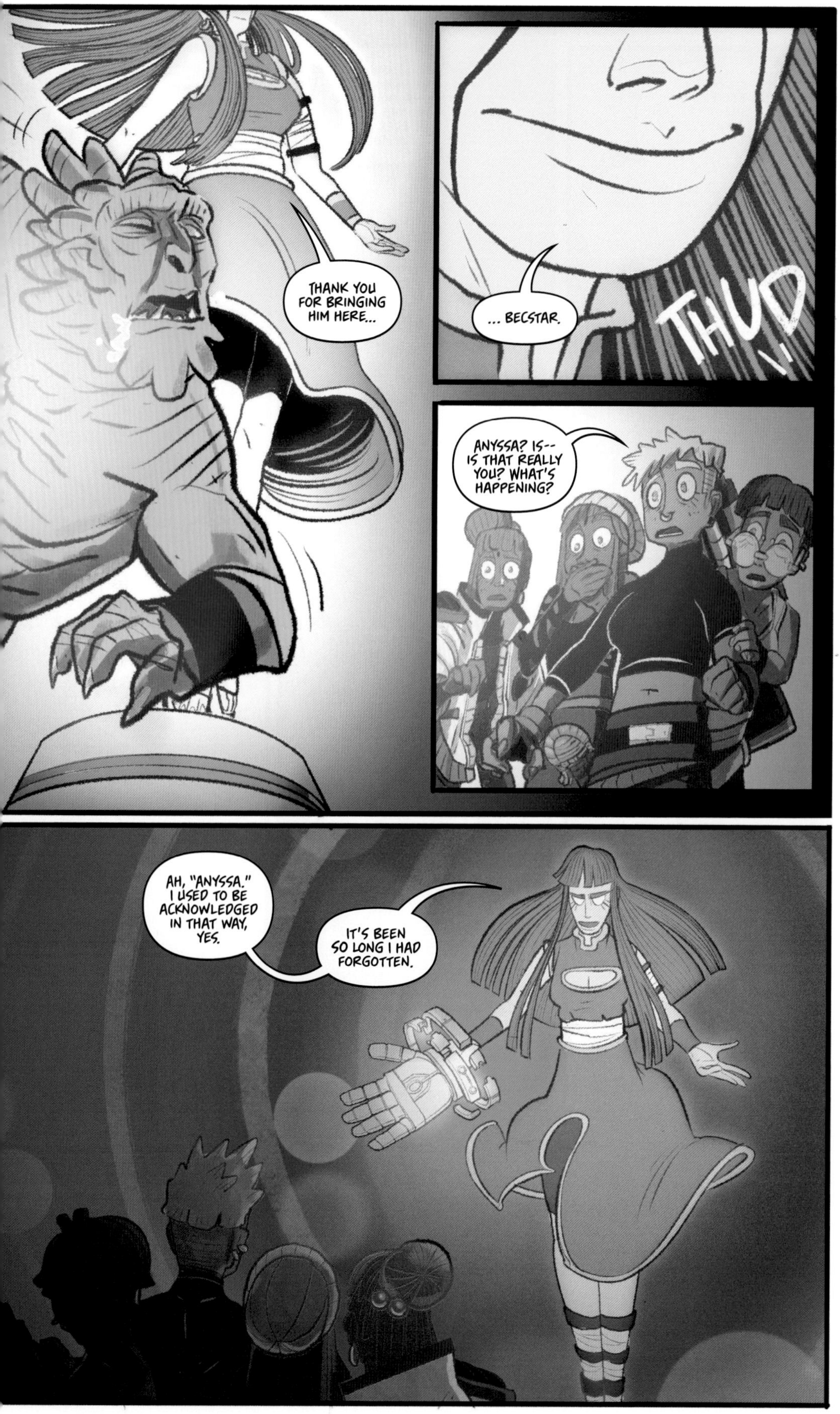
THANK YOU FOR BRINGING HIM HERE...
... BECSTAR.
THUD
ANYSSA? IS-- IS THAT REALLY YOU? WHAT'S HAPPENING?
AH, "ANYSSA." I USED TO BE ACKNOWLEDGED IN THAT WAY, YES.
IT'S BEEN SO LONG I HAD FORGOTTEN.

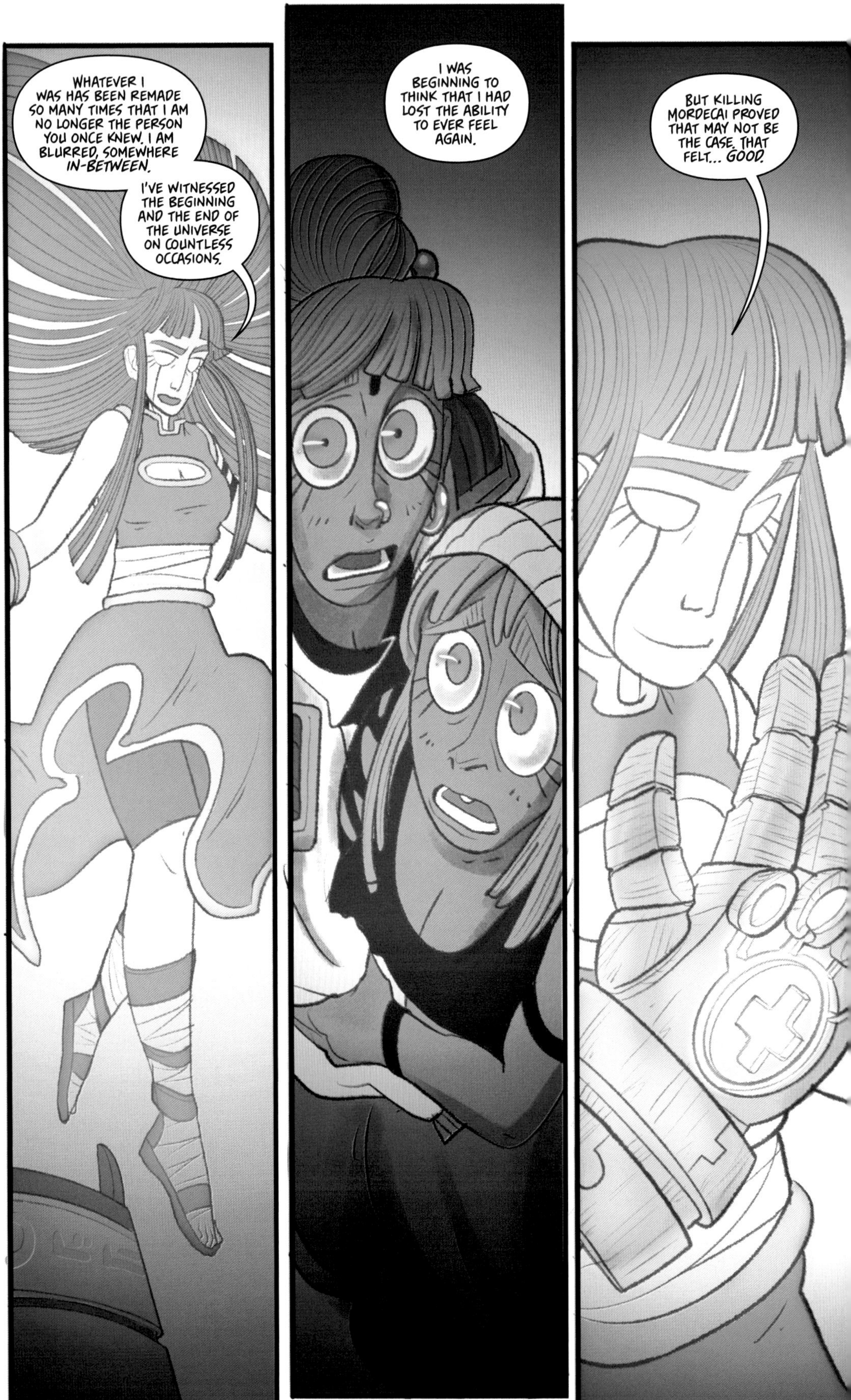
WHATEVER I WAS HAS BEEN REMADE SO MANY TIMES THAT I AM NO LONGER THE PERSON YOU ONCE KNEW. I AM BLURRED, SOMEWHERE IN-BETWEEN.
I'VE WITNESSED THE BEGINNING AND THE END OF THE UNIVERSE ON COUNTLESS OCCASIONS.
I WAS BEGINNING TO THINK THAT I HAD LOST THE ABILITY TO EVER FEEL AGAIN.
BUT KILLING MORDECAI PROVED THAT MAY NOT BE THE CASE. THAT FELT... GOOD.

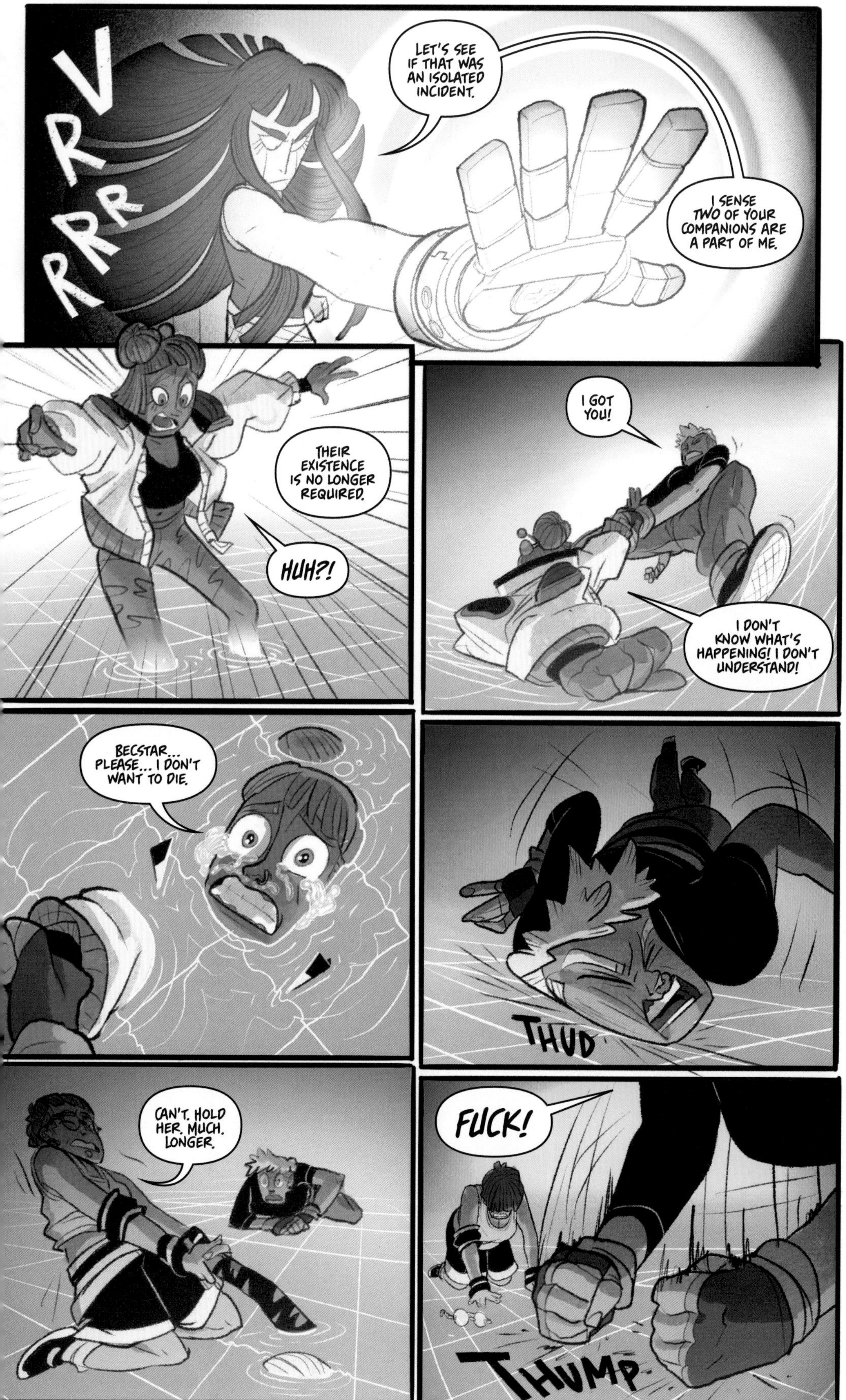
VRRRR
LET'S SEE IF THAT WAS AN ISOLATED INCIDENT.
I SENSE TWO OF YOUR COMPANIONS ARE A PART OF ME.
THEIR EXISTENCE IS NO LONGER REQUIRED.
HUH?!
I GOT YOU!
I DON'T KNOW WHAT'S HAPPENING! I DON'T UNDERSTAND!
BECSTAR... PLEASE... I DON'T WANT TO DIE.
THUD
CAN'T. HOLD HER. MUCH. LONGER.
FUCK!
THUMP

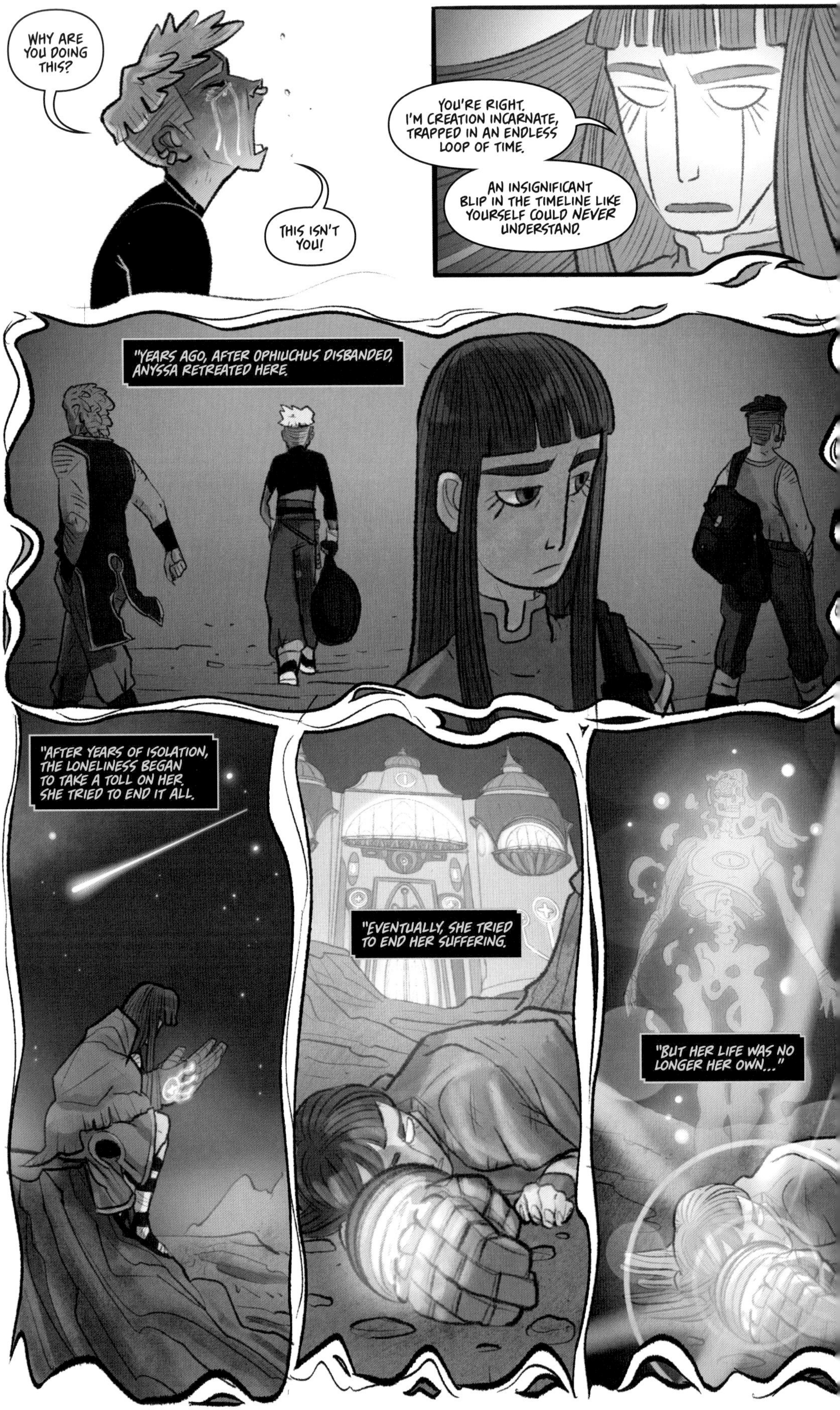
WHY ARE YOU DOING THIS?
THIS ISN'T YOU!
YOU'RE RIGHT. I'M CREATION INCARNATE, TRAPPED IN AN ENDLESS LOOP OF TIME.
AN INSIGNIFICANT BLIP IN THE TIMELINE LIKE YOURSELF COULD NEVER UNDERSTAND.
"YEARS AGO, AFTER OPHIUCHUS DISBANDED, ANYSSA RETREATED HERE.
"AFTER YEARS OF ISOLATION, THE LONELINESS BEGAN TO TAKE A TOLL ON HER. SHE TRIED TO END IT ALL.
"EVENTUALLY, SHE TRIED TO END HER SUFFERING.
"BUT HER LIFE WAS NO LONGER HER OWN..."

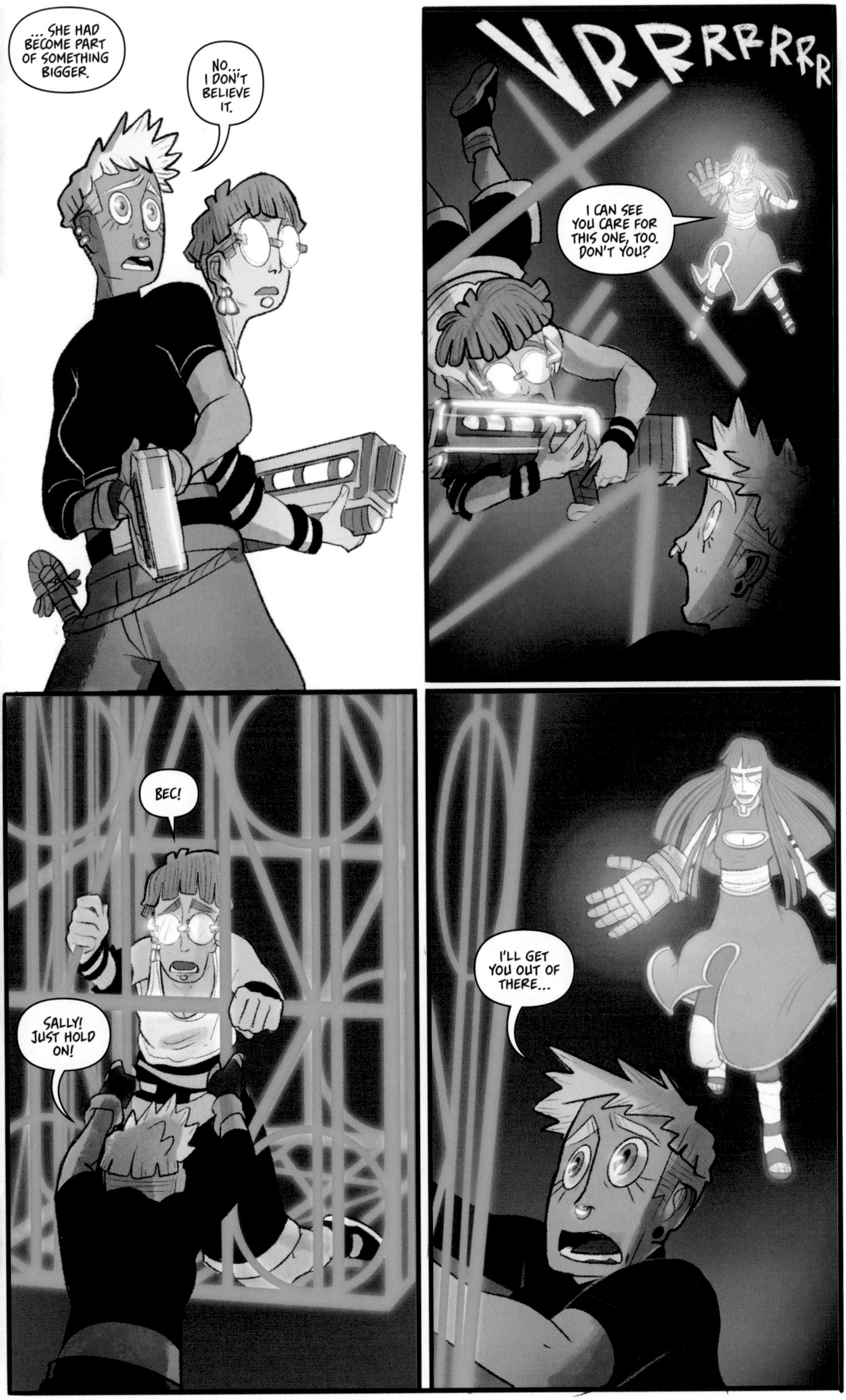
... SHE HAD BECOME PART OF SOMETHING BIGGER.
NO... I DON'T BELIEVE IT.
VRRRRRRR
I CAN SEE YOU CARE FOR THIS ONE, TOO. DON'T YOU?
BEC!
SALLY! JUST HOLD ON!
I'LL GET YOU OUT OF THERE...

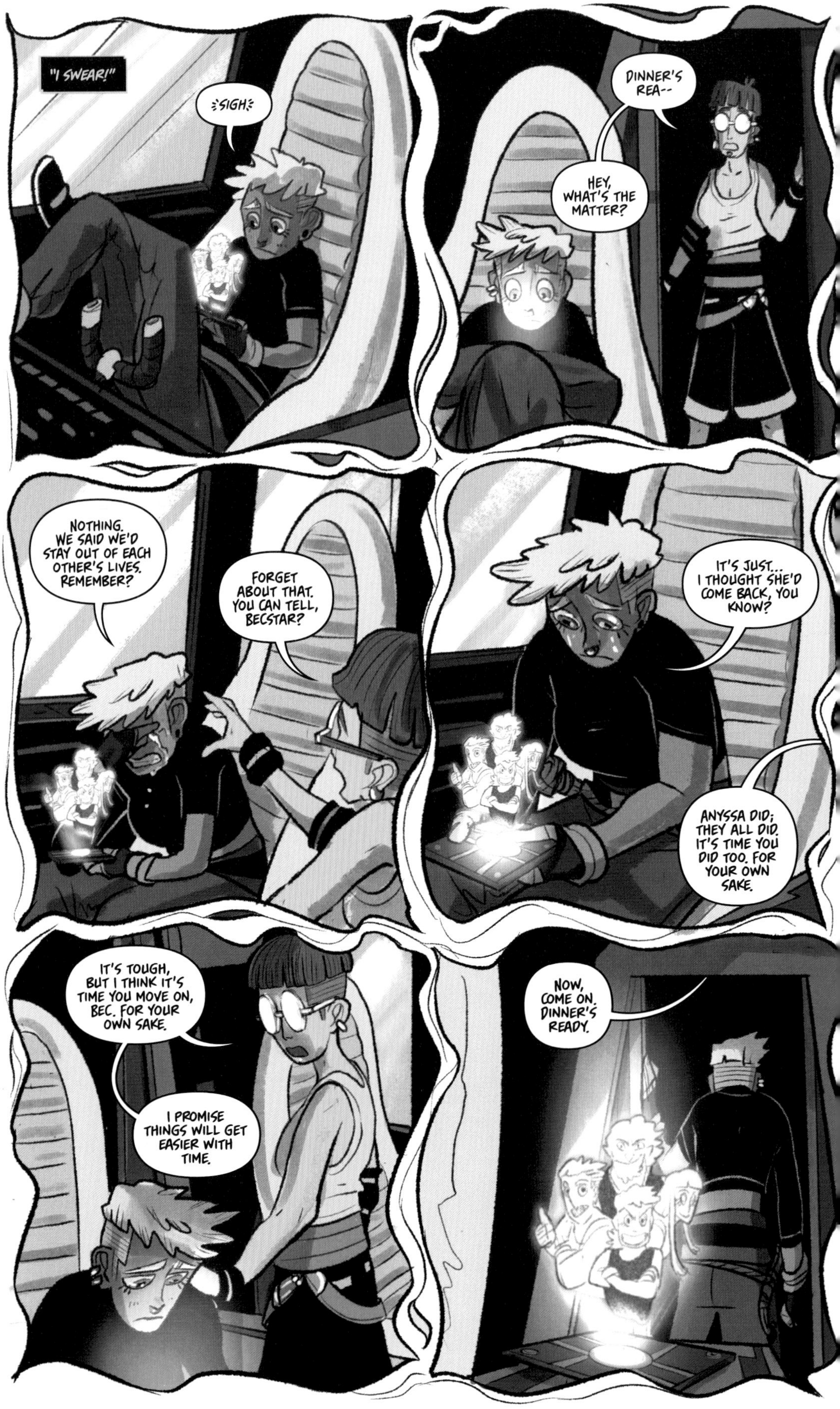
"I SWEAR!"
SIGH
DINNER'S REA--
HEY, WHAT'S THE MATTER?
NOTHING. WE SAID WE'D STAY OUT OF EACH OTHER'S LIVES. REMEMBER?
FORGET ABOUT THAT. YOU CAN TELL, BECSTAR?
IT'S JUST... I THOUGHT SHE'D COME BACK, YOU KNOW?
ANYSSA DID; THEY ALL DID. IT'S TIME YOU DID TOO. FOR YOUR OWN SAKE.
IT'S TOUGH, BUT I THINK IT'S TIME YOU MOVE ON, BEC. FOR YOUR OWN SAKE.
I PROMISE THINGS WILL GET EASIER WITH TIME.
NOW, COME ON. DINNER'S READY.

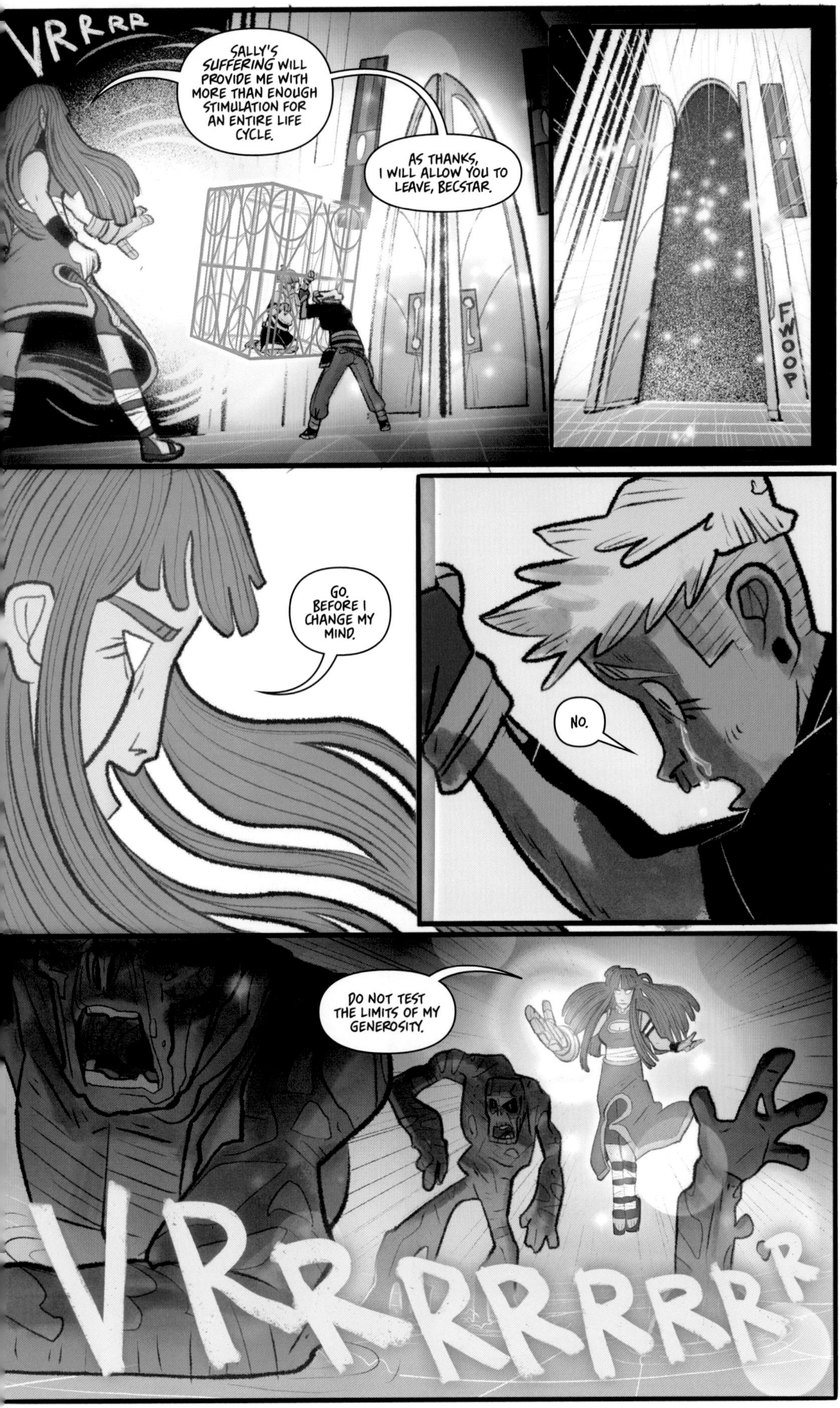
VRRRR
SALLY'S SUFFERING WILL PROVIDE ME WITH MORE THAN ENOUGH STIMULATION FOR AN ENTIRE LIFE CYCLE.
AS THANKS, I WILL ALLOW YOU TO LEAVE, BECSTAR.
FWOOP
GO. BEFORE I CHANGE MY MIND.
NO.
DO NOT TEST THE LIMITS OF MY GENEROSITY.
VRRRRRRRR

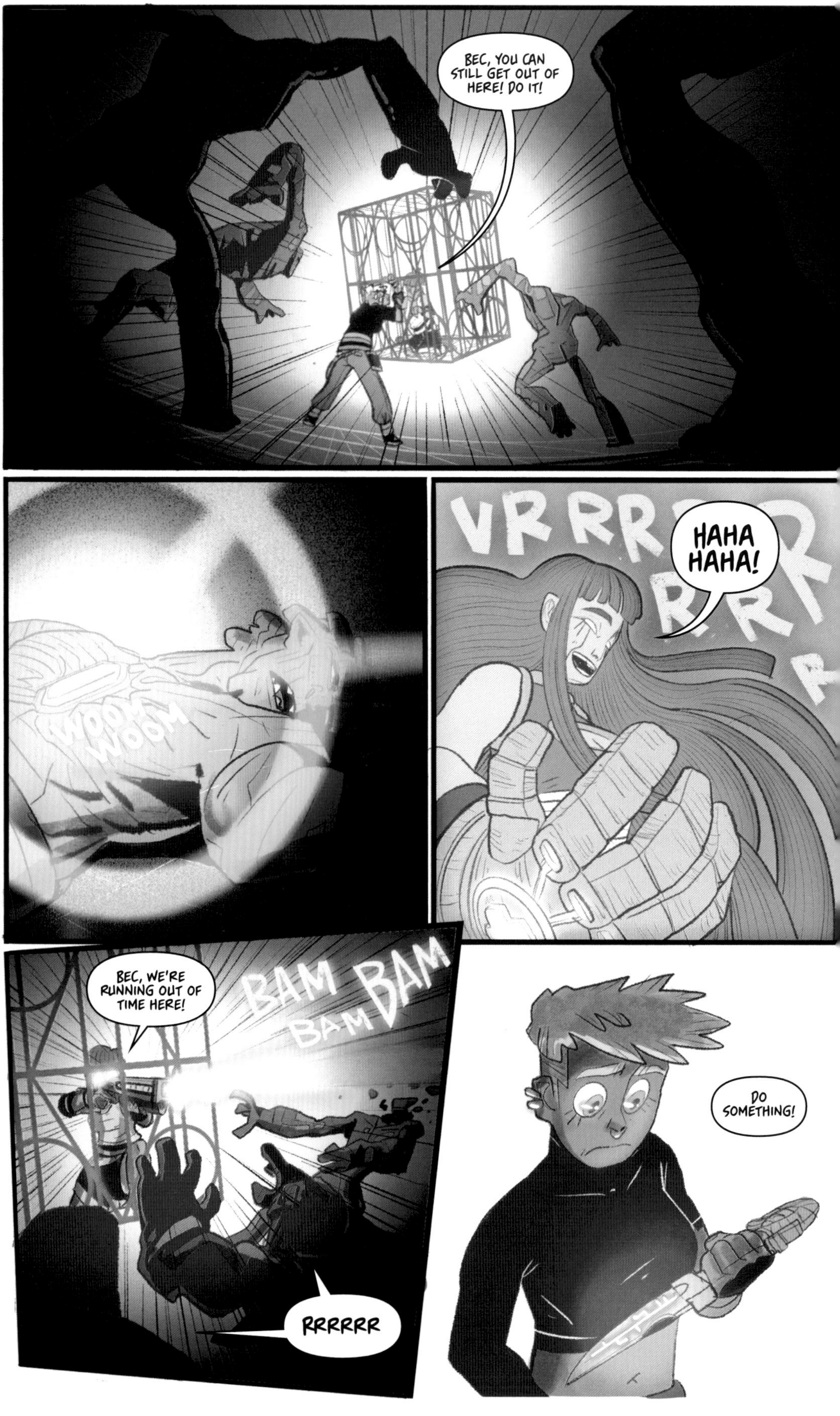
BEC, YOU CAN STILL GET OUT OF HERE! DO IT!
WOOM WOOM
VRRRRRRRR
HAHA HAHA!
BEC, WE'RE RUNNING OUT OF TIME HERE!
BAM BAM BAM BAM
RRRRRR
DO SOMETHING!

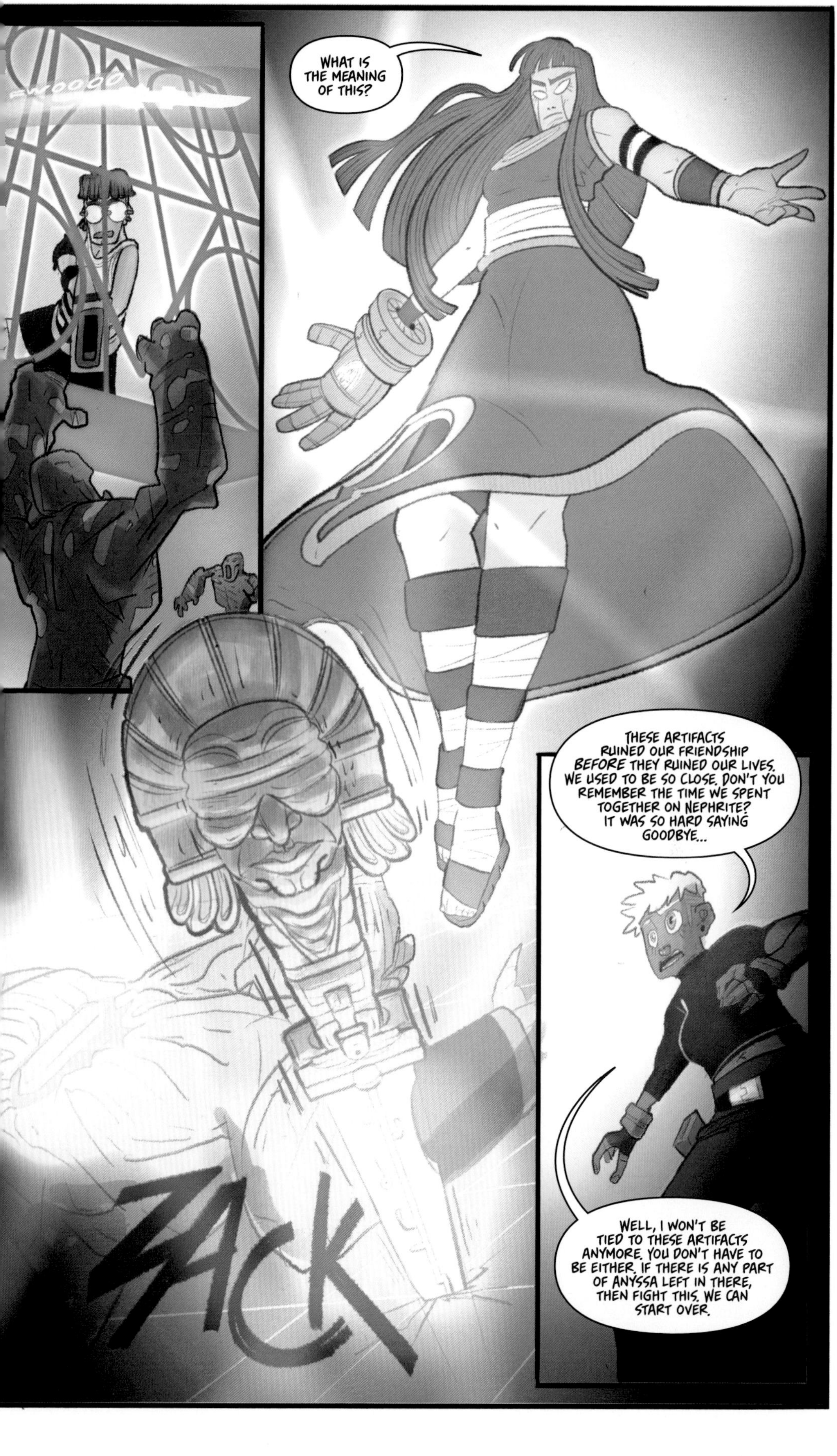
FWOOOO
WHAT IS THE MEANING OF THIS?
ZACK
THESE ARTIFACTS RUINED OUR FRIENDSHIP BEFORE THEY RUINED OUR LIVES. WE USED TO BE SO CLOSE. DON'T YOU REMEMBER THE TIME WE SPENT TOGETHER ON NEPHRITE? IT WAS SO HARD SAYING GOODBYE...
WELL, I WON'T BE TIED TO THESE ARTIFACTS ANYMORE. YOU DON'T HAVE TO BE EITHER. IF THERE IS ANY PART OF ANYSSA LEFT IN THERE, THEN FIGHT THIS. WE CAN START OVER.

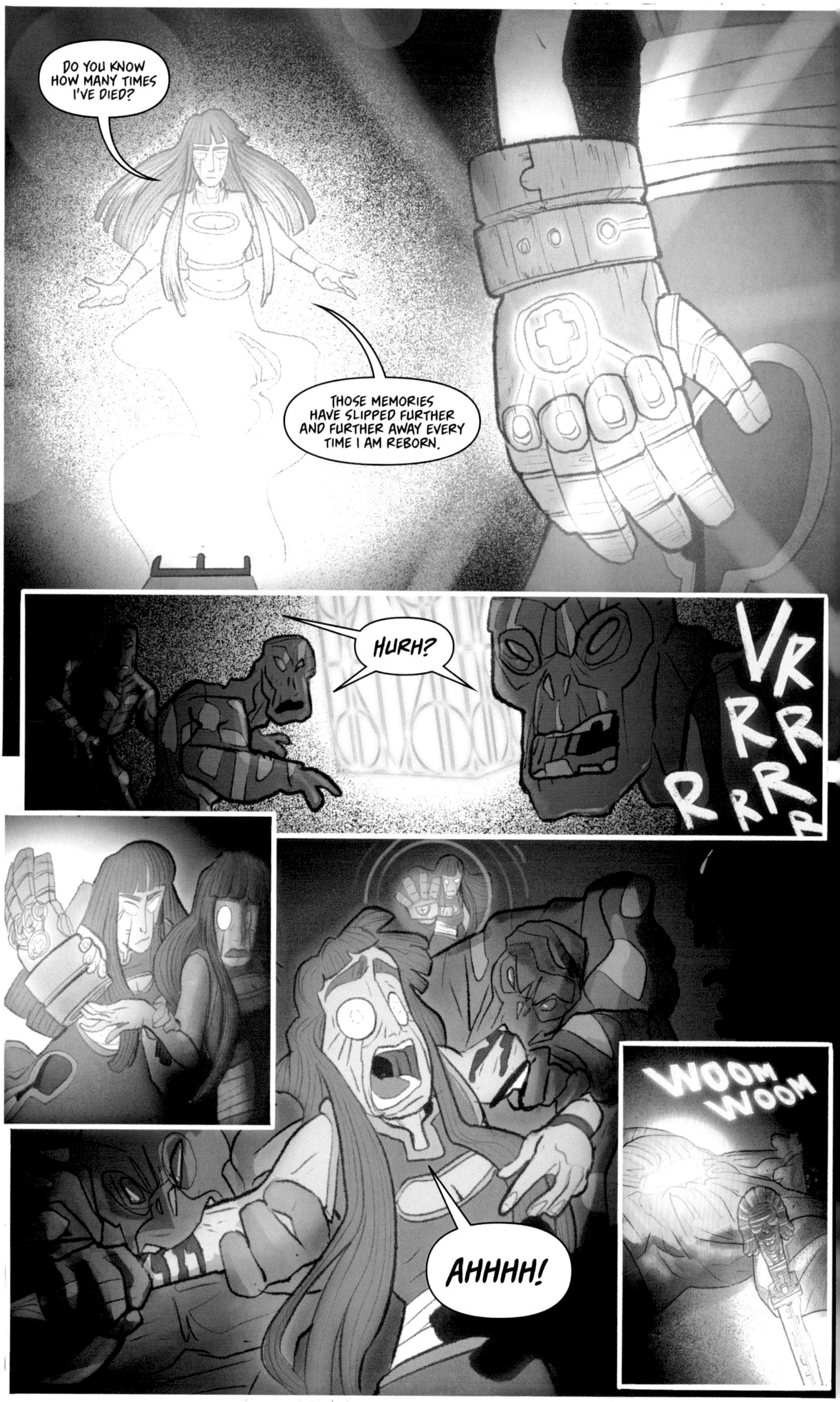
DO YOU KNOW HOW MANY TIMES I'VE DIED?
THOSE MEMORIES HAVE SLIPPED FURTHER AND FURTHER AWAY EVERY TIME I AM REBORN.
HURH?
VRRRRRRRR
AHHHH!
WOOM WOOM

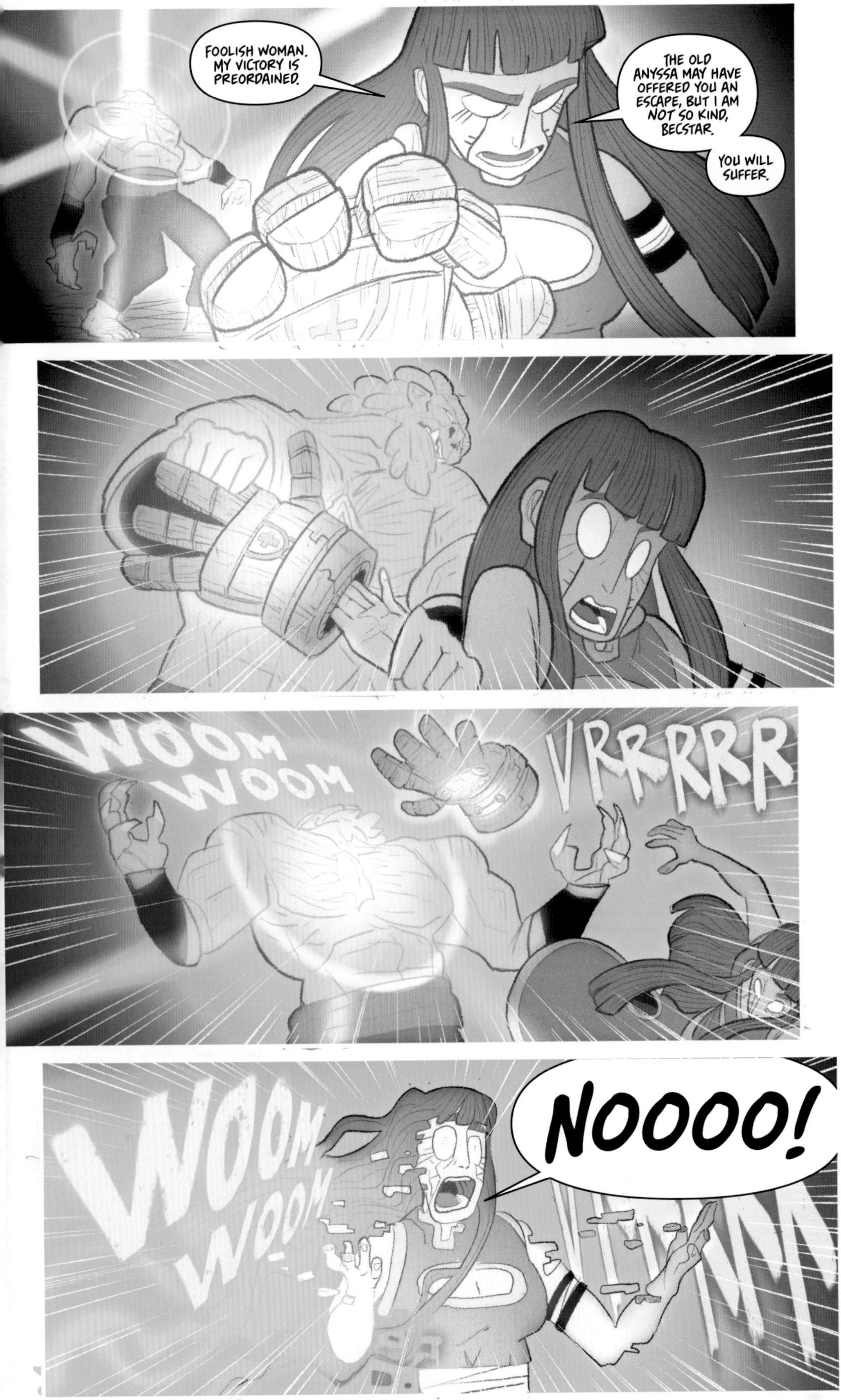
FOOLISH WOMAN. MY VICTORY IS PREORDAINED.
THE OLD ANYSSA MAY HAVE OFFERED YOU AN ESCAPE, BUT I AM NOT SO KIND, BECSTAR.
YOU WILL SUFFER.
WOOM WOOM
VRRRRR
WOOM WOOM
NOOOO!

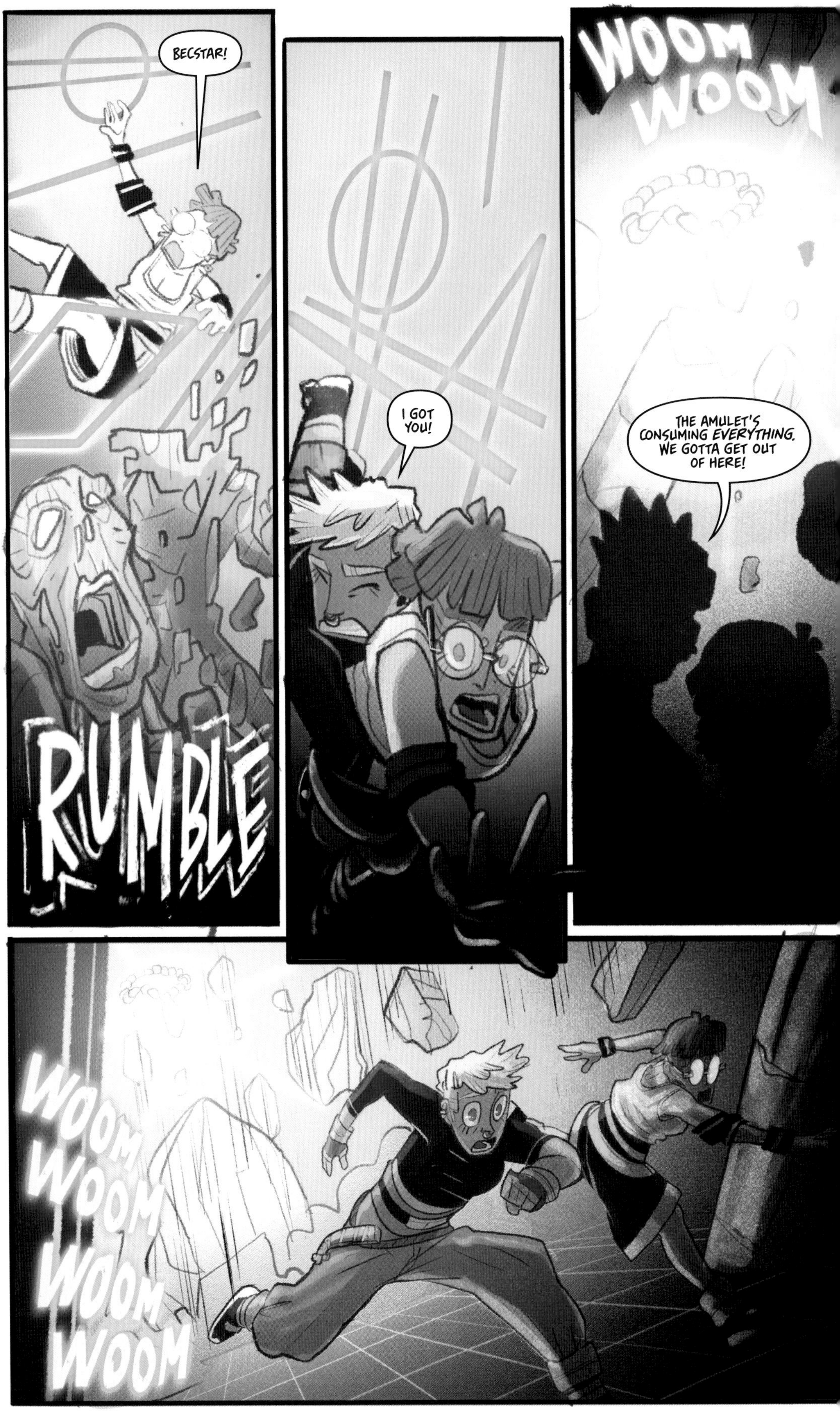
BECSTAR!
RUMBLE
I GOT YOU!
WOOM WOOM
THE AMULET'S CONSUMING *EVERYTHING*. WE GOTTA GET OUT OF HERE!
WOOM WOOM WOOM WOOM

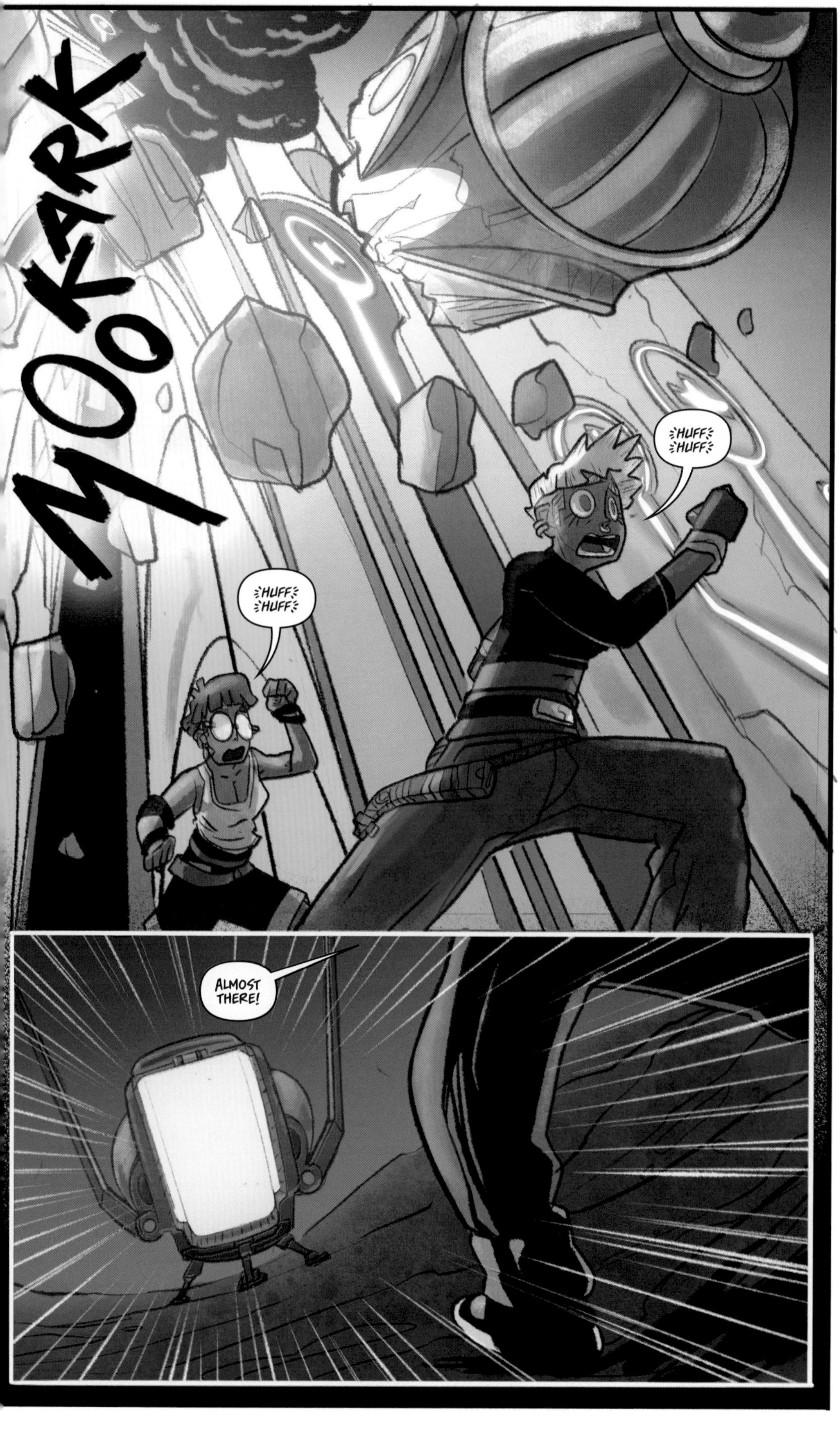
MOOKARK
HUFF HUFF
HUFF HUFF
ALMOST THERE!

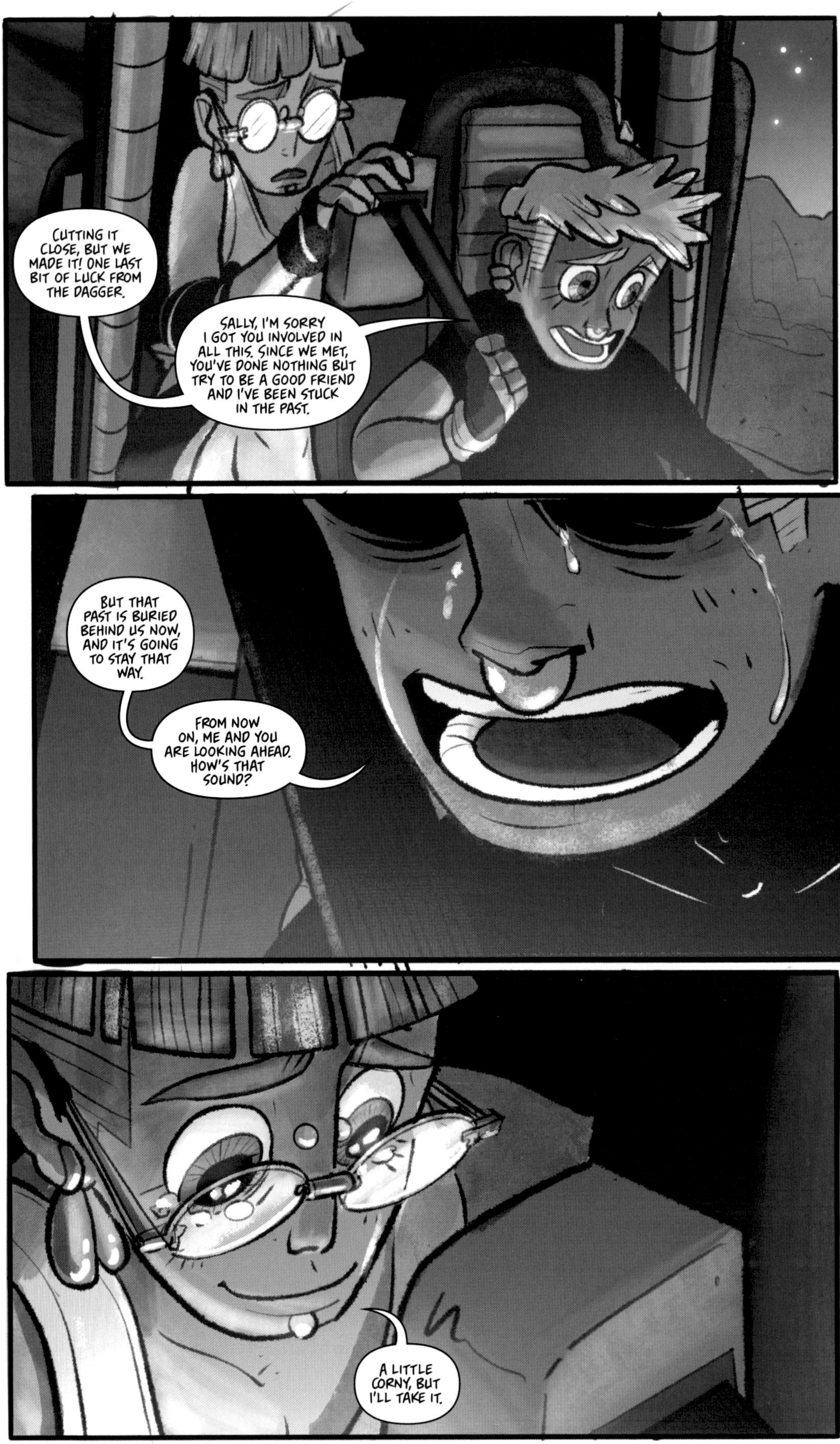
CUTTING IT CLOSE, BUT WE MADE IT! ONE LAST BIT OF LUCK FROM THE DAGGER.
SALLY, I'M SORRY I GOT YOU INVOLVED IN ALL THIS. SINCE WE MET, YOU'VE DONE NOTHING BUT TRY TO BE A GOOD FRIEND AND I'VE BEEN STUCK IN THE PAST.
BUT THAT PAST IS BURIED BEHIND US NOW, AND IT'S GOING TO STAY THAT WAY.
FROM NOW ON, ME AND YOU ARE LOOKING AHEAD. HOW'S THAT SOUND?
A LITTLE CORNY, BUT I'LL TAKE IT.

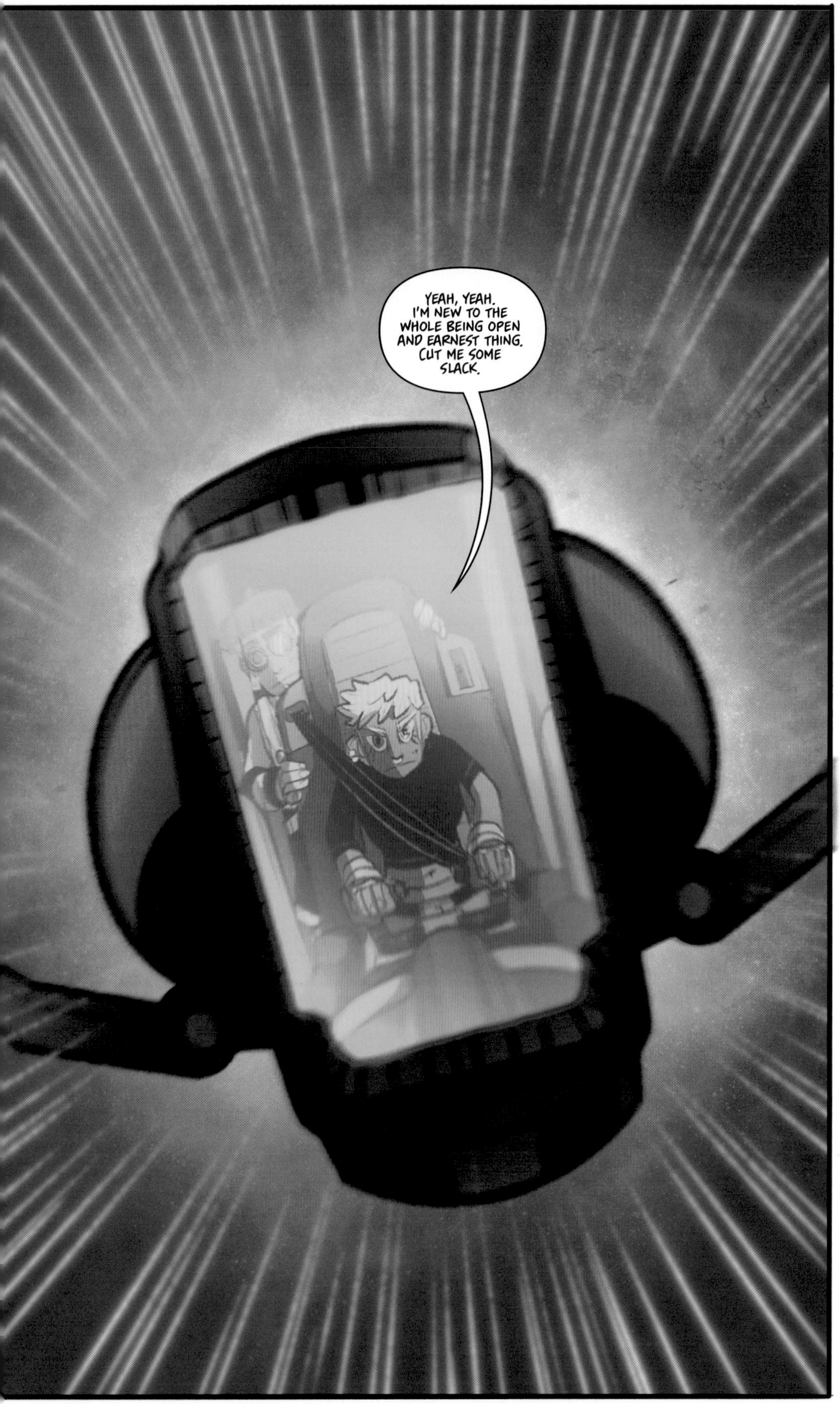
YEAH, YEAH. I'M NEW TO THE WHOLE BEING OPEN AND EARNEST THING. CUT ME SOME SLACK.

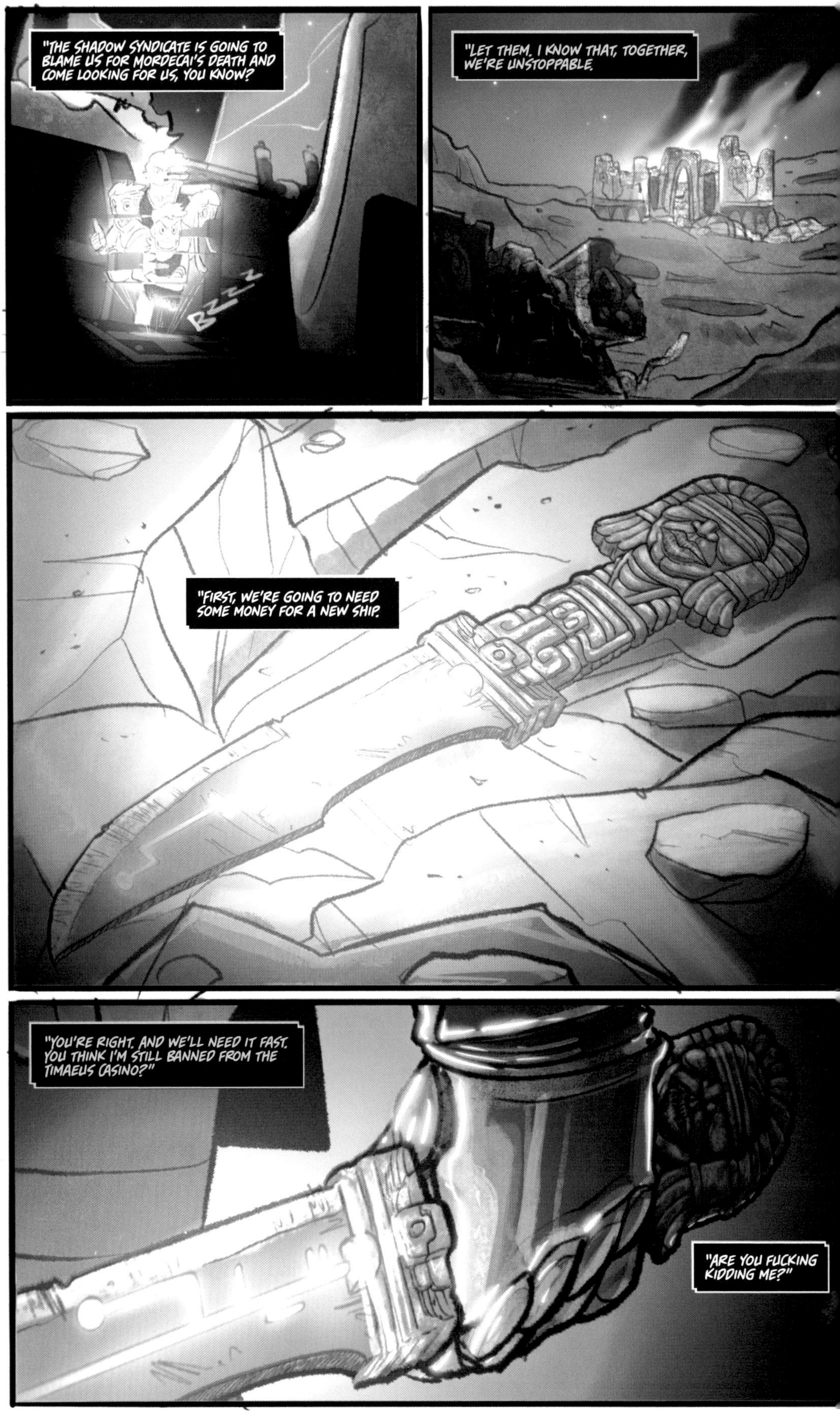
"THE SHADOW SYNDICATE IS GOING TO BLAME US FOR MORDECAI'S DEATH AND COME LOOKING FOR US, YOU KNOW?
"LET THEM. I KNOW THAT, TOGETHER, WE'RE UNSTOPPABLE.
"FIRST, WE'RE GOING TO NEED SOME MONEY FOR A NEW SHIP.
"YOU'RE RIGHT. AND WE'LL NEED IT FAST. YOU THINK I'M STILL BANNED FROM THE TIMAEUS CASINO?"
"ARE YOU FUCKING KIDDING ME?"

_CONCEPT ART

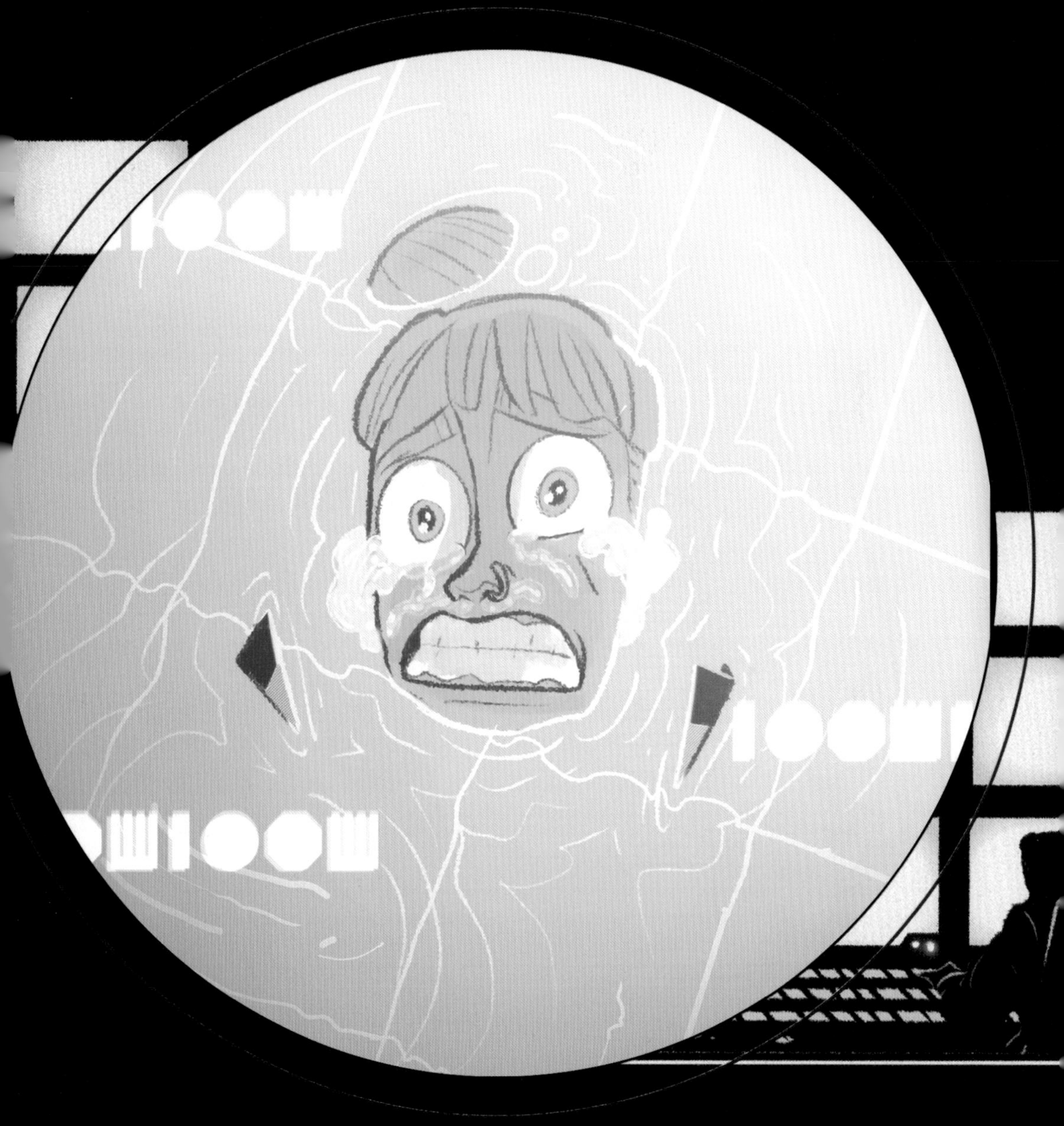

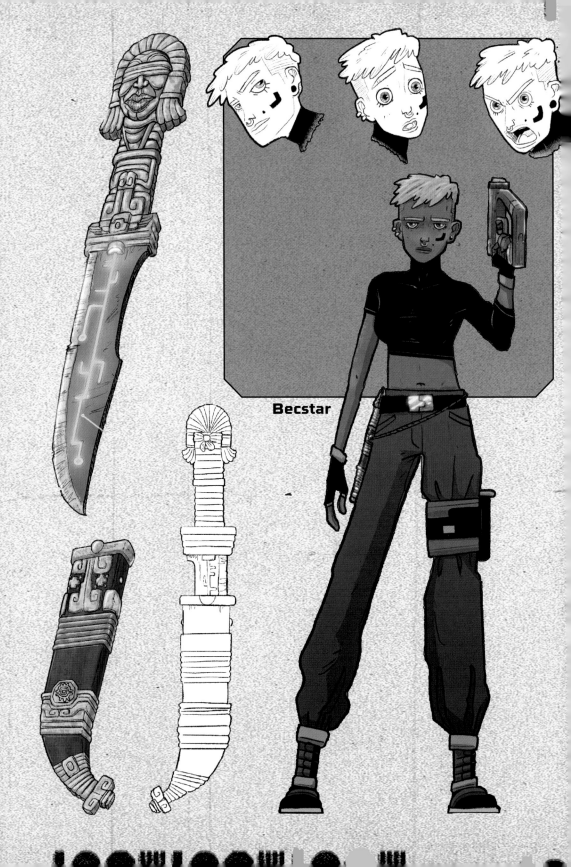

Becstar

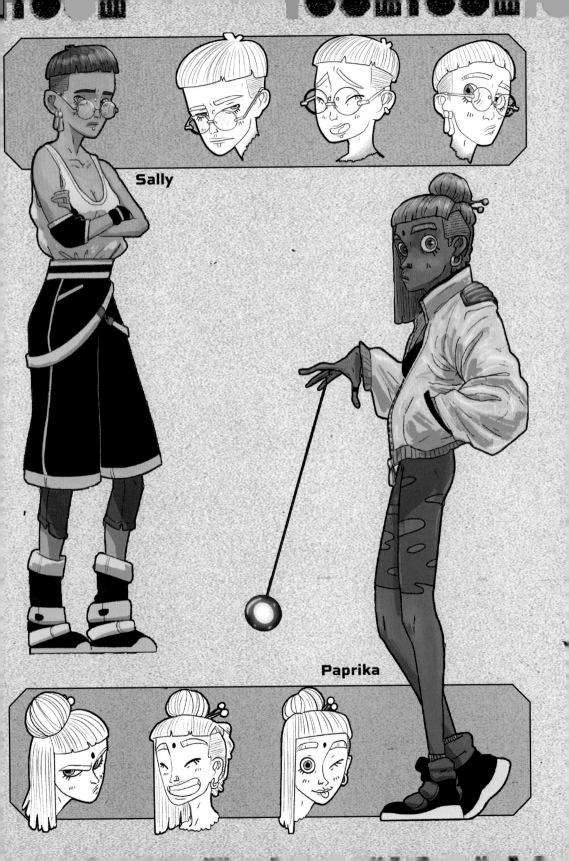

Sally

Paprika

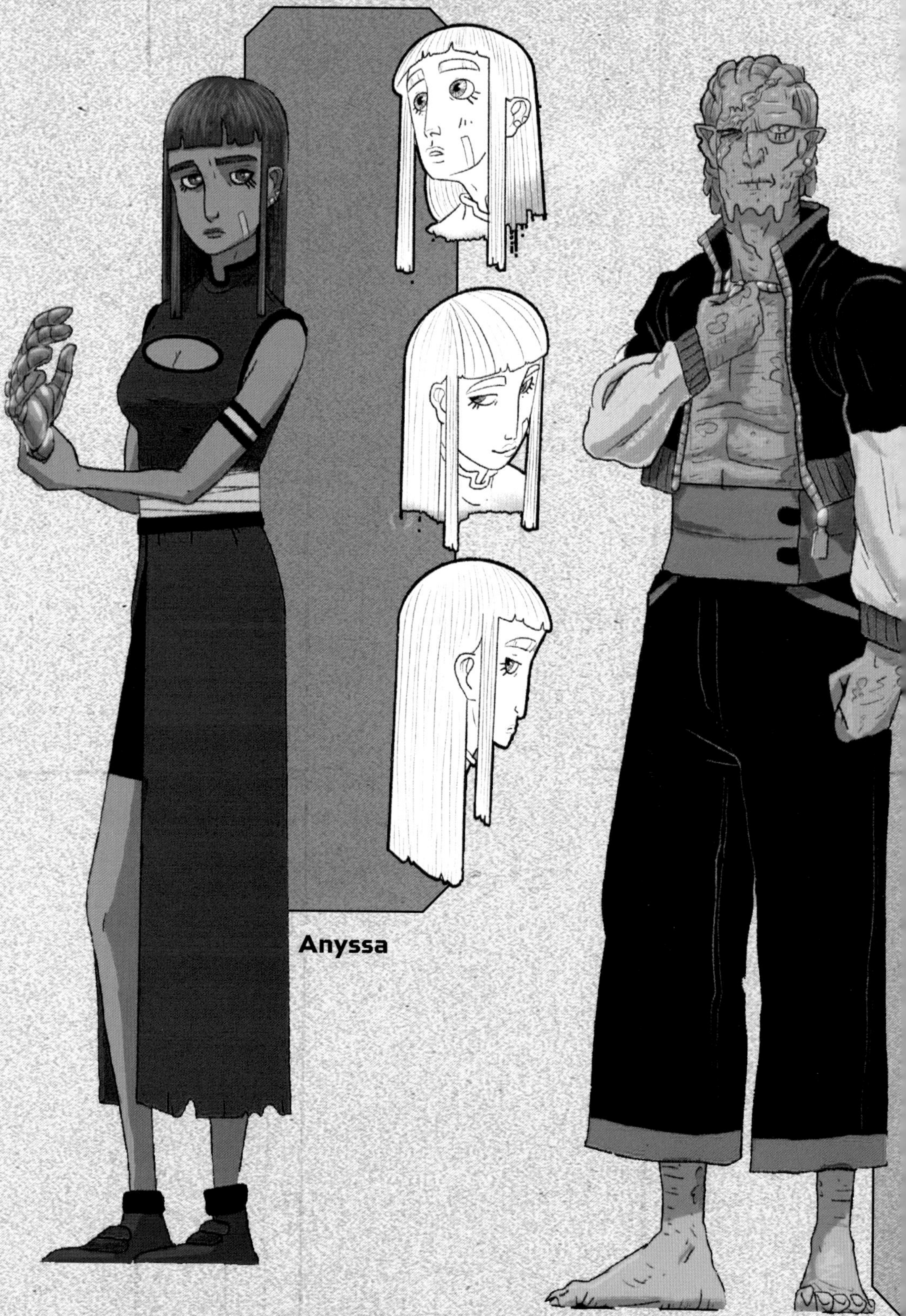
Anyssa

Mordecai

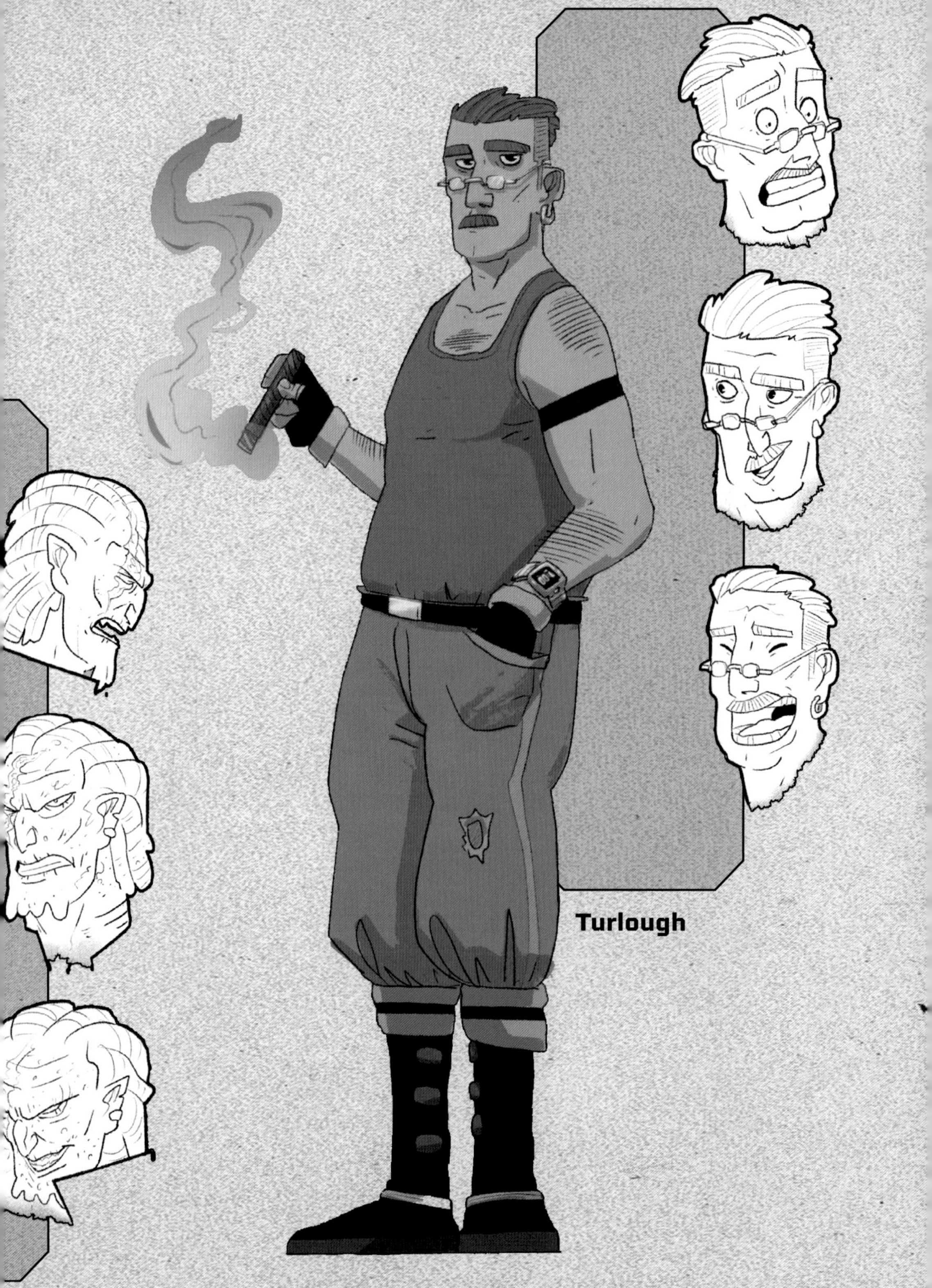

Turlough

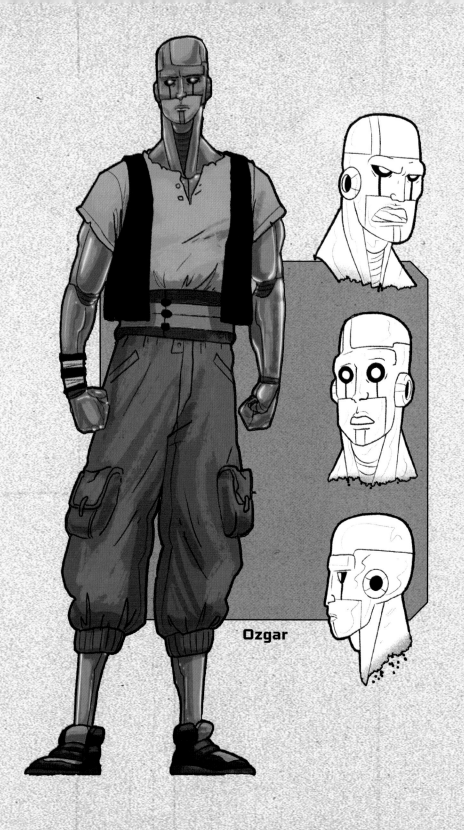

Ozgar

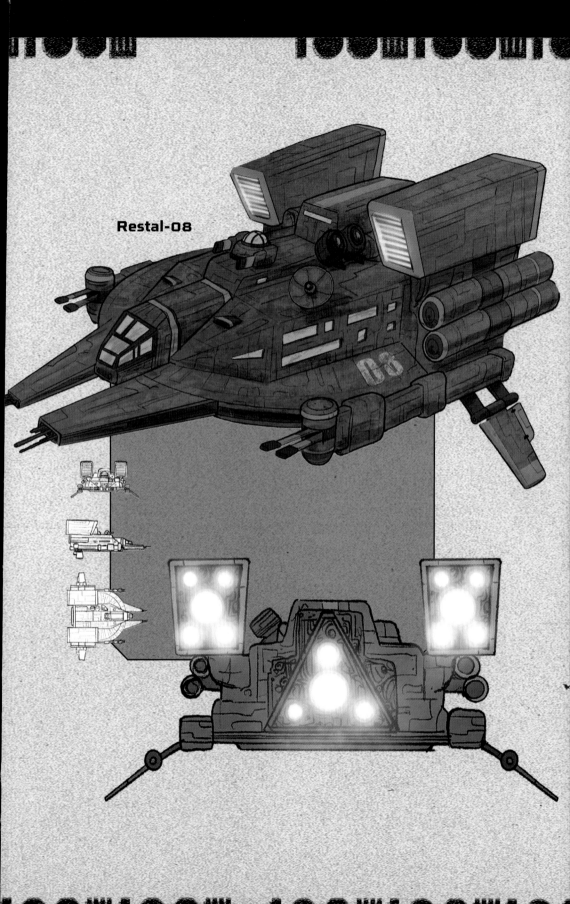

Restal-08

Becstar #1 Variant Cover
Lorenzo Colangeli

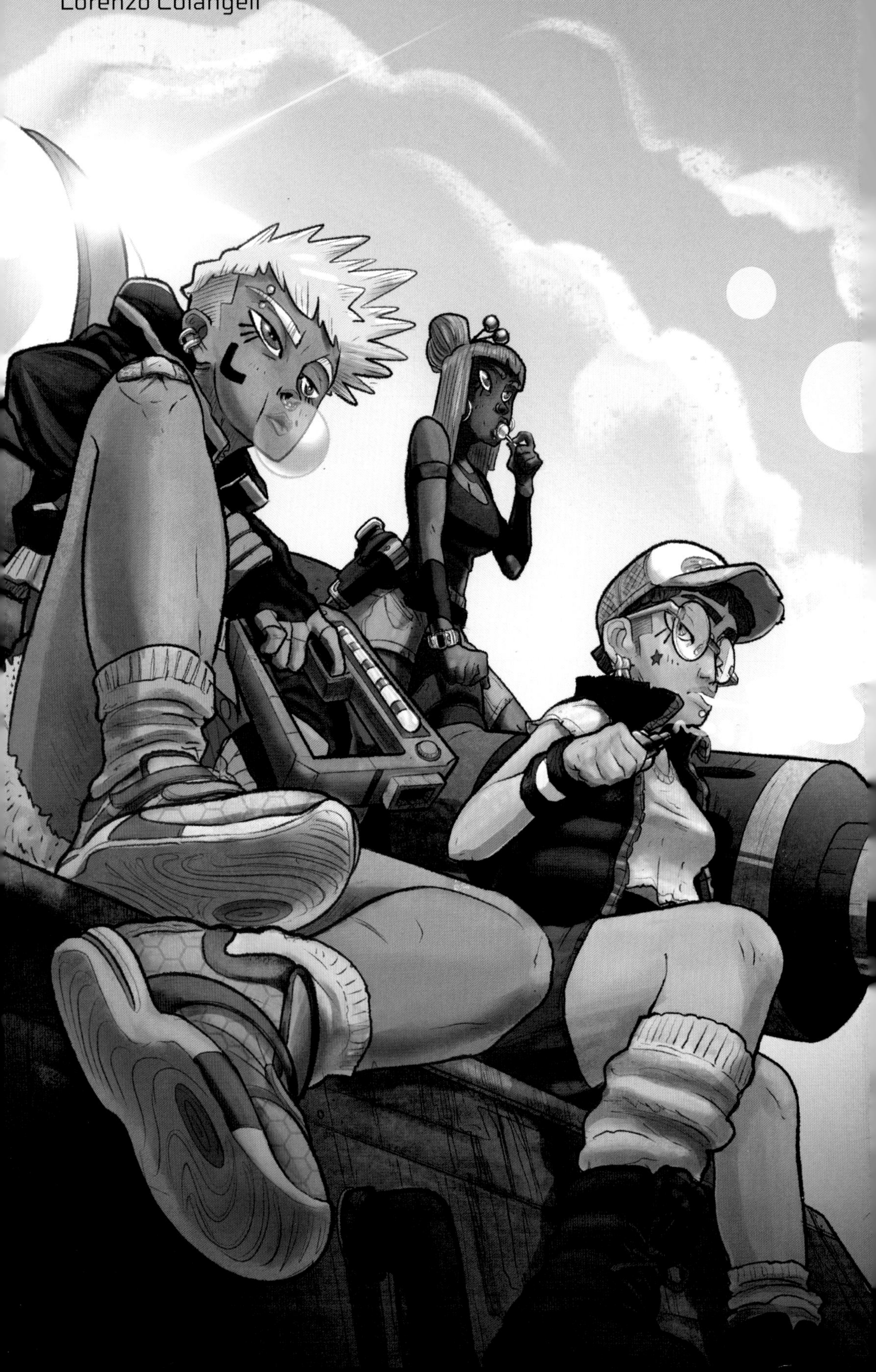

Betstar #1 Variant Cover
Fabian Lelay

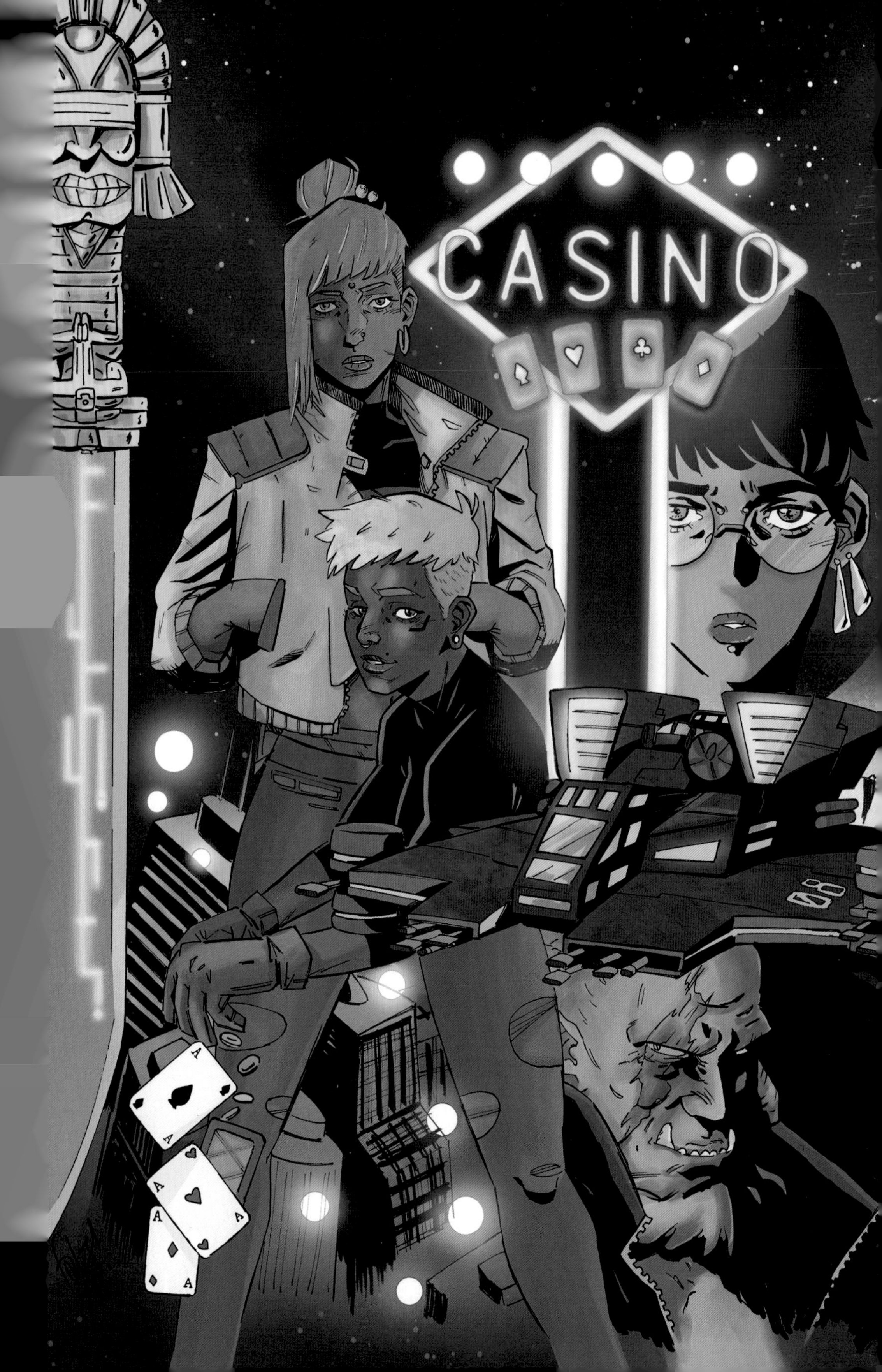
CASINO

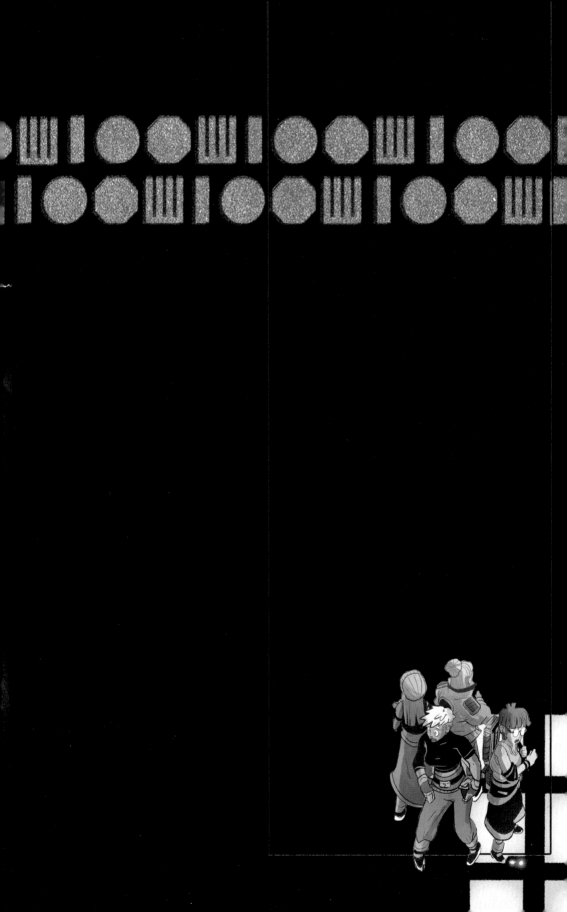